St. Petersburg

Also in the series:

Buenos Aires by Nick Caistor
Berlin by Norbert Schürer
Oxford by Martin Garrett
Frankfurt by Brian Melican
Prague by Andrew Beattie

St. Petersburg

Neil Kent

Interlink Books

An imprint of Interlink Publishing Group, Inc.
Northampton, Massachusetts

First published in 2018 by
INTERLINK BOOKS
An imprint of Interlink Publishing Group, Inc.
46 Crosby Street, Northampton, Massachusetts 01060
www.interlinkbooks.com

Library of Congress Cataloging-in-Publication Data available

ISBN 978-1-56656-046-7

Cover Image: © Batarina Yuliva/Shutterstock

Printed and bound in United States of America

Contents

Introduction

*Z*ayachy Ostrov (Hare Island), on which the first foundations of St. Petersburg were laid in May 1703, after Russia's Tsar Peter the Great conquered Ingria from Sweden, was situated on swampy land in the midst of the River Neva, and would have seemed to many an unlikely spot to establish a new city. Indeed, few if any at that time could have expected St. Petersburg to become in only a few short years Russia's western capital and today Europe's third largest city (some five million inhabitants in 2012), surpassed only by Moscow and London. Yet the ruler of Europe's most extensive empire knew what he wanted to achieve and used all his military, political, and economic might to achieve it despite the many obstacles. Nor was cost, measured in material wealth and human lives, an issue as he had no hesitation in establishing this "city built on bones" very close by to where the Neva meets the Gulf of Finland.

Why did he do this? After all, Moscow, the old capital, established in the early twelfth century, was far more salubriously situated on heights above the Moscow river in the Russian heartland. It also had links by a variety of waterways to the White Sea coast in the north and the Black Sea littoral to the south, making it Russia's most important trading hub. What it did not have, however, was direct access to the sea, the Baltic Sea, central Europe's most important body of water, which ships crisscrossed in all directions, leading not only into the North Sea but through that western body of water into the Atlantic Ocean and Mediterranean Sea themselves, both of which provided access to the rest of the world. The site of St. Petersburg also had connections by water inland, through Lake Ladoga just to the north, and eventually by the River Volga toward Moscow and the south. This new city would become the "window to Europe," a maritime gateway to the world as well as to the interior of Russia itself.

The removal of the principal seat of government from Moscow also meant that Peter had created a space in which he could implement his reforms to the military, bureaucracy, and Church, while disempowering the boyar nobility of the old capital, who stood in opposition to these moves. All now became subject to the virtually all-powerful autocrat of the Russian state, who held all the reins of authority. Moreover, he could draw upon his travels and experiences abroad in both London and Amsterdam, where he had learned about the latest maritime technology and the importance of trade and industry in the successful development of an ambitious state, not least with respect to its economy and military. He also witnessed the latest innovations in architecture and city planning, which came to play a major role in his vision for St. Petersburg and explains the key role he gave to foreign migrants in its construction and design.

Peter had arrived in London in January 1698, nominally incognito, giving him a freedom he would not otherwise have enjoyed on a state visit. He took up residence at Sayes Court in Deptford, in a house owned by the author and diarist John Evelyn, and close to the shipyards which so fascinated him. His three-month visit proved memorable, if not for the best of reasons. The house was wrecked, with floors smeared in grease and ink, the woodwork so badly damaged that three floors had to be replaced. Even the bed linen was "tore in pieces" and the housekeeper lamented the burden thrust upon her by "a house full of people right nasty." The great architect Sir Christopher Wren surveyed the property in the tsar's wake and recorded the value of the damage at £350, including "twenty fine pictures very much tore and all brakes broke," a sum never recovered from Peter.

Yet there were beneficial sides to the visit, such rowdiness notwithstanding, a fact of which King William III of England was fully aware. He received him with great warmth, keen for the country to benefit from Russian trade, especially in pitch and potash, so necessary for England's navy, as well as in tallow, famed Russian leather, luxurious furs, and rich resources of grain.

One of the first things Peter did when he arrived in St. Petersburg in June 1703, after the conclusion of his successful war with

Sweden, was to name the city after his patron saint Peter, but the reference to the tsar himself and his glorious role was clear enough. Yet he chose a Germanized version of the name rather than a Russian one, perhaps as homage to the German Baltic noble families who held sway along the eastern Baltic littoral, or perhaps as an auspicious reference to the German Hansa cities of old, the mercantile network along the Baltic and North Seas that had created such great wealth. It retained this name until 1914, when, at the beginning of the First World War, Russia wished to expunge itself of any German associations, much as the royal family of England, from the German House of Saxe-Coburg-Gotha, changed its name to Windsor in 1917. The city's name was then Russified as Petrograd. Later, in the wake of the Bolshevik Revolution of 1917 and in tribute to Lenin, who was instrumental in establishing the Soviet state, it was renamed Leningrad, in 1924—after his death. By then, Joseph Stalin was increasingly assuming the reins of power, but the city, which had ceased to be the capital in 1918, retained this name until the dissolution of the Soviet Union itself and the establishment of the Russian Federation in 1991. It then reverted to its original name, St. Petersburg, and has enjoyed an almost imperial revival ever since, with the Constitutional Court and other organs of state returning to the city.

During its well over 300-year history St. Petersburg has faced many threats—war, political upheaval, fire, flood, and communist neglect—but the greatest of these was the bombardment and blockade during the Second World War, otherwise known in Russia as the Great Patriotic War, when much of the city's fabric was destroyed and over a million of its inhabitants lost their lives. Yet it resisted and survived and today welcomes visitors from all over the world attracted by the beauty of its architecture, meticulously restored and preserved, the luminosity of its skies during the "white nights" of summer, and the fairy-tale beauty of winter when it is blanketed in snow.

The big question is now how the city will retain and preserve its historic beauty and charm while embracing the high-tech infrastructure required of a vibrant and developing city in the modern global world. As St. Petersburg urbanist Svyatoslav Murunov puts it: "It's the classic question of how to preserve and develop at the same time," lamenting that "The historic center of St. Petersburg is mummified. It's not developing and it's even deteriorating; it has viruses like commercial advertising and high-rise construction that ruin the view." The challenge for Peter the Great's city is to avoid the architectural chaos of Moscow while preserving its rich heritage, a challenge which is far from resolved.

1 | Contours
Geography and Nature

When Peter the Great established his gateway to Europe on the forested lowlands of the eastern coast of the Gulf of Finland in 1703, he chose an unimpressive locale. Although the site was at the confluence of various waterways, most importantly of the River Neva where its delta opens out into the gulf, it was a swampy place, insalubrious and fraught with difficulties for the laying of firm building foundations. Little could even he have anticipated then that some 300 years later it would extend to an area to just under 234 square miles (a little less than 606 square kilometers). Divided into eighteen administrative districts, metropolitan St. Petersburg now includes such formerly distinct suburbs as Kronstadt to the east, Pavlovsk, Peterhof, and Pushkin to the south, and Sestroretsk and Zelenograd to the north. These latter two formerly independent towns were until the Russian conquests of the Second World War under the sovereignty of Finland, Russia's neighbor on the northern shore of the Gulf of Finland.

The flatness of the terrain (the highest point in St. Petersburg is Orekhovaya hill, in the south, at 577 feet or 176 meters), surrounded by so much water—the Sestra, Okhta and Izhora rivers also pass through the city—has made it vulnerable to surges from these as well as from the Gulf of Finland, meaning that flooding has occurred regularly, a problem only recently addressed by the construction of the St. Petersburg Dam in 2011. This was an engineering project that had taken over 32 years to complete. Over the previous centuries only the addition of up to four meters of topsoil had served to hinder these frequent inundations, which nonetheless took place with alarming frequency, a situation further complicated by the presence of the Lakhtinsky Inlet and the Suzdal Lake in the north of the city, as well as the Sestroretsky Inlet just beyond.

With its northern latitude at about 60°N, just under seven degrees south of the Arctic Circle, St. Petersburg is one of the world's most northerly metropoles, a fact reflected in its long winter nights and long summer days. Yet despite its location, the Gulf Stream, carried through the Baltic Sea and Gulf of Finland, moderates the city's climate and makes it warmer than areas only a few miles inland, but also windier and more humid. Its summers tend to be considerably cooler than Moscow's, its winters warmer. Nonetheless, the average winter minimum is in the region of –9°C (16°F), with a record low temperature of –35.9°C (–33°F). The River Neva freezes in late autumn and tends to thaw only in late March or even April. Moreover, the city is often covered by a blanket of snow, which, bearing in mind the dampness of the climate, can accumulate in drifts one or two stories high. When the thaw sets in, streets can be awash with water, making walking treacherous, a danger heightened by the phenomenal icicles which form perilously on many buildings in the spring, claiming several lives each year when they fall upon passing pedestrians. St. Petersburg is thus really an ice queen among Europe's great cities, with frost present for almost two-thirds of the year. Yet when it is hot it is truly hot, and temperatures during the summer of 2010 reached 37.1°C (98.8°F), far from the average summer high of 23°C (73°F). Average precipitation per year is in the region of 600–750 millimeters (23–30 inches), September being the rainiest month. Humidity is almost always high, on average some 78 percent and skies for at least a third of the year are overcast with clouds.

Not surprisingly, then, agriculture around St. Petersburg was relatively poor in the homeland of the Ingrians, a Finnic-speaking people related to the Finns, some of whom still live in scattered villages among its forests. Yet through the will and military might of Peter the Great, St. Petersburg's lasting foundation was secured, and despite the most devastating attacks inflicted during the Second World War the city remains proud of the fact that it never capitulated to any of its enemies, among whom the Swedes were the earliest and most threatening.

The River Neva

While Sweden's last attempt to recapture the site of St. Petersburg failed in 1708, five years after its initial foundation, a number of other threats continued to hang over the new Russian capital, vulnerable not only to military incursions but also the onslaughts of nature. Among these the most devastating were floods from the Neva and the Gulf of Finland. These inundations were a constant and terrifying menace for the low-lying settlement, built as it was on a water-logged swamp. In the very year of its foundation, in August 1703, a major flood wrought havoc in St. Petersburg, the first of many that were to follow in its wake, those of 1777, 1824, 1924, and 1955 being the most devastating. Charles Whitworth, British Ambassador to the Russian court in the early eighteenth century, left the most memorable recollection of a flood in a reminiscence first published in 1758:

> The floods in autumn are very inconvenient, sometimes rising suddenly in the night to the first floors, so that the cattle are often swept away, and the inhabitants scarce saved by their upper stories, on which account they can have no magazines or cellars, nor is the ground practicable for digging, the water coming in at two foot depth. The river is seldom or never clear of the ice before the middle of May, and the ships cannot hold the sea any longer than the end of September, without great danger.

Worse was to follow, when one of the most severe floods was recorded on September 10, 1777. It rose to a height of 3.6 meters (twelve feet) and the Empress Catherine the Great, Russia's most powerful and able autocrat, witnessed the event from her newly constructed Winter Palace, situated precariously on the banks of the Neva. She wrote about it to her philosopher friend, the German diplomat Baron Friedrich Melchior Grimm:

> I was in a sound sleep, when a gust of wind woke me at five o'clock in the morning. I rang the bell and was told that the water was up to my wing of the palace and seemed likely to inundate it. I, therefore, fled to the Hermitage. The view of the Neva seemed to me to be like that which must have accompanied the destruction of Jerusalem.

Yet for all its seemingly hellish power, the Neva was Janus-like since it could also show a side that seemed positively heavenly, at least during the so-called white nights of summer when the sun seemed hardly to set. As an English visitor Andrew Swinton wrote lyrically during a more clement period during the empress' reign:

> In the Summer evenings, when the weather is calm, the citizens of Petersburg delight in sailing upon the Neva in their pleasure boats... The company are seated in the stern, under a canopy of silk, or other stuff, and have with them musicians or frequently the party themselves perform upon different instruments. The rowers are all chosen among such of their servants as have the best voices, and either sing in concert with the instruments, or without them... When the concert is ended, the audience upon the streets go away, repeating the songs, and echoing them into every quarter of the city.

The Neva would continue to show its alternating malevolent and benevolent sides through the centuries, fortunately the latter more often than the former. Yet the floods remained a serious problem: that which occurred on November 7, 1824, was the worst the city ever experienced. Flood waters rose to a height of 4.21 meters (13 feet, 9 inches), the highest level ever recorded. A resident of the Palace Embankment, Count Vladimir Sollugub, wrote in his memoirs:

> One could hardly distinguish between river and sky... Then, all of a sudden, the embankment vanished. There was just one tumultuous, bubbling sea between the fortress and our house. We found ourselves in highly dangerous circumstances... Buckets, tubs, barrels, furniture, coffins, and the simple crosses which had been washed from the Smolensky Cemetery all now drifted by.

On the other side of the Neva, Maria Kamenskaya, the daughter of Count Fedor Tolstoy, recorded her own impressions. A witness of the flood from her family home on Vasilyevsky Island, she remembered how the entire household, tenants and servants, had sought refuge on the second floor and in the attic, where "...the complete hopelessness led the servants to panic. In a state of terror our cook Fedor rode the waves in Mama's wooden bath, paddling for dear life with a spade..."

Though multitudes died in this frightful flood, many of St. Petersburg's inhabitants were ultimately saved by the efficiency of General Count Alexander von Benckendorff, Tsar Alexander I's aide-de-camp, who, with his staff, dashed about establishing an infrastructure of rescue and relief to lessen the general suffering. For these efforts he was eventually rewarded with a diamond-encrusted snuffbox by the emperor himself.

Health and Mortality

With its burgeoning population of some 70,000 inhabitants by the 1730s, St. Petersburg was a notoriously insalubrious city and remained so throughout the eighteenth century and beyond. Epidemics visited the capital regularly and life expectancy was low relative to many other European cities, and much lower than in the surrounding countryside. Smallpox, in particular, was especially destructive, and Tsar Peter II (1715–30), Peter the Great's grandson and heir, died of the contagion as a very young man after a reign of only three years. Yet some foreigners, even medical men, were impressed by the state of the city's cleanliness at a time when other European cities had even fewer hygienic amenities. The Englishman Dr. John Cook wrote enthusiastically that "the common people may have no pretext for leaving nastiness in any part of the streets; convenient places are built upon the banks of the river and its canals." St. Petersburg was, moreover, laid out with wide streets, unlike the cramped ones of ancient European cities where epidemics, poor sanitation, and fires wrought havoc. A variety of sanitary institutions were rapidly established, the Medical Chancery being one of the most important, situated on what would become one of the city's most prestigious thoroughfares, Millionnaya Street. Of particular importance for the warrior tsar Peter the Great was the wellbeing of his fighting men, and so he established two hospitals on the Vyborg side of the city across the Neva to provide for their medical needs. As Cook wrote:

> One is for the army, the other for the fleet. They are joined together, completing three sides of a very large square. In the middle of the side facing the river Neva, is a fine church for the use of both hospitals; the wards are very well contrived; the building is two storeys high, and covered galleries go quite round both hospitals, so as any person may walk without being exposed to the injuries of the weather. At each corner of each hospital is a noble theatre, and dissecting chamber.

St. Petersburg continued to grow, and by the 1750s the population had risen to over 95,000. Nonetheless, the demography was hardly positive because the ratio of male to female with respect to birth rates was 60 to 40 percent in favor of the former. Moreover, most inhabitants lived on the poverty line and their numbers had to be constantly replenished by immigrants, voluntary and involuntary, both from within Russia (92–94 percent)) and the rest from abroad. Of the population just over two thousand were of noble status and a similar number were merchants; the majority was made up of serfs and the urban poor.

Among the most prominent of foreign nationals were the British, who came to play an especially significant role in the improvements of health and hygiene, at least in court circles, later in the eighteenth century. Dr. Thomas Dimsdale, for example, visited the city twice by invitation of Catherine the Great, first in 1768, when he came to inoculate her, her son and heir apparent the Grand-Duke Paul, as well as much of the Russian court. He returned thirteen years later to do the same for the next imperial generation, Paul's son, the future Tsar Alexander I and his brother the Grand-Duke Konstantin.

Catherine took a wider view of the health of all of her people—and not just the military—than Peter the Great had done. For example, she had a hospital built to accommodate indigent expectant mothers from whom future generations of Russian workers would stem. It was specifically laid down that "All of the pregnant women who arrive to give birth should be given immediate access and not be made subject by the door-keeper to questions relating to who they are, whether in the day or at night." Ivan Ivanovich Betzkoi, the illegitimate son of Field Marshal I. U. Trybezkoy, was appointed director and modeled the establishment on similar institutions in Strasbourg, Vienna and Bologna, a situation unheard of in Moscow, the old capital, at this time.

Military hospitals, of course, continued to be given high priority, a state of affairs that was hardly surprising bearing in mind the importance for the empress of fighting men in her military campaigns along the Black Sea littoral. When a British prison reformer returned to the city in 1789, he noted that, although the prisons had hardly improved, conditions for invalids from the navy and army had, at least for those 534 inmates now accommodated in their hospitals. With praise, he noted:

> A new and splendid hospital has been erected just out of the city, and opposite a fine canal: the rooms are spacious, lofty and clean, and had been lately white-washed. The patients were of both sexes, in separate summer lazaretts in the adjoining court; the rooms and beds were clean and neat. Men and Women prisoners come here every day; the latter to wash and clean the rooms, the former to remove what is offensive from the outside sewers of every room.

Yet despite such provisions, in 1789, that fateful year for much of Europe, mortality rates remained high (but in line with those of London and Stockholm) and the city could not sustain itself without new arrivals from outside. The statistics are stark: whereas some 6,200 children were born that year, more than 8,400 people died. Even fifty years later the situation had hardly improved. The arrival of cholera in the 1830s, a new epidemic which came with the steamship and railways (since victims of the disease now lived long enough to transmit the contagion further), cost many lives in repeated waves, a situation which was only ameliorated in the twentieth century with well-constructed sewers and plumbing. So St.

Petersburg's mortality rates remained poor—not only among the highest on the European Continent but in Russia, too—during the later nineteenth century. In 1860 one in 23.6 people died each year, compared to one in 40 in London, one in 36.5 in Berlin and one in 35.1 in Paris. Only Tula out of all Russian cities, home of the armaments and samovar industries where accidents were prevalent, had a higher mortality rate. Moreover, mortality rates in different parts of the capital varied enormously according to their prosperity. Whereas the rate in the most elegant central districts was less than 17 per 1,000 inhabitants in 1870, that in the outlying industrial Narva area was almost three times higher, more than 50 per 1,000.

City in Flux

Poor mortality rates reflected the fact that residential space was expensive and limited. Even the lowliest housing and working spaces were hardly cheap, a situation aggravated by the exponential movement of ex-serfs from the countryside, after Tsar Alexander I's Emancipation Proclamation in 1861. Landlords strove to make the smallest nook and cranny turn a profit. This situation the novelist and short-story writer Nikolai Leskov (1831–95) used rich imagery to depict in his short story, "The Peacock," about a landlady who determines to exploit the poor, "on the well-founded calculation that numerous little flats can be let for more money together than large ones, not least because the poor, who always live together in great numbers, demand neither 'tasteful' accommodation, nor even cleanliness."

In truth, it was food which was even scarcer and about which the poor immigrants from the countryside were most concerned: famines remained a serious problem in many parts of the Russian Empire throughout the period, if not in the capital itself. The famine of 1891 led to the deaths of more than twenty million people in the south of Russia, propelling many more among the displaced rural population into St. Petersburg. When the harvest of 1906 failed once again there was a renewed influx into the capital, leading to even more severe overcrowding and a further breakdown in hygiene and sanitation. The consequence was hardly surprising:

the outbreak of numerous epidemics which raged throughout the nineteenth century. Those in 1892–93 were especially vicious: typhus and cholera spread north-westwards from the Caspian Sea region throughout Russia and into the heart of the western capital. One possible victim was Peter Ilyich Tchaikovsky (1840–93), one of Russia's greatest composers (formerly it was maintained that he died by suicide, unable to cope with his homosexuality and its possible public revelations, but in recent years this has been largely discounted). Nor did the situation improve with the advent of the twentieth century. A later epidemic of cholera carried off almost half a million people throughout the country in 1909, thousands of whom died in St. Petersburg alone. Typhus was also a formidable scourge: a quarter of all young men in St. Petersburg who died in the city before the advent of the First World War—when the city's population was just under two and a half million—succumbed to it. Thus, the city's mortality rates in the early twentieth century, though much improved over those of the previous century, remained unusually high for European cities: one in up to 35.1 people died each year right up until the revolutionary period began in February 1917, toward the end of the empire's devastating involvement in the First World War.

The city's continued susceptibility to floods, together with its perennially poor water system, have led to other ailments which persist even today, such as giardia, caused by a waterborne parasite, even if projects undertaken in recent years with British assistance have been implemented to address the situation.

Suicide rates were also high in this beautiful but unforgiving capital. In 1908 alone, 41 schoolchildren killed themselves in a single month and newspapers made a great deal of it, bemoaning this modern type of "epidemic."

Yet the real trials of St. Petersburg (renamed Petrograd in the wake of anti-German feeling after the outbreak of the First World War, in which Russia fought against Germany) occurred when wartime shortages wrought havoc on the city's infrastructure, which suffered an almost complete collapse during the February and October Revolutions of 1917—the first parliamentary republican, the second Bolshevik. To make matters worse, the ensuing civil war (order was only restored in 1921) led to further devastation, and thousands died from famine, disease, and civil strife. Matters only slowly improved after the establishment of the Soviet state, when the city was renamed Leningrad in 1924 in honor of Vladimir Ilyich Lenin (1870–1924), the Bolshevik revolutionary leader who instigated the October Revolution and ruled the fledgling Marxist state with an iron hand.

The Second World War (discussed in Chapter 5) brought about a catastrophic blockade of Leningrad by the besieging Germans from 1941 to 1944. It was the most disastrous siege of any city on record, in which over a million people died through a combination of starvation, disease, cold, and enemy action. It took years of Herculean postwar labor to bring the city back to normality, albeit at the cost of heavy industrial pollution, much of which is still present and exacerbated by the fumes of traffic. Yet in recent decades, and especially after the collapse of the Soviet Union in 1991, the city has begun to enjoy a revival which gathered pace after the reestablishment of public order in the wake of the lawless years of the 1990s.

Today it is one of the world's most beautiful and culturally rich metropoles, surrounded—beyond its soulless late twentieth-century suburbs—by a leafy ring of forests dotted with restored palaces and churches, coastal resorts and sanatoriums, as well as the suburban villas and summer *dachas* of its more prosperous citizens. For that reason and because of its immensely rich cultural life, including opera, ballet, concerts, and theater, not to mention its world-famous art collections, one of the world's most inhospitable geographical areas has become a magnet attracting discerning international visitors from the four corners of the globe.

2 | Streets
How the City Grew

The transformation of a swamp, where the Neva pours into the Gulf of Finland, into one of Europe's most beautiful cities was an amazing accomplishment. Yet St. Petersburg was built upon the bones of conscripted soldiers and serf laborers, tens of thousands of whom died in the process. And even before anything could be accomplished, its military defense had to be secured.

Among the first initiatives undertaken to support the establishment and growth of St. Petersburg was the construction of its defensive fortifications. Since military threats to Peter the Great's new capital remained significant throughout his reign—he only conquered the formerly Swedish-ruled region in 1703—his wider military campaigns were integral both to its establishment and development, as well as to Russia's existential survival. The construction and improvement of new and existing fortresses (previously built by the Swedes) and other defensive infrastructure were essential, especially since for almost a generation after St. Petersburg's foundation Russia was a country at war. Having begun three years previously, the Great Northern War (1700–21), in which sprawling Russia was pitted against Sweden, led to the deaths of up to 30,000 on the former's side in the region, and if the whole of the tsar's military campaigns are taken into account elsewhere, the total rises to over 40,000.

However, as lethal as this conflict was, an even greater war was being fought at the same time—against the physical elements, geographical as well as meteorological: some 70,000 people died during the city's initial period of construction. Aleksey Tolstoy (1883–1945), Soviet-era author and relative of Leo Tolstoy, creator of the late nineteenth-century epic novels *War and Peace* and *Anna Karenina*, later wrote in his famous biography, *Peter the First* about this terrible fact, noting without exaggeration that one could say the city's foundations were literally embedded among the bones of those who had built it. This was a situation which also had resonances in his own time when the violence of the revolutionary period, civil war and blockade of Leningrad during the Second World War led to waves of destruction which even dwarfed those early ones. While some of his prose focuses upon the early days of St. Petersburg, other pieces highlight the sacrifices, voluntary and involuntary, made during the building of the White Sea Canal, which provided a lifeline to the city from the Arctic Ocean, its only means of breaking the stranglehold of its German blockade during the Second World War. This aid was carried south from Murmansk along the White Sea Canal (the construction of which had cost so many lives of Gulag prisoners) and thence southward toward Leningrad. This was not the first time Russians in the area were existentially threatened. Already, in the time of Peter the Great, when Russia wrested the area from Sweden, they had had to contend what seemed at the time to be the overwhelming might of their enemy. Yet Sweden had been defeated by a costly but skillful use of local waterways to the west to provision Russian forces.

After a bloody encirclement the way was free from Lake Ladoga to the open sea. An endless flow of wagons and masses of workers and prisoners from the East poured in. Axes clanged and saws gnashed. Here, at the ends of the earth, an incredible flood of working people arrived, who would never return home in order to defend the gateway for trade to the Russian state and for the construction of a fortress with six bastions.

Peter the Great's foothold on the Gulf of Finland had been maintained, and seemingly endless numbers of conscripts and serfs arrived to construct the city, whatever the odds of survival. For all the earliest building works required the presence of countless construction workers. As early as 1704, only one year after the city's foundation, the government ordered a levy of some 40,000 conscripts, mainly serfs but also prisoners, to come to the city. While only about 30,000 actually arrived, those who did worked in harsh physical circumstances from dawn until dusk in both the icy cold of winter and the blistering heat of summer. The warmer months, from April until September, were the most productive, although the marshy terrain on which the city was built was especially waterlogged and unhealthy during this period. Nor were autumn and winter much better, as epidemics then took their toll as workers labored from six in the morning to six at night. There was also always a shortage of able-bodied men and increasing duress was required to ensure that there was an adequate supply of labor. Alongside the impressment of serfs and conscription of soldiers, Swedish prisoners-of-war from the ranks and common criminals also made up the numbers.

Even so, the whole process was arduous in the extreme and a marvel for its time. Before any building work even commenced, the marshes had to be drained and the appropriate piles for supporting the buildings driven deep into the unstable subsoil. Mortality, rather than escape or recalcitrance, was the greatest enemy: some 150 construction workers died on average each year from 1703 to 1715, totaling almost two thousand during that period alone. It was only toward the end of the latter decade that mortality gradually diminished in the wake of the more attractive working conditions introduced to encourage more efficient hired labor. Yet even then conditions remained harsh, terms of employment rigorous, and the standards of construction as laid down by government decree not merely demanding but often highly impractical under the circumstances.

In fact, Peter the Great's urban vision bordered on the fantastical, the utopian. No expense was spared and he asked the famous French landscape designer Jean-Baptiste Alexandre Le Blond, a former student of André Le Nôtre, who worked at the Palace of Versailles, to design an urban plan. Though originally based on the form of an ellipse and grandiose in scale, the design changed and the tsar was ultimately obliged to content himself with a more modest and simplified plan. The layout of the city remained rudimentary at best and even its most important buildings were eventually compelled to conform to a simpler layout and design than had initially been envisioned.

For example, Peter's first residence was built of wood rather than of more costly materials like brick and stone, though it was painted to look like them. Not surprisingly, most of the other early buildings of the city were also made of wood, an abundant commodity in a region covered with rich forests of spruce and pine. Sometimes even more humble building materials were utilized, including clay, which could cheaply be sourced in the vicinity and which was employed to construct the so-called *mazanka* (a traditional Russian wattle-and-daub house).

These problems notwithstanding, St. Petersburg grew and prospered. By 1710–11, the city had acquired 8,000 inhabitants, composed of 750 to 800 households. Many of these were of foreign origin, hardly surprising since even in Peter the Great's navy at this time almost all officers and many common sailors were Dutch, and many other nationalities were also employed or enlisted, including English, Scots, and Swedes.

The City Plan and Grid System

To begin with, Peter needed a plan, and as he himself put it, the "city was to be laid out 'in the manner of the Dutch' with regular blocks and straight canals penetrating the territory of the city at right angles to each other." Thus was born the rectilinear grid of the new city which rapidly became Europe's most rationally laid out capital, in diametric opposition to old Moscow, with its confusion, chaos, and narrow, twisting streets. Writing of the long, straight avenue known as Nevksy Prospekt, Harold Williams observes in *Russia of the Russians* (1914):

> Peter's idea of cutting through the forests on the left bank of the Neva some straight avenues called "prospects," or "perspectives," has received a brilliant justification in the Nevsky. There the Nevsky is something tense and exhilarating in the very straightness of this fine, broad thoroughfare, something that tempts the adventurous though heavily-padded coachman to drive his splendid horses at headlong speed, scattering humble cabmen before him.

At the early eighteenth-century stage, the three principal parts of the city were Vasilyevsky Island to the west of the Neva, what is now called the Petrograd Side with the adjacent little island on which the Peter and Paul Fortress is located, and most importantly the eastern Nevsky area, where Nevsky Prospekt is still the city's longest street and most prominent feature. This is the beginning of the overland road link from the new capital to Novgorod, Moscow, and the provinces, evoking what the author Andrei Bely in his novel *Petersburg* (1913) called "the measureless immensity" of the Russian Empire and "the orphaned distances of the provinces." It begins at the Admiralty, on the Neva, and carries on to Vosstaniya Square, where the Moscow Railway Station is located, after which it makes a small turn, carrying on to the Alexander Nevsky Monastery, also founded by Peter, on the far eastern end of the city, a length of nearly 4.5 kilometers (three miles).

For all Nevsky Prospekt's importance, however, the city's plan and grid are determined by even more significant geographical features, namely the rivers and canals which flow through its western side. These, including the Moika and Fontanka rivers, as well as the Griboyedov and Kryukov Canals, meander through the urban landscape, breaking up the otherwise strict formality and logic of its street plan. Crisscrossed by an elaborated system of bridges, some of startling beauty, these waterways still define St. Petersburg to a degree that even its main thoroughfares cannot rival. A boat ride on them under blue skies during the summer remains one of the most delightful experiences available to a visitor, as magnificent palaces and mansions glimmer on either side, making the city a rival even of Venice in this regard.

St. Petersburg's layout is also characterized by one other feature, well-known to readers of Dostoyevsky but treasured too by others who become aware of them—its courtyards. Numbering in the hundreds and of various shapes and sizes, they are intrinsic to the city. It has been said that throughout its history residents or visitors, even terrorists and political outcasts wishing to avoid being seen by the authorities, could make their way through them from one end of the city to another without ever needing to walk along a street or alleyway. Among the most intriguing were those, now demolished, across the canal behind the Mariinsky Theater, or near St. Isaac's Cathedral, where Dostoyevsky set the scene for the murder by the character Rodin Raskolnikov in his novel *Crime and Punishment*. Thus the city of St. Petersburg is a palimpsest in which rational planning and grids are almost defeated by local geography, both natural and manmade, but which merge together in an intriguing synthesis.

With respect to Vasilyevsky Island, it is the so-called "lines" that create its principal grid. These streets run parallel to one another, intersecting the Sredny (Middle) and Bolshoi (Large) Prospekts and following the straight course of the Neva, from the 1st Line to the 29th Line. These begin at the eastern end of the island where the main, larger branch of the Neva meets its smaller tributary by the Palace Bridge. Originally envisaging the island as the heart of the city, the Italian architect Dominico Trezzini (1670–1734) designed the area from the 1st to the 25th Line as early as 1716–18, planning to construct a series of embanked canals suitable for the city's transport, as well as creating a visual appearance that would have made St. Petersburg a veritable Venice of the North. Only four canals came to be built in the end, however, and streets took their place. Today it is one of the busiest parts of the city, full of historical buildings and monuments along the University Embankment which runs along its Neva shore. This embankment is also the site of the Twelve Colleges, now forming the heart of St. Petersburg State University, which by virtue of their own grid-like arrangement create the impression at a distance of one palatial edifice. Such an approach would be utilized a century later in the British architect John Nash's work at Regent's Park in London.

The Petrograd Side (the first word reminding us that it is Peter's City), now a largely residential area, was constructed in a less regulated manner, containing as it still does the first dwelling erected in St. Petersburg for Tsar Peter himself, an elaborate wooden cottage only sixty meters square which combines both traditional Russian and Dutch elements. He lived here for five years, from 1703 to 1708, and the dwelling, now located at 6 Petrovskaya Embankment, still contains much of its original inventory. With its interior walls painted to appear as though made of brick, the flammable structure nonetheless survived the bombing of the Second World War. This public museum is enclosed within a red brick cocoon-like structure to preserve it from the elements. Otherwise, the area enjoyed major residential development with imposing villas and blocks of apartments during the later nineteenth century. Its most famous landmark, however, is probably the cruiser *Aurora*, which remains permanently docked along the Petrogradskaya Embankment, from which in October 1917 the first shots of the Russian Revolution were fired at the Winter Palace. Today it is a museum.

Hard Labor

During the second decade of its existence the urban infrastructure of St. Petersburg began to enjoy development of astonishing modernity. In 1714 the city's first post office was designed by Trezzini, a single-story building constructed at a site adjacent to the Trinity Landing Stage on what was then called the Great Meadow but has now long been known as the Field of Mars. The postmen employed in this fledgling postal system, though, had no easy task, since there would be no regulated system of addresses in St. Petersburg for another thirty years.

Yet despite this and other weaknesses, St. Petersburg was becoming a recognizably European city. The paving of streets began as early as 1715 with Nevsky Prospekt, then as now the most important thoroughfare in the metropolis. Within ten years, many of the city's principal streets were laid out and it was Le Blond who was given the onerous task of organizing street lighting for the new capital: by the 1720s, 595 lanterns were dotted about the city, lit by hempseed oil produced by the local and recently established Menshikov-Yamburg factories. The lanterns' durability and efficiency were extraordinary and most of them remained in function for some 140 years. The 64 lantern men who first serviced them became a familiar sight, the memory of which survived for decades.

The creation out of a swamp of such an extensive city required above all labor, and this would long prove a major difficulty, for the incentives were few for workers who came voluntarily. Indeed, the need for laborers was virtually unlimited, whether free or bonded. In any case, even the former were granted few rights in comparison to such workers in other European cities. For instance, they had no freedom to choose where in the new capital they were going to live, since such matters were laid down by law according to one's position—ethnic, social, and religious—within society. Each such community was allotted its own *raion* (borough). Craftsmen, for example, were obliged to live on today's Petrograd Side, while from 1716 the nobility and merchants were settled on Vasilyevsky Island.

The French were one target group. In 1717, Peter the Great returned to Western Europe, visiting France partly for political reasons but also to encourage the immigration of skilled French craftsmen and their families to the new capital. In the wake of this visit some two hundred arrived in St. Petersburg, the majority of whom were artists, carpenters, actors, dancers, and pastry cooks.

Working hours were long, conditions hard, and the climate oppressive—damp and freezing for at least half the year, mosquito ridden during the warmer period. Ever larger factories accommodated the workers, and the length of their working day was dictated by the availability of daylight. In the winter, this period was as short as seven hours, but in the brighter months it increased, extending to eighteen hours at the height of the summer, the so-called "white nights" period.

Child labor also played a significant role. Even the sons of master craftsmen were registered as working in their respective workshops and factories when they were as young as nine. Of course, their working conditions depended on the positions of their fathers in the social and economic hierarchy, and those toward the bottom of the social scale had a life that was usually arduous in the extreme, not least because they also had to compete with the labor of serfs. These bonded laborers, tied to specific owners and usually bound to their land, were not chattels in the American sense, according to which African slaves were held in bondage in the Americas. Their labor and freedom of movement were, nonetheless, under strict control. Yet by the end of the reign of the Empress Elizabeth (1741–62), a daughter of Peter the Great, much of the work formerly done by serfs in the city came to be carried out by more productive paid workers. Prisoners, too, continued to play a major part, since a significant portion of the population in these early days (and as they were to be even into the second half of the twentieth century) were such, the majority ordinary convicts but many also prisoners of war or guilty of political crimes, real or imaginary.

The Twelve Colleges

Of course, a great European metropolis needed brains as well as brawn and so one of the early priorities was to establish an efficient administrative bureaucracy. The so-called Twelve Colleges (1722–42) were established to this end, with Trezzini commissioned as architect. He had previously been hired to design the Alexander Nevsky Monastery (discussed in Chapter 9) but his work there had been curtailed. These new colleges formed a vast and concatenated palace-like structure some 383 meters (1,250 feet) in length which housed a variety of government ministries and remains today a lasting monument to Trezzini's late style.

Situated on the University Embankment, the complex has accommodated the seat of the St. Petersburg State University and some of its faculties since 1819. This university had originally been founded by Peter the Great in 1724, and its first rector was Gerhard Friedrich Müller (1705–83), a German academician, historian, and ethnographer. In the eighteenth century, however, the colleges accommodated the Holy Synod, which administered the Russian Orthodox Church after Peter abolished the office of the patriarch, as well as ten governmental ministries and the Senate itself until other buildings were constructed later in the century to house them. An eclectic mix of Western European Baroque architectural elements, this huge complex rests upon a plainly rusticated base and is surmounted by a row of Baroque gables which seem to be inspired by the seventeenth-century Stock Exchange of the Danish King Christian IV in Copenhagen, built by the Flemish-Danish architects Laurens and Hans van Steenwinkel from 1619–24. This link is perhaps not as surprising as it might seem, for Russia's greatest

European ally throughout the seventeenth and eighteenth centuries was Denmark, a country which shared the same dominating goal of keeping Sweden, Russia's arch enemy, politically and militarily on the defensive. The colleges remained unfinished at Trezzini's death, but his son-in-law Giuseppe completed the building, adding a gallery-like structure to the rear.

Industrial Developments

Russia's new capital needed an industrial infrastructure as well, and to this end Peter the Great encouraged the arrival of Western European industrialists. Two of the earliest were the Dane P. Marsenius and the Dutchman F. Akema, who had already built four factories in the Kashirsky District of Moscow. More important, though, were the British, who would remain among the most prominent industrial entrepreneurs in Russia in general, and in St. Petersburg in particular, until the 1917 Revolution forced their flight. They established themselves on what soon came to be known as the English Embankment, where the Anglican Church of St. Mary and All Saints was constructed (today an adjunct to the Rimsky-Korsakov Conservatory of Music). This was set up in a mansion originally built for Count B. P. Sheremetev which had been acquired by the English-owned Russia Company in 1723 and underwent the first of many major reconstructions during its life as a church, a function it would serve until the Bolsheviks enforced its closure, sending its Anglican priest into captivity. But the British were noteworthy in another regard: education, and they were among the first in St. Petersburg to establish a traveling library which, continuously enlarged over the following decades, boasted some ten thousand volumes during its heyday, making it the largest English library in Russia.

The church was not the only hub of English social life in St. Petersburg. One of the centers of British social life, at least for those of aristocratic background, was the English Club, a branch of which also opened in Moscow. Founded in 1770, it welcomed both British and Russian male members until the Revolution led to its closure and the murder of many of its members. However, the English Masonic Lodge or "Perfect Union" flourished only briefly, succumbing to a number of political pressures which caused its early demise, in part because of the Enlightenment and irreligious values it propagated to the dismay of the Russian Orthodox Church.

Yet the British were a highly significant community in the new capital, predominantly because of their influence on industrial development. Among major industrialists was the Scot Charles Bird (1766–1843). He arrived in Russia in 1786 and established a factory which in 1805–06 provided materials for numerous bridges in the city as well as figures for the new palaces of the Senate and Holy Synod, the famous bas relief for the pedestal of the Alexandrovsky Column and other decorative elements for the Admiralty, the Mikhailovsky Castle, and St. Isaac's Cathedral. These "British" contributions notwithstanding, however, Anglo-Russian relations during this period were by no means always smooth and could frequently be highly volatile and fraught with hostility. The Commercial Treaty of 1797 and Tsar Paul's anti-French stance initially served to foster improved Anglo-Russian relations. Yet after the latter realigned himself more closely with Napoleon, they rapidly deteriorated, culminating in May 1800 with the suspension of diplomatic contact. An embargo was imposed upon all British merchandise while the tsar, now envisioning assistance from the new French emperor, contemplated Russian imperial expansion eastwards toward British India. This, as we shall see in Chapters Four and Eleven, would prove his undoing, and perhaps even his death.

By then, within the space of just four generations, St. Petersburg had become one of Europe's most important cities, with a population of some 192,000 inhabitants in 1784. Yet it was a city, then as now, of extraordinary contrasts—luxury and destitution could be found not only in the same districts or streets but in the same buildings, with the rich living on the lower floors and the hungry poor in the attics. It was also a city of great cosmopolitanism, with foreigners continuing to be welcome throughout the imperial period. Nor were the British the only ones prominent on the social and commercial scene. In 1793 at least eight hundred Frenchmen lived in the city, 63 of them merchants, making St. Petersburg the city with the second largest French community in the empire (Moscow had nine hundred at the time).

The Merchants' Court

If industry was a new but important component in the development of Russia and St. Petersburg, trade was even more so and had long cemented Russia to its Western European neighbors—British and Dutch in particular. This dated back to the sixteenth century when the principal trade route was along the northern coast of Norway, down to the White Sea at Arkhangelsk, and by river transport down to Moscow. Thus mercantile activity already played an enormous role in the earliest years of St. Petersburg's foundation and one of the most significant architectural projects during the reign of Catherine the Great was the construction of the vast *Gostiny Dvor* or Merchants' Court, a prototype shopping mall situated in the heart of the city on the corner of Nevsky Prospekt and Sadovaya Street. Although the initial plans had already been provided by Francesco Bartolomeo Rastrelli, the French architect Jean-Baptiste Vallin de la Mothe (1729–1800), who had come to St. Petersburg in 1759, assumed the commission which came not from the crown but from the merchants of St. Petersburg themselves. Rastrelli's plans had favored the monumental, but Vallin de la Mothe preferred a more low-key neoclassical design for this quadratic complex, composed of covered arcades on all four sides. The Doric order, the most humble of the classical orders, was chosen for this highly bourgeois building which laid no claim to aristocratic pretensions. As usual with such projects involving funds from many individuals, it took many years to complete and only opened for business in 1785 with more than a hundred shops. Today it remains one of the most important shopping complexes in St. Petersburg.

New Holland

Yet another important development for both the defensive security and mercantile prosperity of St. Petersburg was New Holland, a vast naval complex with storage and shipbuilding facilities. Built on a triangular artificial island created for this purpose at the intersection of the Neva and several canals in 1720 (hence its name), most of it was constructed by the Russian architect Ivan Korobov who built a series of warehouses, the entrance to which led through a monumental gate in Baroque style, all carried out from 1732 to 1740. However, in 1765 another Russian architect Savva Chevakinsky, together with Vallin de la Mothe, was employed to redevelop the site using red brick rather than the less durable wood previously deployed, the latter providing a new monumental gateway in a fashionable early neoclassical style with Tuscan columns of red granite imported from Finland, then under Swedish sovereignty. Known as the Great Arch (1765–88), it rises majestically over the canal providing access to the site, a veritable monument to the economic success of that age. Although the complex's present appearance is largely the result of nineteenth-century accretions, including a former naval prison and construction basin, it will doubtless change again when the current redevelopment, to include hotel accommodation, a conference center, restaurants, and shops, is completed.

Yury Felten

Yury Felten (original name Georg Friedrich Veldten, 1730–1801) was an architect of German immigrant extraction who by the mid-1750s had come to rival Vallin de la Mothe with respect to the favor he enjoyed in Russian court circles. Born in St. Petersburg, he had studied not in France or Italy, but in Tübingen within the German Holy Roman Empire, before being taken on as an apprentice by Rastrelli. Felten left his mark, in particular in the construction of the South Neva Embankment, with its still-lustrous red granite. He was also increasingly busy in the restoration and construction of a number of palaces, imperial as well as aristocratic. Together with Vallin de la Mothe, he built the Southern Pavilion of the Small Hermitage in 1764–67. He also constructed the eccentric Chesme Palace, built to commemorate the Russian Navy's victory over the Turks in 1770 in the Bay of Chesme. Atypical of Russian architecture of the period, it looks to the revivalist eighteenth-century English Gothic for inspiration, as does his Church of St. John the Baptist at Chesme. Other works include the picturesque Upper Swan

Bridge from the 1770s, adjacent to the Winter Palace, and he also assisted others in different *métiers* when his skills were required. For example, he provided the foundations on which Étienne Falconet's monumental *Bronze Horseman* statue of Peter the Great, in its commanding position on Senate Square, came to rest.

The Napoleonic Period

Giacomo Quarenghi (1744–1817) was another of the later generation of Italian architects who continued to have a profound influence on the architecture of St. Petersburg, especially during the period of the Napoleonic Wars under Tsars Paul and Alexander I. Among his most noted Palladian works is the so-called Manège, built in 1804–07 on St. Isaac's Square to accommodate the horses of the prestigious Imperial Regiment of the Horse Guards.

With the turn of the nineteenth century, St. Petersburg grew by leaps and bounds, with some 220,000 inhabitants recorded in 1800. This increase in population continued throughout the early years of the nineteenth century, and by 1813 the city had no fewer than 285,000 residents, of whom at least 35,500 were foreigners. These included many British, among them William Hastie, noted for designing the so-called "Police Bridge," which spanned the River Moika on Nevsky Prospekt.

Most foreigners throughout this period were men, and indeed, the ratio of the sexes remained as unbalanced as it had been in the eighteenth century in all levels of society. With respect to Russians, many of these were newly arrived men from the countryside who came to find work, hoping to escape from rural poverty but with their wives more or less abandoned in the countryside. In consequence, the male proportion of the population remained high, some 62–65 percent of the total.

The various markets were the meeting places where many of these new arrivals gathered to seek work, buy food, and socialize. St. Isaac's Square, in particular, was a hub of activity where at four in the morning many urban working men and peasants came to offer their labor. There was also a market for the purchase, sale, and hiring out of serfs, many of whom had been imported from the country-side for that purpose.

Most of these working people, free or serfs, lived on the edges of the city in tenements or other basic housing near the outlying factories. Two families frequently shared one room in densely packed, poorly ventilated slums, with minimal privacy provided by a curtained partition. For those even poorer, as many as thirty people might be accommodated in a single room, obliged to share no more than eight wooden beds among themselves and frequently sleeping in shifts. Other furniture was usually scarce, at most a simple wooden chair, cupboard, and bench. The time available to spend in these tightly packed rooms was in any case limited, as factories generally expected their workers to arrive by five in the morning and to work until darkness fell. Saturday was the day for bathing—still the case in much of rural and small town Russia today—in local sauna-like bathhouses. Sundays were strict days of rest with church attendance required at Orthodox liturgies, which usually lasted several hours (see Chapter 9), and subject to frequent fasts, not always the result of church calendars.

Urban Infrastructure

As the nineteenth century progressed St. Petersburg rapidly adopted much of the urban infrastructure to be found elsewhere in European cities. Gas street lighting was introduced in 1835 and within four years there were 204 lamps throughout the center of the city, in particular at key sites including Palace Square, Nevsky Prospekt, the Admiralty, and Liteiny Prospekt.

New bridges were also spanning the Neva. Its first permanent crossing, the Annunciation Bridge, designed by the Polish engineer Stanisław Kierbiedz and decorated by Alexander Brullov (1798–1877), opened to traffic in 1850. Later, in 1855, it was renamed Nikolayevsky Bridge, only to acquire in 1918 the name of the revolutionary hero of Sebastopol in 1905, Lieutenant Pyotr Schmidt. From 2006 it has been known by its original name which denotes a no-longer-existent chapel there formerly dedicated to St. Nicholas and built by another well-known Russian architect of the period,

Andrei Stackenschneider (1802–65), in 1854. The Soviets demolished the chapel during the bridge's reconstruction in 1936–38.

The improvement of water provision and sanitation was another major development. Already in the time of Catherine the Great two public water-pumping stations were built on the Neva by the St. Isaac's and Resurrection Bridges to provide much of the water needed for drinking, cooking, and washing. Carried away by customers or their servants in tubs or barrels, the water was distributed throughout St. Petersburg. Few further developments followed until, during the second quarter of the nineteenth century, matters improved dramatically. By 1849 there were 37 public pump-houses, whereas in 1827 there had been only two for the whole city—an increase of over eighteenfold. Moreover, by the 1850s St. Petersburg had at least a thousand water carriers who purveyed water from pumps scattered about the city. The colors of the barrels distinguished their appropriate usage. The white barrels contained relatively clean drinking water from the Neva; less pristine water, in yellow barrels, came from the more polluted River Fontanka, while the liquid in the aptly colored green barrels was taken from the more stagnant canals and so was definitely not drinkable. There were also numerous wells in the city, 1,320 by 1839. Yet as the century progressed it became apparent that the further development and capitalization of water treatment and distribution were necessities. To this end the St. Petersburg Water Pipelines Joint-Stock Company was established in 1858. By that year the city's population had grown to half a million. The company oversaw the construction of the prominent 54-meter (175-foot) water tower on Shpalernaya Street, built by the architect Ivan Merts and the engineer Ernest Shubersky. As such it was one of the key features in the city's new water and sewerage system introduced in 1863, which, however imperfectly, looked for its inspiration to that of London, which in turn was only recently renovated in the wake of a disastrous cholera epidemic.

By 1881 the infrastructure of water in the capital had improved dramatically. At least five thousand houses, that is, half the housing stock, now had running water. Moreover, by 1889 the initial technical problems which had troubled the city's new water system had been overcome as a network of water filters came into function. Still, many of the poor, crammed into the upper floors of tenements, remained without, so it was only at the turn of the century that running water on tap became available throughout the city. Electricity was also introduced, and by 1884 Nevsky Prospekt was illuminated by it.

Becoming Modern

Peter the Great's dream had been to make St. Petersburg an important center of shipping in Europe and the most important in Russia. Within a century of his death this had become a reality, and by 1830 there was a thriving shipping industry in the western capital, supported by some 2,500 paid workers as well as by thousands of serfs. Trade was booming and the Swiss-Italian architect Luigi Rusca (1758–1822) built the Feather Lane Portico (1802–06) on Nevksy Prospekt, near the Merchants' Court—really a prestigious entrance to the trading houses behind—as well as remodeling parts of the Winter Palace. He, in turn, influenced another Italian architect, Giovanni Lucchini, who built a series of warehouses (1826–32) in the vicinity of the Stock Exchange, suitably large and imposing for their purposes. This construction was in part facilitated by the introduction of platinum from the Ural Mountains used for coinage from 1828 until 1845.

The number of factories in the city increased, in particular those powered by steam, which increasingly came to depend on skilled wage-workers rather than poorly motivated serfs. Some were designed in ever more eclectic architectural styles, evincing the influence of Konstantin Ton (1794–1881), a native of St. Petersburg who had built the Cathedral of Christ the Savior in Moscow in a so-called Russo-Byzantine style, a building blown up by Stalin but rebuilt during the post-Soviet period. A student of the Academy of Art, he had studied, like so many architects and artists before him, in France and Italy, returning home to reinterpret what he had seen in a style deemed by the national romantic movement to be appropriate for Russia. In St. Petersburg he submitted a design for the St. Catherine's Church in the Kolomna district, but his most famous work actually completed was the Church of the Annunciation (1843–49) and the Nikolaevsky Railway Station (1849–51), today the city's Moscow Station. The Passage Shopping Arcade on Nevsky Prospekt (1846–48) was also designed in a neo-Renaissance style by the Russian architect Rudolf Zheliazevich. Even today, it is one of the city's most important arcades. It opened its doors in 1848 and included a hall for literary and other cultural events, now used as a theater. All these developments were indicative of the role the capital had assumed by becoming one of Europe's largest and most important cities. By 1890 its population had almost doubled in comparison to just over thirty years before, and it retained its highly cosmopolitan mix, with 15 percent of its residents of foreign birth. All this vast population was accommodated by the turn of the century in more than 22,200 homes, palaces and hovels, among the best and the worst in the whole of Europe.

Transport was immensely important for Russia, economically, socially, and culturally. Thus the arrival of the railway was of great significance in the country, the world's largest. In particular, the importance of the rail link between St. Petersburg and Moscow, the two Russian capitals, cannot be underestimated. So the opening in St. Petersburg in 1851 of the Nikolaevsky Railway Station, named in honor of Tsar Nicholas I and designed by Konstantin Ton, took on great symbolic importance. A highly eclectic building, its style combines traditional Russian architectural elements such as double-arched bays with those of the Italian Renaissance and Baroque. In 1843 the first omnibus came into service along Nevsky Prospekt, while the tram arrived in September 1907, its cars produced by the British firm Brush. Since in the early 1900s they were the only form of transport which regularly crossed the Neva in winter, with their rails laid down on the ice. The need to construct permanent bridges across the Neva became apparent if transport communications were to thrive. As a result, a number of temporary bridges were replaced by permanent structures. The old pontoon Palace Bridge, for example, gave way to the present-day cast-iron replacement in 1912–16.

Horseless vehicles were introduced early into St. Petersburg, popular among the country's aristocratic, industrial, and mercantile elite. Yet there was a practical side to the interest in these vehicles and the Russian inventor Fedor A. Blinov (1827–1902) introduced a track car into Russia as early as 1877, in reality a tractor for agricultural use. Then, in 1896, the Yakovlev engine factory and the Freze carriage makers, based in Moscow, brought out the country's first automobile, which ran on petrol. It functioned with a single horizontal cylinder positioned at the vehicle's rear and produced up to two horse power. Hippolyte V. Romanov, in turn, introduced the city's first electric car, the Cuckoo, in 1899. In the following years a range of Russian-built cars were introduced, including the Russo-Balt, one of whose cars won ninth place at the Monte Carlo Rally of 1912 and second place at the San Sebastián Rally the following year, when racing driver Andrei P. Nagel as given an award by Tsar Nicholas II for his services to the industry. Although motor car production continued into and throughout the Soviet period, motor racing—considered an unacceptable bourgeois activity—did not. Yet it was Moscow rather than St. Petersburg (then Leningrad) which was and remained the center of motor car production.

War, Revolution, and Twentieth-Century Decline

On the cusp of the First World War St. Petersburg was a thriving European capital with positive economic, cultural, and social prospects. Indeed, even after the devastating toll of the war, the city, now renamed Petrograd to disassociate it from its former German name, had increased its population since the turn of the century by over 70 percent, to some 2,420,000 inhabitants. Had the First World War and Revolution not intervened, it might have enjoyed a continuation of this economic and social flourishing for decades to come. Instead, a major decline ensued. Two revolutions and a civil war devastated the urban fabric of the city.

Although the First World War did not inflict damage on the city as did the Second, its people suffered greatly and food supplies became scarce as the demands of war on manpower and resources severely undermined Petrograd's logistical infrastructure, leading to numerous strikes and riots, the worst of which erupted on March 8, 1917. This was followed two days later by a general mutiny of troops in the capital, an event that played into the hands of the elected Duma, jealous of its own authority, which ignored the tsar's command to dissolve. His powerlessness to avert a collapse of the imperial regime was now clear to all, even within his own family, and the vacuum was filled by the parties of the political left. On March 12 a Provisional Government was formed under the leadership of Prince Georgy Lvov, who was chairman of the Union of Provincial Assemblies and Municipalities. Three days later, Tsar Nicholas II, a saintly man but poor leader (as even his mother the Dowager Empress Maria Feodorovna admitted in her private diaries), abdicated on behalf of himself and his hemophiliac son Alexey. His brother, the Grand-Duke Michael, was next in the line of succession, but ultimately refused unless a Constitutional Assembly were to acclaim him. This never happened and the jockeying for power continued behind the scenes under the ineffectual rule of the Provisional Government, with factions for and against Russia's continued involvement in the First World War an important factor. Conflict with the Petrograd Soviet (Council of Workers' and Soldiers' Deputies) also undermined military order since the Soviet's issue of the infamous Order No. I challenged the authority of military officers while giving considerable powers to ordinary enlisted men loyal to the Soviet.

This volatile mix was ignited by the arrival from exile in Switzerland of Vladimir Lenin and his Bolshevik entourage at the Finland Railway Station on the Petrograd Side on April 16. They advocated a transfer of power from the Provisional Government to the Soviets and the end of hostilities with Germany (which had provided Lenin with a railway carriage to cross Germany on his way through Scandinavia to Petrograd). He also supported the expropriation of land throughout Russia for redistribution to the peasants and the transfer of industrial ownership to the workers' committees. In these goals he was supported by Leon Trotsky, who arrived in May from New York.

Matters deteriorated in Petrograd and on July 20 Prince Lvov resigned, his role taken over by a socialist, Alexander Kerensky. General Lavr Kornilov, military commander-in-chief, carried out an assault on Kerensky's government which failed, but this enabled the Bolsheviks to further entrench themselves in the capital, which led to the Revolution on November 6 (in October according to the old Julian Calendar). The Winter Palace was stormed but Kerensky managed to escape dressed as a woman and fled into exile. Although the elections to the Constituent Assembly gave the Bolsheviks a minority of the votes in January 1918, their Red troops successfully seized power by force. The opposition—monarchist, democratic republican, even other parties of the left—refused to accept this outcome, leading to a vicious civil war in the country which raged from 1918 to 1920. Petrograd was forced to undergo the greatest political, social, and cultural upheavals it has ever experienced before or since. Ultimately the Bolsheviks or Reds were victorious, despite the military actions of the Allied powers in supporting their enemies, the Whites, and Petrograd was reduced to a satrapy of Moscow. Thousands of "enemies of the people" were murdered during this period and the overwhelming majority of the nobility and large sections of the middle classes fled abroad, carrying only the clothes on their back, on occasion with valuables—which meant death if they were caught—woven into their fabric.

The capital was moved back to Moscow in 1918 and St. Petersburg languished over the following decades—a few workers' housing complexes and factories in the Constructivist style notwithstanding—until the Second World War. The Soviet authorities tried to restructure the former imperial city, now named Leningrad, in line with the new ideology. The spacious apartments that had belonged to the pre-revolutionary middle classes were divided up into the so-called *kommunalki*, communal flats with often entire families sharing single rooms and with one lavatory and bath serving fifteen to twenty people. It is estimated that some 68 percent of Leningrad's inhabitants lived in this way by the mid-1930s. Later, plans were made to resettle some of these in the southern suburbs where new residential complexes were envisioned. Their construction design turned its back on Constructivism, adopting instead the heavy neoclassical style preferred by Stalin. The overwhelming majority of these, however, had to await the postwar years of the late 1940s and 1950s to come to fruition.

German bombardments during the Second World War (discussed in Chapter 5) destroyed virtually all of St. Petersburg's suburbs and much of the inner city, leaving only the shells of buildings standing. Yet the basic street plan remained and the old capital was resurrected in the post–World War years. Many buildings gutted by bombing and shelling were rapidly rebuilt in an extraordinary celebration of skilled labor. What the French visitor, the Marquis de Custine, wrote about the city toward the middle of the nineteenth century became true a hundred years later: "even the edifices that appear the most ancient have been reconstructed but yesterday..." Then, during the final years of Stalin, new stately residences were constructed on the city's outskirts and Leningrad underwent another period of major demographic growth. This lasted for decades. Whereas in the late 1950s it had just under three million inhabitants, by the late 1970s the city could claim over four million.

As a result of this growth and conquests made during the war from Finland, new suburbs joined Leningrad, incorporating territory which formerly belonged to Finland on the Isthmus of Karelia. These included what are today Sestroretsk and Zelenogorsk. All such developments, both to the north and south, required an improved transport infrastructure and to this end the Leningrad Metro underground system, initially designed in the late 1930s, was constructed. Operations commenced in 1955, and the initial eight metro stations rivaled those of Moscow with their elaborate interiors, magnificently decorated with revolutionary themes in marble, bronze, and mosaics. Later stations were more modest in appearance in accordance with the increased focus on quantity rather than quality.

Increased austerity was also apparent in the widespread construction of the *Khrushchyovka*, low-cost, prefabricated blocks of two- or three-room apartments first produced under the leadership of Nikita Khrushchev from the 1960s. While far from the classical dignity and grandeur of Stalinist architecture, they were a vast improvement on the *kommunalka* or communal flat in the sense that they gave families some modicum of privacy. A rush to the suburbs ensued, with commercial centers growing up to serve them. More stylistically sophisticated apartment complexes came to be built during the 1980s, a nod to the architectural beauties of St. Petersburg, but often with shoddy construction standards as the economy of the dying Soviet Union contracted and food rationing was introduced. This was the period of *perestroika* (restructuring) and *glasnost* (opening), introduced under premier Mikhail Gorbachev, who sought to revive the flagging economy of the Soviet Union while liberalizing its political system from within.

Post-Soviet City

With the ultimate failure and fall of the Soviet Union in 1991, Leningrad underwent dramatic changes, especially under the administration of Anatoly Sobchak, its first democratically elected mayor. Controversially at the time, the city was renamed St. Petersburg but other issues were more challenging, not least the growing criminality which reached a peak under his successor, Vladimir Yakovlev, who took office in 1996. Sobchak was later murdered not long afterwards but under the next governor (as the mayor was now called), Valentina Matviyenko, elected in 2003, the city came into its own, with funds provided to embellish it for its tercentenary celebrations that same year. Russia itself, meanwhile resurrected from the ruins of the Soviet Union as the Russian Federation, came under the administration of its first democratically elected president Boris Yeltsin (1931–2007) and he it was who propelled a native St. Petersburger Vladimir Putin (born 1952) into the political limelight. Having studied law in St. Petersburg and then joined the KGB, Putin resigned from the secret service to enter politics in his native city. By 1999 he was appointed acting president as one of Yeltsin's colleagues, and won the 2000 presidential election by a wide margin after Yeltsin had resigned. Two terms of office then followed, during which Russia enjoyed a startling economic recovery and reduction of crime. St. Petersburg, along with Moscow, was a principal beneficiary of this economic upsurge and the city benefited in many ways under his administration. When Putin was obliged to relinquish the reins of presidential power, his close colleague and fellow lawyer Dmitry Mevedyev was elected president. He appointed Putin prime minister in what came to be known as "tandemocracy" because of the closeness with which they collaborated.

It was during this period that the restoration and development of St. Petersburg as a tourist destination became an important priority. Not only many townhouses in the city but magnificent suburban palaces left in ruins by the Germans, like Peterhof and Tsarskoe Selo (discussed more fully in Chapter 12), rose again like phoenixes, attracting many visitors. These include dozens of UNESCO World Heritage Sites, making St. Petersburg and its environs one of the most concentrated places in the world for such monuments of global value. Many historical buildings were turned over to businesses, hotels, and banks, as well as museums.

This renaissance demanded that St. Petersburg's infrastructure of roads undergo major development, partly through the construction of new motorways and a ring road, not only lessening traffic congestion within the city—where the use of the car has increased exponentially, further exacerbating the pollution caused by antiquated industries—but improving links to Moscow to the east and Helsinki to the west. New luxury suburbs have come into being, along with a boom in middle-class condominiums, with a local infrastructure of supermarkets, cinemas, and other amenities. The maritime port, meanwhile, has also experienced a remarkable process of development, providing not only berthing for cruise ships and military vessels but a mercantile trade of about 60,000 tonnes in 2008.

Other forms of economic activity have also thrived in St. Petersburg, even if Moscow remains the heart of Russian capitalism. It has even boasted its own resident billionaire oligarch, Viktor Vekselberg, a native of Ukraine, whose money was initially made in the aluminium industry. Unlike many oligarchs, who prefer to spend their money on football or yachts, Vekselberg took a keen interest in the arts and put together one of the finest private collections of Fabergé jeweled eggs, originally made for the imperial family, by purchasing them from the US Forbes publishing dynasty. The collection is now displayed in the newly restored Shuvalov Palace on the Fontanka Embankment along with 4,000 other works of decorative art.

In 2012 Putin once again entered the electoral fray and was re-elected president for his third term of office. The falling price of oil, one of Russia's principal commodities, in 2014, and the imposition of sanctions on Russian imports by the US and the European Union, who accused Russia of military intervention in Ukraine and the "annexation" of Crimea—accusations vigorously contested by Russia—reversed some of the progress that had been made. Many inhabitants of St. Petersburg suffered economically and the material fabric of the city, always requiring constant upkeep in the damp cold weather which prevails for so much of the year, was undermined. Only recently, as oil prices have stabilized and internal measures were taken to compensate for the sanctions, have matters improved. Despite everything, St. Petersburg remains one of Europe's principal tourist destinations, with more than two million foreign visitors in 2016.

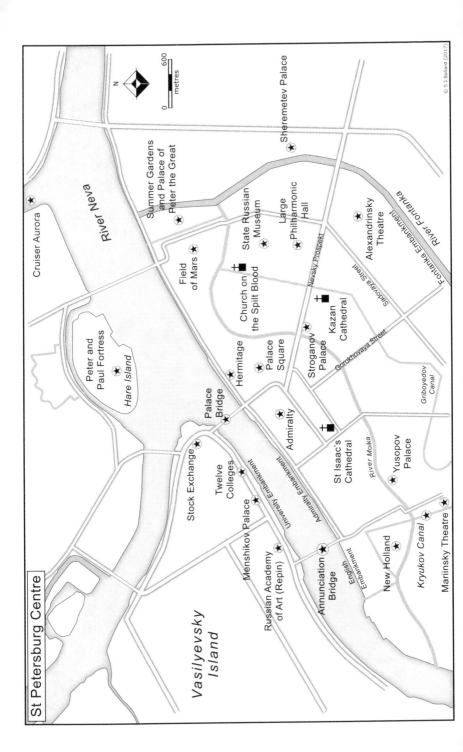

St Petersburg Centre

© S J Ballard (2017)

3 | Face of the City
Iconic Buildings and Architectural Styles

W hile Sweden's last attempt to recapture the site of St. Petersburg failed in 1708, a number of other threats hung over the city, as it was vulnerable not only to military incursions and floods, but to fire. At its foundation there was already an awareness of the danger of fire which confronted cities and towns built of wood. Unlike almost all other Russian cities and towns, the use of fireproof materials, brick and more importantly stone, was encouraged and in many instances required, at least in the heart of the city. But finding the stone that would make St. Petersburg less vulnerable was no easy matter. In 1714 construction in masonry elsewhere in Russia was curtailed so as to make more stone available for building in St. Petersburg. More drastic measures were also taken: vast quantities of stone were levied from 1714 to 1776 from virtually all ships and carts entering the capital, much of which was used to provide the foundations of buildings. Even then, though, the quantity was insufficient and many buildings, especially in outlying areas, continued to be constructed of wood. As a result, fires continued to ravage the city at varying intervals, that of 1736–37 being the worst in this early period.

Yet St. Petersburg was, and remains, one of the world's most resilient cities. It survived the attacks, floods, and fires of its infancy and by 1712 was secure enough for the court to be moved to St. Petersburg from Moscow. The Senate followed in 1713 and the Holy Synod of the Russian Orthodox Church (which had superseded the patriarchate by imperial command as the highest administrative body of the Church), along with the various ministries, was also established in the new capital. Of course there was opposition to these developments in Moscow, former seat of the patriarch, which looked at the new capital with a mixture of disdain and distrust.

It was not so much Moscow that was the fledging city's principal rival—in economic if not in political and religious terms—but the city of Arkhangelsk on Russia's northern White Sea coast. English merchants had been established at this port on the Northern Dvina River since the mid-sixteenth century and it was not about to relinquish its economic privileges lightly. But the autocratic powers of the tsar were not to be underestimated, and when Peter the Great forbade the transport of bread through Arkhangelsk in 1710 there was little the city could do to resist. Three years later the "Autocrat of All the Russias," as the Russian tsar was officially styled, added potash, tar, jute, red caviar, glue, and bristles to a list of banned trade items. This formerly prosperous mercantile port now came to play a decreasingly significant role. By 1725 the new Russian capital, granted highly valuable internal customs privileges, could boast of trade eight times greater than that of Arkhangelsk.

Shipping and trade were now the mainstays of St. Petersburg. In 1720 alone 75 ships visited the city; two years later, their number had grown to 119 and by 1724 to 240. The overwhelming majority of these seagoing vessels were Dutch or British, carrying comestibles and manufactured goods such as sugar, coffee, wine, and fabrics—silk and cotton. Russian fur, skins, linen, and other domestic commodities were exported in turn to far corners of the globe. Eighteen countries were by now trading with Russia directly from various European ports. As the century wore on and despite various economic ups and downs, at least 250 to 300 ships were arriving in the port each year, and taking into account Kronstadt, the naval base situated on Kotlin Island just outside St. Petersburg, during the 1780s and 1790s this number more than trebled to a thousand.

Palatial St. Petersburg

Maritime trade meant the accumulation of wealth and as a result the city's magnates acquired both money and political power, albeit subject to the whims of the tsar. To express their usually newly found and somewhat precarious social positions—they could be exiled or dispossessed at a moment's notice—these magnates frequently built palaces of astonishing beauty, most of which survived their fall. Indeed, these palaces vied in grandeur with those built by order of Peter himself, which embellished the city with its earliest architectural treasures. As early as 1712, one of St. Petersburg's residential jewels stood completed, yet another contribution by the Italian architect Domenico Trezzini to the city's architecture. This was the diminutive Summer Palace of Peter the Great, located on the banks of the Fontanka river near its confluence with the Neva. While its interiors clearly reveal Flemish influences, some French elements are apparent and it is known that the French architect Le Blond himself designed at least one of its rooms.

The palace that was built for the tsar's favorite prince, Alexander Danilovich Menshikov (1673–1729), the city's first governor and a self-made man, was much more splendid, showing the Italian influences which now dominated not only Russian but northern European architectural tastes. It was designed by the Italian-Swiss architect Giovanni Maria Fontana and is an imposing building, the largest palace of its time in the new capital and the first to be built in stone. Even today it retains its magnificence, not least by virtue of its commanding position at University Embankment on Vasilyevsky Island where it operates as a branch of the Hermitage Museum. Its flanking wings were added in the early 1720s by the German Gottfried Johann Schädel and its interiors still reflect the importance of the Dutch influence which continued to dominate the aesthetics of virtually all St. Petersburg palaces of the time. Of particular note in this regard are the tiled interiors of many of its rooms—recently restored—many of which are among the most impressive of their type in all Russia. As such, it bears comparison with the so-called Kikin Hall, built in 1714 for the courtier Alexander Kikin, a favorite of Peter before his disgrace and execution four years later. Menshikov, too, was perceived to have overstepped the mark and his presumed hubris, political as well as architectural, led to his fall after the death of the tsar in 1725. As a result, Menshikov only briefly enjoyed his palace. Falling from imperial favor in 1727, he was condemned for corruption (as still happens in Russia, witness the case of Mikhail Khordokovsky) by the Supreme Council, over which the rival Dolgorukiy family, which governed in the name of the new underaged and short-lived Tsar Peter II, had assumed control. Menshikov's palace was confiscated and in 1729 he and his family were exiled to Beryozovo, in Siberia, just one of millions of individuals throughout the long history of Russia to suffer such a forced eastward migration and captivity. The palace was then given over in 1731–32 to the newly founded military college known as the Cadet School for the Nobility, run by Field Marshal Minich. Offering the finest education in Russia, it provided teaching in a variety of languages including German, French, English, and Latin, along with education in literature, history, mathematics, and physics. The muses were also not forgotten, and both painting and dancing featured prominently, along with the noble martial art of dueling—so lethal to many Russian literary figures of the following century. A splendid library was also provided, lifting the education of young noble officers to a level unparalleled in the history of Russia up to that time.

Meanwhile Peter II died, the victim of smallpox, which claimed so many lives before the introduction of inoculation and vaccination later in the eighteenth century, and with his demise—Peter the Great had already been implicated in the death of his only son—the direct male Romanov line was extinguished. The Empress Anna, niece of Peter the Great, then acceded to the imperial throne and moved the court back to St. Petersburg from Moscow, to which Peter II and his court had briefly retired for a period of three years. Almost immediately, the Dolgorukiys were themselves exiled to Beryozovo, following in the footsteps of the banished Menshikov, only to be eventually executed in the time-honored Russian tradition of new leaders removing political rivals.

Once again, a spate of further new palace building followed in the wake of the re-establishment of the imperial seat in St. Petersburg. This was spurred on by the elevation of the Empress Elizabeth, the younger daughter of Peter the Great, to the throne in 1741, the commencement of a relatively long reign which continued for a generation until 1761. She demonstrated herself to be among Russia's most cultured monarchs and contributed greatly to its development in this regard. Before her ascension to the throne she already maintained her own orchestra and choir and thereby laid the foundations for what would become one of the world's greatest musical cultures. The imperial choir became the stuff of fairy tales after the empress became infatuated with one of its choristers, a former Cossack shepherd named Alexei Rozum (1709–91), who had been discovered singing in his village church by a passing military officer who then brought him to St. Petersburg. There he entered into a morganatic marriage with Elizabeth (such became a custom for Russia's ruling empresses) who elevated him to the nobility as Count Alexei Grigorievich Razumovsky. So was founded a new noble dynasty, members of which flourished in Russia and in the Austrian Hapsburg Empire during the imperial period—Prince Andrey Razumovsky, a diplomat, had a quartet, the centerpiece of which is its majestic march, dedicated to his name by Beethoven in the early nineteenth century.

The tsarina presented her husband with the new Baroque Anichkov Palace, built from 1741 to 1750, largely the work of the Russian architect Mikhail Zemtsov (1688–1743), although Francesco Bartolomeo Rastrelli later made a major contribution to its interior decoration. It remained the seat of imperial favorites throughout most of the eighteenth century: a generation later Catherine the Great gave it to her own paramour and later morganatic husband Field Marshal Grigory Potemkin. On that occasion, the Russian architect Ivan Starov (1745–1808) incorporated a wide range of the neoclassical details into the palace which had become so fashionable by that time.

The Stroganov Palace, built by Rastrelli in 1752–54 on the southeastern corner of Nevsky Prospekt and Moika, is still today one of the architectural highlights of Baroque St. Petersburg. Count Sergei Stroganov, its first owner, was a relation of the Tsarina Elizabeth and the scion of a family whose wealth emanated from the salt mines and foundries of the Ural Mountains. It was later restored in the early nineteenth century by Andrey Voronikhin (who also built Kazan Cathedral; see Chapter 9), who was born a serf of the Stroganov family but was eventually emancipated. Today the palace belongs to the Russian Museum and contains a splendid collection of Lomonosov Imperial Porcelain among other works of art.

Rastrelli's fifty-room Vorontsov Palace was built in 1749–58 for Count Mikhail Vorontsov, another relative of the Empress Elizabeth and who was of special service to her because he had helped her to mount the throne. The site on which it is situated is unusually large, stretching from the Fontanka to Sadovaya (Garden) Street. Whereas the Stroganovs continued to occupy their palace until the outbreak of the Revolution in 1917, the count, upon his retirement, was obliged to sell it when Catherine the Great came to the throne.

Also of note was the Apraksin Palace, constructed on the site where the Winter Palace now proudly stands by the French architect Jean-Baptiste Le Blond from 1717 to 1725. It contained thirty rooms and was a byword for splendor at the time. This monumental Baroque edifice was built for Fedor Apraksin (1661–1728), a relative by marriage of the tsar and a leading admiral who eventually became commander of Russia's newly established Baltic Fleet in 1723. Under his command, the Russian Navy achieved new heights. By the following year it had 141 sailing ships and hundreds of galleys. This enabled it to assume an important naval role in the Baltic for most of the remainder of the century. It successfully took Memel (Tallinn, in today's Estonia) during the Seven Years' War in 1757, and it kept Sweden at bay in the Battle of Högland in 1788 and that off Viborg in 1790. That would prove to be the zenith of Russian naval might, however, for at the Second Battle of Svensksund later that year it suffered a major defeat, with more than 9,500 casualties out of 14,000 men, thereby ending the war. Never again would the Russian Navy assume the Baltic prominence it had enjoyed earlier in the century.

The Admiralty

Originally established by Peter the Great as a fortified shipyard in 1704, the Admiralty building was rebuilt according to a design by Ivan Korobov from 1730. Its unmistakably elegant spire is one of St. Petersburg's most beautiful and conspicuous sights and can be seen from many vantage points throughout the city. The inspiration for its construction came not from Russia but from Holland, where Korobov studied from 1718 to 1727 and where Peter the Great had gone to better appreciate shipbuilding. The navy was, of the course, the pivot upon which most of his military plans with respect to the city were focused and nobody was a more enthusiastic sailor than Peter. As the British naval officer and hydraulic engineer Captain John Perry, employed by the Russian government to survey and supervise the construction of the Volga-Ladoga canal, noted at the time, his courtiers were rarely as keen:

> ...unless some very extraordinary Thing happen to prevent him, he sails and plies to Windward upon the Ice with his said Boats, with Jack-Ensign and Pennant flying in the same manner as upon the Water. But his Lords have no Relish nor Pleasure in those Things, and although they seemingly complement [sic] the Czar whenever he talks to them of the Beauties and Delights of Petersburgh; yet when they get together by themselves, they complain and say that there are Tears and Water enough at Petersburgh, but they pray God to send them to live at Moscow.

The Admiralty which we see today in all its neoclassical glory is, however, a construction of almost a century later, the work of Professor Adrian Zakharov, carried out from 1806 to 1823. With its many statues based on the gods, goddesses, and heroes of classical mythology and history—Neptune, Achilles, Ajax, and Alexander the Great—it is crowned by a commanding tower adorned by 28 stone columns. These support a vast cornice embellished with 28 sculptures representing the four elements of nature—air, earth, fire, and water—as well as the winds and the seasons of the year. Yet what is most intriguing in its decoration is the series of symbols derived from freemasonry, strange at a time when the movement itself was vigorously condemned by both state and Church.

It has been suggested that the statues above the Admiralty's colonnade represent—in units of four—the seasons, the elements, and the points of the compass. To what degree its complex symbolism was obvious to freemasons themselves is still debated, but this secret society had long been established in the city—as far back as 1731—and many saw the reforming values of Peter the Great as in harmony with those of freemasonry. Moreover, both Alexander Stroganov, president of the Imperial Academy of Arts, and Piotr Chekalevsky, its vice-president, were well-known as highly influential freemasons and Western-thinking intellectuals who followed the Swedish rite of the order. As Mikhail Safonov has put it, bearing in mind that the Masonic Lodge in St. Petersburg was named Urania and that the Egyptian goddess Isis figured prominently in masonic cryptic imagery, it is worth considering how "the arched main entrance [is] flanked by pedestals upon which sculptures of nymphs support spheres, and also the figures of the ancient goddesses Isis and Urania on the upper colonnade." Certainly such eminences of the time as Pushkin, the architect Vasily Bazhenov and the powerful military figures Alexander Suvorov and Mikhail Kutuzov, were all freemasons and surely had no trouble deciphering the masonic message.

Third Winter Palace

An important element in propagating the values of the autocratic order in St. Petersburg was the construction of a third winter palace. This most important of commissions was given to Rastrelli and was under construction from 1732 to 1735. A wooden building built for the Empress Elizabeth, it was situated in and around what until 2007 was the Barrikada (Barricade) cinema, located between the Moika Canal and Bolshaya Morskaya Street. A vast structure with over two hundred rooms, its chapel and theater were of particular note, the latter especially favored by the empress. Yet it was its Amber Study (1743), in which numerous mirrors reflected the light of the amber panels, which most dazzled the eye—a harbinger of the later Amber Room of the Catherine Palace of Tsarskoe Selo. So appreciated was Rastrelli's work that it was natural that he should be appointed court architect in 1748, a position which enabled him to carry out other significant projects.

Among these was Rastrelli's last great work, the construction once again of a new winter palace, to be situated, interestingly enough, within the old (or third) Winter Palace. Typical of so many palaces built in St. Petersburg at this time, it was built around a large courtyard, and its construction lasted from 1754 to 1764 at the vast cost of 959,555 roubles. Such an enormous sum was not easy to raise even for a Russian autocrat and so the money for its construction was acquired from a levy imposed on taverns for that purpose. When completed, the 700-room complex was an architectural wonder of the world and a symbol of imperial munificence, its famous Jordan Staircase and grand gallery even now startling in their grandeur. As a result, Rastrelli was elevated to the rank of major general, a rare mark of honor for an architect at this time.

Other work by Rastrelli included the building of the third Summer Palace (1741–44), located in the old Summer Garden of Peter the Great not far from his former summer residence there, where later the Mikhailovsky Castle came to be built. When completed, it contained over 160 apartments and represented the apogee of Italian and French Rococo influence in the city. Nonetheless, it graced the capital for only a few years; it was torn down in 1797 to make way for the construction of Tsar Paul I's beloved Mikhailovsky Castle, a monumental fortress-like edifice so unlike the Rococo-inspired, pastel-colored pleasure palace which had so recently preceded it, and where the tsar would later be murdered in a palace coup (see below).

Age of Science: The *Kunstkammer* of Peter the Great

Starting with Peter the Great, Russian rulers invariably devoted great financial resources to the development of education and culture in their western capital, a keystone in their attempts to bring Russia into line with the other great European powers. One of the most important early seats of learning was Peter's famous *Kunstkammer* (this German term literally meaning "art chamber" was fashionable for such establishments in this period), built in 1718–34 by the architects Georg-Johann Mattarnovy (who favored the incorporation of a central tower, not a typical fashionable feature of this period in St. Petersburg), H. F. Gerbely, Mikhail Zemtzvo, and the Italian Gaetano Chiaveri. It was not merely a museum of often ghoulish curiosities collected by and for the innovative tsar (the first museum in Russia), but also the seat of the newly founded Academy of Science. It moved to its present home later in the century, a building characterized by its imposing blue and white Baroque facade overlooking the University Embankment. Among the *Kunstkammer's* most striking features are its circular theater of anatomy and the astronomic observatory located at the top of the tower, both of which were intended to illustrate the fact that Russia, after many centuries of intellectual backwardness, was joining the first rank of scientifically curious European states. Today the *Kunstkammer* houses two other small museums as well, the former imperial Ethnographic Museum and the Lomonosov Museum, dedicated to the memory of that eminent scientist.

The age of Peter the Great was an era of scientific inspiration for Russia, and architecture was only one area in which this phenomenon expressed itself. Another was the famous expedition of the Dane Vitus Bering, which set off from St. Petersburg, where he himself was first taken into Russian service. Today the straits between Siberia and Alaska which he "discovered" still bears his name and, as such, indirectly gives honor to the tsar who hauled Russia into the modern age. The nation would, moreover, in the next generation have its own scientists and intellectuals who, as we shall see, went on to play important roles in its scientific, cultural and economic development.

In the forefront among these was Mikhail Lomonosov (1711–65), in many respects the father of Russian science. From his office in Peter the Great's *Kunstkammer*, where he worked from 1741 to 1765, Lomonosov helped to bring draughts of fresh air, intellectually speaking, into Russia, encouraging Russian academics and dilettantes to adopt the modern world of scientific hypothesis and verification by experimentation. Not without reason, therefore, it is his statue that was erected at the beginning of the Mendeleyev Line, along which many faculties of St. Petersburg's University, founded in 1819, are situated in the buildings originally designed for the use of twelve government ministries.

Lomonosov's life is fascinating in its own right. Born in the village of Denisovka, to the east of Arkhangelsk, he had first moved to Moscow in 1731 and thence on to St. Petersburg. Once in the new capital, he took up residence at the nearby Praskov-Feodorov Palace, the former home of Peter the Great's sister-in-law.

A man of literature as well as science, Lomonosov was instrumental in reforming the Russian prosody of his time. He was also a talented author and wrote two tragedies, *Tamira* and *Selim*, based on martial historical themes. As the Russian critic V. G. Belinsky put it, his importance for Russian culture should not be underestimated, writing: "our literature begins with Lomonosov: he was its father and mentor; he was its Peter the Great."

Cosmopolitan in a cosmopolitan age, Lomonosov's lifestyle was peripatetic. Returning to Moscow in 1736, he then went abroad to Germany not long afterward, only returning to St. Petersburg in 1741, from where he worked ceaselessly to develop a world-class scientific culture in Russia.

With respect to astronomy, he came to the conclusion that Venus possessed an atmosphere, based in part on his telescopic observations of the planet's transit made at an observatory near his residence in St. Petersburg. He also introduced improved technology for the construction of the telescopes themselves, which was well before its time and not unlike that later associated with William Herschel and his telescope decades later.

In terms of chemistry, Lomonosov recorded mercury's freezing point and devoted much attention to the subject of mineralogy and how it impacted on natural resources such as coal, peat, and petroleum. The peculiar characteristics of such Arctic features as icebergs also intrigued him. All these studies eventually led to his publication, *On the Strata of the Earth*, which appeared in 1763. It also enabled him to postulate the existence of another unknown continent to the south—which we now know of as Antarctica. He became fascinated with the pursuit of a Northwest Passage, even organizing an expedition to the coast of Siberia under the command of Admiral Vasily Chichagov, a passage only successfully achieved in our own day against a background of global warming.

Family Fortunes

While Peter the Great (and his imperial heirs) spared little in supporting men of science in their domains, he himself depended upon others to stabilize and extend the power and influence of Russian autocracy. Among the closest and strongest supporters of Peter the Great was Boris Petrovich Sheremetev (1652–1719), who only in 1706 was elevated to the rank of count although his family had been noted members of the nobility since at least the fourteenth century. Indeed, tradition has it that the Sheremetevs were descended from the Prussian Prince Michael Glanda Kamibla, who emigrated in flight from the Teutonic Knights to Russia, where he adopted Russian Orthodoxy.

The European title of count awarded to Sheremetev had been the first of its kind in Russia when granted by Peter the Great and thus had great symbolic value. He was also elevated to the rank of field marshal for his services during the war against Sweden, in which Russia achieved its conquest of Ingria on which St. Petersburg came to be founded. Boris' heir was Peter Borisovich Sheremetev (1713–88) and his famous Baroque palace on the River Fontanka was built by the serf architect F. C. Argynov in 1750–55, to the designs of Chevakinsky, the architect of the St. Nicholas Naval Cathedral, a glittering Baroque wonder of the capital. The palace also encompassed a theater, and a future generation in the nineteenth century would incorporate a large music room suitable for concerts, designed by the famous Italian architects Giacomo Quarenghi and I. Corsini in 1838.

The Yusupovs were another family that thrived under Peter the Great and, in turn, lent him their support. Said to be descended not only from the Muslim Tatar Khan Edege Mangit but the Prophet Mohammed himself, they entered the service of Ivan the Terrible in the later sixteenth century in the wake of his conquest of Kazan. Two generations later, their descendant Abdul Mirza converted to Russian Orthodoxy. It was the latter's son Grigory Yusupov (1676–1730) who became one of Peter the Great's most important supporters. Head of the College of War, he greatly assisted the tsar in both the Northern War against Sweden and in his military campaigns around the Lake of Azov in the far southeast. His son Boris (1696–1759) was also prominent at court but more in Moscow than St. Petersburg, where he was appointed governor during the reign of the Empress Anna.

But it was during the reign of Catherine the Great that the Yusupovs came to feature most prominently at court. Prince Nikolai Yusupov (1750–1831) was famed not merely for his vast wealth but as a man of intellect and patron of the arts. His correspondence with Diderot, Voltaire, and Beaumarchais was prodigious and deepened his ties to his imperial mistress. He traveled widely and visited the studios of the French painter Hubert Robert and the Italian sculptor Antonio Canova among others. Appointed a senator in the time of the Tsarina Elizabeth, he was appointed director of both the Hermitage and the Imperial Theaters. He also oversaw the empire's production of porcelain and glass. Indeed, it was he who provided the inspiration to produce copies of the Raphael Loggia in the Vatican for the Hermitage, depicting some 52 subjects from the Bible. Later in life he retired to his great estate Arkhangelskoye, near Moscow, which he turned into one of Russia's most magnificent private palaces and gardens, adorned with one of the country's greatest collections of works of art.

Aristocratic Addresses

Of course, Russia's imperial rulers were keen to establish their own great collections, as well as suitable buildings to accommodate them. To this end the French architect Jean-Baptiste Vallin de la Mothe carried out work on the old Small Hermitage (1764–65) adjacent to the Winter Palace, where the Tsarina Catherine the Great kept her magnificent collection of art. With vast wealth spent on one of the world's largest art collections, it came to include some of Europe's most important paintings, many of which can still be viewed there to this day.

Other palaces also underwent major restoration. The Stroganov Palace which was devastated by a fire in the early 1790s was renovated by the noted decorator Andrey Voronikhin (1759–1814). Born a serf on a Stroganov estate in the Urals, he revealed his artistic talents as a youth and was sent to Moscow to train under Russia's greatest architects Vasily Bazhenov and Matvey Kazakov. The brilliance of his architectural gifts and the projects on which he worked enabled him to be emancipated in 1786. The Stroganovs then sent him on an extended grand tour of Western Europe for further studies, after which he returned in 1790. Later, during the early nineteenth century, he would acquire international architectural fame for his masterpiece, the Kazan Cathedral, based on the designs of Bernini for St. Peter's in Rome (discussed in Chapter 9).

The most important palace construction of the period, however, was the renowned Marble Palace, today one of the seats of the Russian Museum and the venue for many contemporary exhibitions of both Russian and international art. Built in 1768–85 between the Field of Mars and Palace Quay for Count Grigory Orlov (1734–83), a favorite of Catherine the Great who had led the conspiracy which invested her with autocratic power, the palace is one of the Italian Antonio Rinaldi's (1710–94) most important constructions. Although neoclassical in style, it clearly shows the influence of the vast Late Baroque Royal Palace of Caserta, outside Naples, built by the architect Luigi Vanvitelli under whom Rinaldi had worked not long before. Trapezoidal in shape, its facades vary in terms of their decorative features, its polychrome marble plates which mask the Karelian granite beneath making it one of the most striking buildings in the city. It was extraordinarily costly in terms of its building materials and the expenses involved in bringing them to St. Petersburg. No fewer than 28 varieties of marble were utilized, imported not from Italy but from the far-flung reaches of the Russian Empire: Karelia in the case of the pink pilasters, the Ural Mountains in that of the white capitals and festoons and the blue-gray veined marble panels. The marble used for the ornamental urns came from near Tallinn, in present-day Estonia. With cost no object, some of the most famous craftsmen of the period were employed on its interior decoration, including the Italian painter Stefano Torelli (1712–84) and the Russian sculptors Fedor Shubin (1740–1805) and Mikhail Kozlovsky (1753–1802).

After Orlov's fall from grace the still uncompleted palace was let to another favorite, Stanisław August Poniatowski (1732–98), Poland's last king, and finally to the Grand-Duke Constantine Pavlovich and his heirs. It was one of them, the Grand-Duke Constantine Nikolayevich, who commissioned the palace's last major renovation, by Alexander Brullov in 1844–51, which, except for Rinaldi's grand staircase, altered the interiors dramatically, bringing in many elements of eclecticism so fashionable throughout Europe in the middle and late nineteenth century.

Another architectural landmark of this period was the Tauride Palace (1783–89) near the Smolny district, designed by Ivan Starov and built for Prince Grigory Potemkin. Its monumental temple-like façade embodies the simplicity of the Palladian style and stands in contrast to the more opulent interior. However, when the young British traveler Lionel Colmore visited the city in 1790, its uncompleted state made an unpleasant impact upon him, even if its gardens left a favorable impression. He wrote:

> The finest skeleton of a house (for there is nothing but bare walls) is Prince Potemkin's; it is but one story, but there is no end to the rooms, and they are all as immense as himself. There is one gallery two hundred feet long, with a double row of fifty pillars on each side; one of the sides opening into a winter garden, so large, that there are several walks in it, with a temple in the middle, in which is a statue of the Empress. In summer the window-frames are taken out, and the whole thrown open to a large English garden, where there are a piece of water, shrubberies, temples, ruins, &c.

After Potemkin died, Catherine made weekly autumnal visits there and continued to develop its gardens, in particular its winter garden, originally designed by William Gould. He had been invited to St. Petersburg to provide garden design due to the international fame of his work at Ormskirk, in Lancashire. Despite the fact that the site now houses the city's Botanical Gardens, the English imprint he put upon the surrounding gardens remains to this day, and not without justification he has been called the "Repton of

Russia," an allusion to Humphry Repton who left his mark upon so many English stately home gardens of that period.

The contents originally intended for the Tauride Palace were dispersed, however. Among the most famous was the Peacock Clock, a horological masterpiece by the London clockmaker James Cox, which is today one of the most prominent treasures of the Hermitage Museum (discussed in Chapter 7).

The Mikhailovsky Castle

Another Italian, Vincenzo Brenna (1747–1820), made a significant contribution to the face of St. Petersburg under the sponsorship of Tsar Paul I, Catherine the Great's obstreperous son, in the form of the Mikhailovsky Castle (later known as the Engineer's Castle). It was built on the site of the orangery of the third of the Summer Gardens. Initially Vasily Bazhenov had been asked to carry out the work on the site of Rastrelli's now demolished wooden Summer Palace, but the tsar favored the Italian. The results are a monumental, fortress-like complex, the stucco exteriors of which are painted a vivid pinkish orange. In early February 1801 Paul and his family took up residence there, with Carlo Bartolomeo Rastrelli's statue of Peter the Great, commissioned by the Empress Elizabeth, finally positioned in front of it.

Yet their stay was to be short-lived. The tsar, whose behavior had become not only a social but a political embarrassment, was murdered by dissident officers and courtiers in his bedroom on March 12, 1801. It was hardly an assassination in the usual sense of the term, since the highest reaches of government supported the intervention. The British government was also said by many to have been implicated. His son Alexander then succeeded to the throne of the Romanovs.

Not surprisingly in view of the events which took place there, no imperial personage ever chose to live in the palace again, and in 1820 it was given over to the army's School of Engineering. It was immortalized by Alexander Pushkin, his ode "Vol'nost" characterized by the haunting memories of regicide the castle has continued to evoke:

When on the dark Neva the star
Of midnight makes the water gleam,
When carefree eyelids near and far
Are overwhelmed with peaceful dream,
The poet, roused with intellect,
Sees the lone tyrant's statue loom
Grimly asleep amid the gloom,
The palace now a derelict.

Later another palace complex, again dedicated to St. Michael, arose in the heart of St. Petersburg, on what was formerly known as Mikhailovsky Square, but since Soviet days has been called Arts Square. Work on this majestic neoclassical Mikhailovsky Palace (1819–25) was directed by the Italian architect Carlo Rossi (1775–1849) and is notable for its majestic portico of Corinthian columns facing the square. On either side of this main block are two flanking wings with pavilions at each corner. Behind, overlooking the English gardens, the facade is adorned by a twelve-column Corinthian loggia. The interior is equally striking, its central feature being the grand central staircase which sweeps upwards from the ground floor to the public rooms above. In 1890, through imperial largesse, it was converted into a museum by the Russian architect Vasily Svinin. As part of the State Russian Museum it now houses some of Russia's most important works by native artists over the centuries, its only rival in this sense being the Tretyakov State Gallery in Moscow. Among its treasures is its vast collection of ancient icons, some from the studio of the painter and saint Andrei Rublev (c.1360s–1427).

Krestovsky Palace

Another palace of considerable note was the so-called dacha reconstructed on Krestovsky Island by the noble Beloselsky-Belozersky family, who bought the land from the Razumovsky family in 1803. The original hunting lodge had been built by Count Münich in the first half of the eighteenth century, but the Beloselsky-Belozerskys employed the architect Andrei Stackenschneider, already favored by Tsar Nicholas I. Rather than utilizing a contemporary style he took his inspiration from the Baroque designs of Rastrelli.

The dacha became their year-round residence in the 1880s after they sold their grand palace, also by Stackenschneider, on the banks of the River Fontanka in the heart of St. Petersburg (see below). The precarious state of their finances had forced the sale and as matters worsened Major General Prince Konstantin Esperovich Beloselsky-Belozersky entreated Tsar Nicholas II in 1903 to take the dacha, as well as his mines in the Urals, into a trusteeship. Although this proved successful and enabled the prince to salvage a certain portion of his resources and emigrate abroad before the revolutionary curtain fell, it reflected poorly on the imperial government for the public at large. As for the dacha itself, it fell victim to a German shell during the Second World War. However, it has recently been rebuilt by a property developer, using historical documents to ensure some degree of architectural accuracy.

The Stock Exchange

Among the most iconic buildings built in St. Petersburg during the first decade of the nineteenth century was the Stock Exchange (1805–10)—the Naval Museum from 1939 to 2010—a splendid edifice gracing the southern shore of the Neva by the eastern point of Vasilyevsky Island, in front of which are situated the famous pair of rostral columns. The terracotta columns, fueled by oil, served as beacons for the river's shipping and are studded with the prows of ships. The building itself had been planned as far back as 1783, but it was the Frenchman Thomas de Thomon who carried out the work to completion, choosing a Greek Revival style with respect to the plan and exterior derived from the Greek Temple of Hera at Paestum, south of Naples, in Italy. De Thomon's design features a total of 44 Doric columns on a red granite base, with a statue of "Neptune with two rivers – the Neva and the Volkhov" above the portico.

Conflagration at the Winter Palace

For visitors and residents of St. Petersburg alike, there was something diabolically beautiful about Russia's great capital, which had arisen from a swamp, full of magnificent architectural and artistic treasures, yet constructed with so much human suffering and sacrifice. This was a theme that has been part and parcel of its identity from its establishment and one which would continue through the Second World War to this very day. As Poland's most famous poet Adam Mickiewicz (1798–1855) wrote in his poetic drama *Dziady* (*Forefathers' Eve*):

> While Rome was built by human hands,
> And the gods constructed Venice;
> Anyone who gazes upon Petersburg
> Can entertain no doubts:
> It was the Devil who built this city.

Certainly it must have seemed on the fateful evening of December 17, 1837 that the devil was reclaiming his own when a major fire broke out at the Winter Palace just as the imperial family were attending the theater. It raged for two days and destroyed much of the building. There was time, however, to save much of its contents which were removed to Palace Square by regiments of the Imperial Guards. A famous anecdote relates that when Nicholas I saw a soldier attempting to salvage a looking glass firmly nailed to a wall, the tsar himself ordered him to abandon it and save his life. But the soldier persisted until his sovereign, still carrying his opera glasses, threw them at the looking glass, shattering it. "I told you it couldn't be saved!" Nicholas is said to have exclaimed, and the guardsman's life was saved.

A major restoration took place almost immediately afterwards. This made no attempt to restore the original interiors by Rastrelli but was carried out in a stylistically eclectic style characteristic of the spirit of that age. An exception, though, was the famed Jordan Staircase, which leads to the Rastrelli Gallery: structurally undamaged, it was faithfully restored according to Rastrelli's intentions by the Russian architect Vasily Stasov (1769–1848).

Tatyana Kukushkina, in her article "The Strange Feeling of a Full Stomach" provides a colorful account of the aftermath of the fire:

> By this time, the palace was a veritable city in itself, with some three thousand people performing a multitude of diverse activities, each with their own perquisites, not least of which was the tradition that palace servants were generally given the leftover food from the imperial tables. A negative consequence of this practice became apparent after the fire when the remains of countless dinners were found to have accumulated in the palace attics, causing both a great stench and a health hazard: not only leftover food was uncovered but animals feasting on the remains were discovered as well. On Rastrelli's instruction the enormous floor area of the Winter Palace attics had been covered with a thick carpet of felt for insulation. Plank walkways had been laid over the top of the carpet, and over the years small branches appeared, as if spontaneously, running off these walkways toward the eaves and ending in little stalls, pens, cages or lockers. Living in these, while being fattened for the table, were geese, turkeys, sheep and even pigs. So, above the heads of the imperial family there was something that can only be described as little short of a barnyard. This amazing fact emerged only during the fire. In its wake, witnesses recalled that the cries of the unfortunate creatures could sometimes be heard above the roar of the fire.

A variety of other more modest renovations took place in the following decades, and during the 1890s the sculptures embellishing the balustrade of the Winter Palace were recast in copper, in substitution for the original stone ones which had deteriorated over time.

Fire was indeed a major threat to the fabric of the city and to facilitate the handling of such outbreaks a tower was erected, attached to a building which later became the city's municipal duma. On its crown a device was placed that provided warnings of outbreaks of fire. It would later also serve another highly important purpose, namely as the starting point of an optical telegraph system which was begun in 1839. When completed in 1854 it was the world's longest, some 1,200 kilometers (750 miles), spanning the western plains of the Russian Empire from St. Petersburg to Warsaw.

Restoration problems, then as now, remained a serious issue for this fragile stucco covered city, afflicted not only by fires but buffeted by snow, wind, ice, and rain for so many months of the year. As a young British aristocrat Richard Bourke put it on a visit in 1845,

> I suspect the long winter of the north is an excellent friend to the tribe of masons, plasterers, &c.; for a town whose buildings are composed exclusively of brick and plaster is not likely to escape unscathed the attacks of six months of frost. Marble statues lose their noses as well as the inhabitants, and the skin equally peels off the faces of churches and Christians.

The New Hermitage

The famed German neoclassical architect Leo von Klenze (1784–1864), a native of Lower Saxony, was given the job of designing the New Hermitage Palace, which he did from 1839 to 1852. He opted for an eclectic neo-Renaissance style for what became the first purpose-built building intended to house a public museum in Russia. It was Giacomo Quarenghi, however, who constructed the famed Raphael Loggia, lying along the eastern facade of the New Hermitage, which strives to replicate the original one in the Apostolic Palace in Rome, where popes traditionally reside. The copies of Raphael's works which adorn its walls were painted by the Italian artist of Austrian extraction Cristopher Unterberger (1732–98).

The palace's most striking feature is its extraordinary portico composed of gray granite sculptures designed by Alexander Terebenev (1815–59) and sculpted with the assistance of some 150 serf craftsmen. These are in the form of ten monumental *atlantes*, columns in the shape of muscular men alluding to the Titan Atlas, the classical figure from Greek mythology famed for his physical strength since he was purported to carry the world on his shoulders. The use of such figures was unusual in Eastern Europe. Vasily Stasov, in turn, designed the top floor of the South Pavilion of the Small Hermitage, built from 1840 to 1843.

Stackenschneider's Legacy

Andrei Stackenschneider, whom we have already encountered, and who had previously won a stipend from the court which had enabled him to travel extensively in the cultural centers of Western Europe, received the commission to build the Mariinsky Palace (1839–44) for the Grand-Duchess Maria Nikolaevna. Situated opposite St. Isaac's Cathedral, it is constructed of a ruddy brown sandstone quarried in the vicinity in an eclectic style in which Renaissance and Baroque elements are combined. Today it is the seat of the government of St. Petersburg and its great rooms are among the most beautifully restored in the city. As such, it is the principal backdrop for the monumental equestrian sculpture of Tsar Nicholas I by the Baltic German Baron Peter Klodt von Jürgensburg (1805–67), who had already achieved fame with his statue of the fabulist Ivan Krylov, exhibited in the Summer Garden in 1855.

Another great building looking rather older than it really is is the Beloselsky-Belozersky Palace (1846–48), in reality a major neo-Baroque reconstruction of a previous building by Stackenschneider, situated on the far corner of Nevsky Prospekt by the Fontanka, across from the Anichkov Bridge. The original much smaller building, in a French Baroque style, had been built in 1747 for Prince Mikhail Andreevich Beloselsky. However, it was first in the nineteenth century that the palace took on its monumental proportions and appearance. For then Princess Elena Pavlovna Beloselsky-Belozersky instructed Stackenschneider, otherwise working exclusively as court architect for Tsar Nicholas I, to undertake a thorough reconstruction. This clearly looks back to the work of Rastrelli in the previous century, in particular his Stroganov Palace, and again the funds to pay for the work were derived from the Stroganov family's industrial activities in the Urals.

As we have already seen, the Beloselsky-Belozersky family ultimately preferred to live in its palatial home on Krestovsky Island and the palace on the Fontanka was eventually purchased by the imperial family, becoming a residence for the Grand-Duke Sergei Alexandrovich and his consort Elisabeth who again remodeled the structure, introducing old "Slavic" elements, in particular in the chapel. Grand-Duke Sergei, who had taken on the office of governor of Moscow, was assassinated at the Kremlin by a terrorist in 1905. Thereafter the palace was inherited by his widow and then by her ward Grand-Duke Dmitry who sold it on the eve of the Revolution. In the wake of the Revolution and until 1991 the palace served as the offices of a local Soviet, undergoing further restorations to repair war damage in 1954. Now a museum and concert venue, it suffered major fire damage in late February 2012 and is undergoing a major restoration.

Stackenschneider also carried out a new project, that of the Pavilion Hall at the Small Hermitage (1850–58), with its eclectic mix of Gothic, Renaissance and Oriental features. Shortly afterward he went on to design the New Mikhailovsky Palace (1857–61) on the Palace Quay. Built for the Grand-Duke Mikhail Nikolaevich, its neo-Rococo Grand Salon is a room of considerable opulence. Then Stackenschneider built the New Hermitage in 1864, after which time the art collection was opened to general public.

The indefatigable Stackenschneider was also responsible for the construction of another important St. Petersburg mansion, the famed three-story Nikolaevsky Palace (1853–61), which became the residence of the Grand-Duke Nikolai, the sixth child of Tsar Nicholas I. It was eventually given over in 1894 to a school for daughters of the nobility, the Xenia Institute for Wellborn Young Ladies, one of whose pupils left her vivid impressions of school days there. As Marta Aleksandrovna Almedingen (1898–1971) wrote in her English-language autobiography of 1963, after living in England for many decades where she worked as an author, particularly of children's books:

> At certain functions in the great panelled white hall it was easy to imagine yourself plunged into the court life of the late eighteenth century... The palace, for all its enormous size, was beautiful. The sweep of that regal, gray marble staircase, curving off to the right and the left, must have been an architectural marvel. We played in halls, their high ceilings supported by Corinthian pillars, their walls covered with most exquisite paneling. We read and studied in rooms with lovely mirrors, framed in the scrolled and carven fantasies of great artists. We slept in dormitories, their walls covered by delicate frescoes... The exquisite staircase... swept down to a hall where a gigantic Cerberus of a porter, magnificent in scarlet and gold, stood on duty. The great front doors, splendid with carved wood and panes of cut glass, were nearly always closed.

After the Revolution it was given over to trade unions which renamed it the Palace of Labor and dramatically altered much of the interior. Today is used as a theatrical venue often for folk dancing troupes, as well as offices for a variety of businesses.

The Nikolaevsky Palace was built not far from the city's first permanent bridge crossing the Neva, first named the Annunciation Bridge (1843–50) in honor of the church formerly situated at what is today Truda Square. The latticework arches which supported it greatly appealed to Petersburgers for their aesthetic qualities. Its cast-iron railings were designed by Alexander Brullov, while its lanterns and pavilions were the work of Leonid Noskov. As an astute contemporary wrote, "During the day, it looks transparent, as if it were composed of filigree, light as a wave, but at midnight illuminated, it becomes an immense mass which fuse together two cities."

With its 331-meter length and 24-meter breadth, it was the largest bridge in Europe at the time it was constructed and still today provides the most direct route to reach the imposing Russian Academy of Arts (see Chapter 6), situated at its far end on Vasilyevsky Island.

Many leading figures of the world of the arts at this time were nonetheless not enamored of these new and elaborate buildings.

Alexandre Benois (1870–1960), son of the court architect Nicholas Benois and himself a famous stage designer and art critic, wrote in *Mir iskusstva* lamenting the state of modern architecture. For him, its "pathetic parodies" of the German Renaissance, French Rococo, and Gothic were signs of the moral turpitude of the age. It was *moderne*, a Russian form of art nouveau, with its outrageous organic elements which he most condemned, an architectural and artistic symptom of the diseased decadence of his time.

Modern Trends

As the turn of the twentieth century approached and until the advent of the First World War, a great number of urban mansions and villas were constructed for prominent figures from the prosperous middle classes and from the world of the arts—music, art, and dance. Among the most prominent is the villa of Matilda Kshesinskaya (1872–1971), the prima ballerina of the Mariinsky Theater who worked closely with Marius Petipa, and mistress of Tsar Nicholas II while crown prince before his marriage, and who has recently become the subject of a controversial film *Matilda* (2017), directed and produced by Aleksey Uchitel. She later had intimate relations with two other members of the imperial family, for one of whom it is quite likely she bore a son. The villa was one of the most admired of its time, a supreme Russian interpretation of the Viennese Secessionist movement, as initiated by the famed Austrian architect Otto Wagner. Built by the German Alexander von Hohen at what is today 2–4 Kuybysheva Street on the Petrograd Side, it is lavishly decorated with ornamental ironwork and an eclectic mix of stone rustication or decorative masonry. In 1917 the Bolsheviks made it their headquarters, turning it later into a Museum of the Revolution. Today it houses the Museum of Political History, which focuses upon leading Russian political figures of the pre- and post-revolutionary periods.

The Chaev Mansion at 9 Rentgena Street was built for Sergei Chaev, an engineer involved in the construction of the Trans-Siberian Railway, by the Russian architect Vladimir Petrovich Apyshkov

(1871–1939) and is a highly important example of its type, antici-
pating as it does early architectural development toward the design
aesthetic of functionalism—with the emphasis on the purpose of the
building. As such, it reflects the ideas expressed in his seminal work,
The Rational in the Latest Architecture, published in 1905. His geometric modules, in particular his circular one, are combined in a way that
derives more inspiration from the United States than from Central
Europe: there is a picture gallery on the first floor and a cylindrical
conservatory brimming with tropical plants is also incorporated into
the house. Even so, more traditional features are still evident today,
most strikingly a parapet which crowns the building, although the
statue of a female nude in the Russian *moderne* (art nouveau) style
fashionable at the time has long since disappeared.

Russian neoclassicism, however, found its own revival in the
Polovtsov Dacha (1911–13) situated on Kamenny (Stone) Island,
commissioned by the diplomat Alexander Polovtsov, who had married the adopted daughter of the millionaire banker Alexander von
Stieglitz, one of Russia's most powerful financiers. Its exterior was
inspired by classical architecture from the age of Alexander I, while its
interior was especially noted for its so-called Gobelin Gallery adorned
by five French tapestries of great historical and artistic importance.

Perhaps a swan song of the imperial age, though, was the mansion of Ivan Aleksandrovich Fomin (1872–1936) built for Prince S.
S. Abamelek-Lazarev in 1913–15 on the Moika in the heart of the
city in a neoclassical style which clearly harks back to the early nineteenth century. Less than two years after its completion, the entire
political, economic, and social edifice of the old regime collapsed,
sweeping away the Romanov dynasty but leaving intact a marvel-
lous architectural legacy.

Commercial Palaces of the Industrial Age

During the later nineteenth century and into the twentieth commercial architecture in St. Petersburg reached its zenith. To the western side of the Merchants' Court, Luigi Rusca, a native of Lugano,
built the famous Feather Bed Line Portico (1802–06), characterized by its austere Doric portico, an embellishment to the essentially

eighteenth-century shopping complex. Doubtless the most iconic of such buildings, however, is the art nouveau Singer House, built by the Russian architect Pavel Suzor (1844–1919) in 1902–04 for the Russian branch of the Singer Sewing Machine Company. Situated at the corner of Nevsky Prospekt and the Catherine Canal (now Griboyedov Canal), its glass cupola with a metal framework surmounted by a globe is, along with the spire of the Admiralty, St. Petersburg's most famous rooftop image. On the cutting edge of modern technology at the time, its combination of a reinforced concrete frame, steel girders, plate glass windows, and fireproofing made it the mercantile showpiece of northern Europe. Suzor dealt with over a hundred projects in the imperial capital, including a remodelling of the Ushakov Building at 54 Nevsky Prospekt on the corner of Malaya Sadovaya Street, in which the famous confectionary shop of F. Ballet was located. Soon, however, with the advent of war and then revolution private commercial commissions became a thing of the past. Not until the late twentieth century, first with foreign-built hotels under *perestroika* in the late 1980s and privatization in the wake of the collapse of the Soviet system, did such initiatives revive; nor when they did, did their architectural qualities ever attempt to rival those of the imperial years. To be sure, the architecture of imperial St. Petersburg was never cozy and warm, but it was coldly fascinating. As the British novelist Somerset Maugham observed of the city's buildings in *A Writer's Notebook* (first published in 1949) when he visited St. Petersburg on a political mission late in revolutionary 1917: "There is something exquisitely strange in their architecture; the decoration is very simple and yet gives a sensation of being ornate; they remind you of a Dutch lady of the seventeenth century, soberly but affluently dressed in black. There is something prim about them, but not at all demure."

Palace of Workers

Building largely came to a halt with the advent and unfolding of the 1917 Revolution and the civil war which followed. Then architects such as Igor Fomin (1904–89), Ivan Fomin's son, reinvented themselves as architectural foot soldiers of the new socialist order.

In this context, his design for a Palace of Workers provided a model of what new types of public buildings were to be the priority of the new regime in the former capital now demoted to the state's second city, its reputation permanently tarnished by all the glories of its imperial associations. He could draw on his father's early work, Novy Peterburg on Goloday (now Dekabristov) Island, which looks back to Palladian classicism. It was built in 1911, the initiative of a British investment company which conceived of a vast housing development for the rising middle classes. Only one building there was actually completed and still stands today. Igor Fomin's residential design for the working classes, however, was never actually completed, though he did complete the Vosstaniya metro station in the city center during the 1930s. In any case, such monuments to Bolshevism today find few admirers in Russia, except for American and European intellectuals still fascinated by left-wing political idealism. Even such an undoubtedly left-leaning intellectual visitor as the Jewish-German Stefan Zweig (1881–1942) could still write with a grudging admiration, almost despite himself, in his *Travels to Russia*, recording his visit to the city in 1928, that

> There is nothing here of the architectural confusion which presses in Moscow all styles and costumes into one singled masked ball of stone. No! One notices it immediately, that here one single autocratic will has wished forth a city and formed it precisely in his mind's eye: its lord and founder, Peter the Great. His model was Amsterdam, but, three hundred years ago, with the presentment of Russia's great territorial expanse, he extrapolated its dimensions into the American; where there were small canals, here flowed broad ones, where there were European streets, here there were grand boulevards, radiating out from vast squares.

Yet the city had lost its previous dynamism: Soviet energies were now lavished on Moscow which had become the unrivaled seat of political, economic, and military power. As a result, St. Petersburg/Petrograd, from 1924 renamed Leningrad, became a "petrified city," more like a theater, but one in which "the light has been extinguished, the actors departed," as Zweig put it. To many of the nostalgic, it was as if the old capital had fallen into a slumber from which it would take over seventy years—a lifetime—to reawaken. However, awaken it did, but not until it had endured the horrors of war, blockade, and famine (see Chapter 5).

Architectural Revival

Despite the ravages of war, some historic mansions survived. Count Roman Vorontsov's palatial dacha, midway between Peterhof and Oranienbaum on the Gulf of Finland, had been set to be demolished in 1989 to make room for a new housing complex. It was spared, however, and converted into a church in 1999. The building which his daughter Princess Yekaterina Vorontsova-Dashkova, president of two academies, had designed for the Kiryanov estate also remains, a gem amidst the twentieth-century architectural horrors of the Narva district. Its chief fame today rests in the fact that the "Venetian Don Juan" Giacomo Casanova lived there during his visit to the Russian capital.

Today the Peterhof Road contains a collection of of UNESCO World Heritage sites (discussed in Chapter 12), just as the city of St. Petersburg itself does.

Alexander Solzhenitsyn (1918–2008), who won the Nobel Prize for Literature in 1970, wrote in "City on the Neva":

> What joy that nothing more can be built here! No squeezing a wedding-cake skyscraper into Nevsky, no slapping together a five-story box by the Griboyedov Canal... What a delight to wander down these avenues today! But it was with clenched teeth, cursing, rotting in murky swamps, that the Russians built this beauty. The bones of our ancestor packed and melted together, hardened into palaces—yellowish, grayish-brown, chocolate, green.
>
> Terrifying to contemplate: our unwieldy, perishing lives, all the eruptions of our discord, the moans of those shot dead and the tears of wives—will all this, too, be entirely forgotten? Will all this, too, give rise to such finalised, eternal beauty?

This, however, is no longer the case.

The ex-Lieutenant Schmidt Bridge, reconstructed during the 1930s after the demolition of much of its structure in 1929, recently underwent a major renovation which has kept its original famous piers and, along with its original name of Annunciation, restored its original appearance, except for the small chapel which Andrei Stackenschneider had built. Yet its otherwise historically accurate appearance masks the deployment of the latest technology and its added breadth of thirteen meters.

Already in the 1980s Leningrad had begun to undergo a modest revival. Even then the renowned local poet Joseph Brodsky in his *Less Than One* could extol its beauties, but with a twist in the tail:

> There was a city. It was the most beautiful city on the face of the earth. With an immeasurably gray river, which hung over its tributaries like the grey sky did over the river. Splendid palaces stood along the river which such wonderfully formed facades ... with the appearance of a giant mollusc named civilisation. Which was dead.

In 1991, the Hermitage Theater underwent a major renovation. This was followed by restorations of the city's most important theaters, including the Mariinsky, Alexander, and Mikhailovsky to name the most important (see Chapter 8). The old Yeliseyev Mansion, from 1919–22 the House of the Arts, was transformed in 1997 into the lavish Taleon Club and then the Taleon Imperial Hotel in 2003, one of a number of major palaces and mansions restored by the company which owns them and which also formerly published a cultural magazine of considerable note, viewable online (see Further Reading). That year, the tercentenary of the founding of St. Petersburg, witnessed the completion of a number of urban renovations which brought the city back to a higher standard of restoration than it had enjoyed since imperial days. Not only were palaces refurbished and repaired, but other practical features of the city's face were given a makeover. This remodeling soon included the World of Water Museum, housed in Merts and Shubersky's watertower, which brings to wider public attention the central, if often forgotten, importance of the city's infrastructure for the supply of suitable water to its millions of inhabitants. Despite the devastation of revolution, war, famine, blockade, and deliberate neglect, St. Petersburg had unquestionably once again become one of the world's most beautiful cities.

FACE OF THE CITY

4 | Rulers and Ruled
The Romanovs

The imperial Romanov dynasty was established in 1613, when the boyar (Muscovite noble) Mikhail Romanov assumed the throne of Russia by invitation after the chaotic Time of Troubles which followed the death of Tsar Boris Godunov (today remembered in Mussorgsky's eponymous opera), who had controversially seized power after the extinction of the original Rurikid dynasty. Mikhail's grandson Peter eventually succeeded to the throne after the death first of his father Alexey and then his older brother Fedor. This he did at first with his half-brother Ivan—who was ill and co-tsar in name only—until the latter's death in 1696. Peter then became "Autocrat of all the Russias" and immediately went about consolidating his power.

Peter the Great's capture in 1702 of Oreshek, a wooden fortress first built by the Prince of Novgorod in 1323 at the convergence of the Neva and Lake Ladoga, just north of what is now St. Petersburg, ended not only ninety years of Swedish hegemony but opened the door to a whole new era of Russian imperial history. The tsar could now fulfill his ultimate dream: the foundation of a new city: a port on the Gulf of Finland, a gateway to the Baltic Sea and the heart of Europe. Almost immediately Peter ordered the construction of his first fixed home there, the log house painted to look as if it were constructed of brick at what is now 6 Petrovskaya Embankment, on the Petrograd Side of the Neva. The work was finished within just three days by the soldiers of the Semyonovsky Regiment.

The tsar also saw to it that those who had assisted in the military victory were reconfirmed in their military and administrative positions. The Scotsman Robert Bruce, for example, a key figure in his military success, continued to play a prominent role in the newborn city's survival, not only supervising governmental and residential construction but also in continuing to secure its defense, especially after Sweden attacked its recently lost territory—in vain and for the last time, it would turn out—in 1704 and 1705.

His first priority was, of course, defensive in nature, and he ordered the construction of yet another imposing fortress, this one to ensure that Sweden would never again assert sovereignty over the lost province of Ingria. To achieve this aim Peter looked to the West, as he almost invariably did throughout his reign, for the cutting edge in engineering expertise, and he hired the Frenchman Joseph-Gaspar Lambert de Guerin to carry out the work. The plan was then taken over by Domenico Trezzini, who had studied under the famed architect Francesco Borromini and had worked on fortifications for Russia's old ally Denmark, as well as in Moscow. When completed, the new Peter and Paul Fortress—the tsar himself gave it its name—on Zayachy Ostrov (Hare Island) encompassed a six-sided fortification at the corners of which six towered bastions were situated. As such it was the first construction in Russia to introduce bastions as defensive elements and became the model for others throughout the Russian Empire and beyond.

First built of wood in 1708, it was reconstructed in stone in 1715–17 and, after further additions, was finally completed in 1732. Daunting though its appearance was, however, it never actually came under enemy fire. Instead, it became tsarist Russia's most notorious prison, sequestering for over three centuries some of the most prominent political opponents of the crown and government, as well as, during the period following the October Revolution, members of the imperial family and their supporters.

The Peter and Paul Fortress was just one attempt to secure the western sea approaches to St. Petersburg, the direction from which all serious threats seemed to emanate. Thus the tsar personally designed Kronshlot Fortress, the first fortification to be built on the western side of Kotlin Island, 32 kilometers (20 miles) west of St. Petersburg, where the Russian flag was raised on May 7, 1704. This the tsar had done in commemoration of the anniversary of the foundation of his new city the year before. However, unlike the Peter and Paul Fortress, this defensive complex had come under attack by Sweden before the following month had passed, and the tsar became all too aware of its weaknesses. Although the assault failed and the Swedes admitted defeat, Peter decided that further improvements to it required greater professional knowledge than even he possessed. This he found in Trezzini, and as a result the fortress of Kronshlot, located near Kronstadt, Russia's first line of defense in the eastern Gulf of Finland, became a resounding success: no foreign navy was ever bold enough to attempt another direct assault and it has successfully guarded the city from foreign maritime attack to this day.

Imperial Rule

St. Petersburg, like Imperial Germany, was not founded on liberal democratic principles but, as Bismarck put it with respect to the Second Reich, on blood and iron. Seemingly endless toil in brutal conditions, leading to the death of tens, if not hundreds, of thousands of people was unavoidable in securing its foundation. Most of those who contributed to its construction were forced laborers. Moreover, for those free and even from the nobility, it was the tsar, his ministers and military who set the tone of society and the enforcement of his autocratic wishes. Within the first generation, and unusually for European cities at this time, an urban police force was established to maintain general public order. Its first chief was appointed by Peter the Great in 1718. He was António Manuel de Vieira, from Amsterdam, whose father was a Sephardic Jew, but who had converted to Russian Orthodoxy. He was given the Russian name and title of Count Anton Devier and given the hand in marriage of none other than the daughter of Prince Menshikov, one of Peter's closest friends, whom it was said Devier had seduced. He was eventually appointed to the Senate only to fall foul of Menshikov during the brief reign of Peter II, after which he was exiled to Yakutia in Siberia before regaining imperial favor and resuming his role as chief of police until his death in 1745.

His experience was hardly typical of others of Jewish background in imperial Russia. Jews were generally forbidden to settle or even come to Russia during the reign of Peter the Great and his three successors. Under the Empress Anna, a Jewish merchant

Baruch Leibov was burned at the stake for the alleged ritual murder of an Orthodox girl as well as the attempt to convert a Russian naval captain.

Prisons also characterized the capital from its earliest days, in particular the Peter and Paul Fortress. One of the most famous of the early prisoners incarcerated there was the Tsarevich Aleksei (1690–1718), Peter the Great's only son and heir, accused by the tsar of plotting against him. He died in the fortress in June 1718, but countless others would take his place in its cells well into the post-revolutionary period of the Bolshevik regime. Today it is a fascinating museum of both tsarist and Bolshevik political horrors. Yet its Baroque gateway, framing the principal entrance to the complex, is an aesthetic masterpiece. Flanked by Doric pilasters and surmounted by scrolls, it is one of the city's architectural highlights, carried out to the designs of Trezzini.

Along with crimes against the state, the Russian autocracy did all in its power to crush other forms of criminality with punishments of such severity that they shocked visiting Western Europeans. Counterfeiting was already a serious problem even before the Petrine period and the state dealt with it with extreme brutality. Russia's legal code of 1649 demanded draconian measures against counterfeiters:

> Coiners who dare to make copper, tin or steel coins, or in their production venture to add copper, tin or lead to the silver, thereby causing losses to the sovereign's treasury are to be executed for these crimes by such actions by having molten metal poured down their throats.

Despite such penalties, counterfeiters persisted over the following decades and more than 7,000 were executed, while a further 1,500 had their hands chopped off. Less serious crimes—at least those which did not threaten the financial stability of the state—were punished by lengthy terms of imprisonment, the fate of most convicted criminals. For the most serious of these, the Peter and Paul Fortress remained one of the most notorious of Russian jails.

When a British reformer visited it in 1781, he noted that up to 35 prisoners were accommodated per cell, heated but poorly ventilated by two small window openings—not unlike cells in Kresty Prison in today's St. Petersburg. Most inmates of the Peter and Paul Fortress were put to work on construction projects there, but a few privileged individuals were employed in the governor's garden in remuneration for which he gave them flour. The British visitor found the part reserved for debtors particularly lamentable:

> The prison for debtors consists of four vaulted rooms communicating with one another, and furnished with stoves and barrack-beds. The prisoners are never permitted to go out of their rooms. They subsist by alms, received from passengers in little boxes placed before the windows; but government supplies them with wood for fuel. One told me, he had been confined for five years, for a debt of fifteen roubles; and another, four years for twenty-five roubles.

Court Life

Tsar Peter II (1715–30) reigned only briefly after he succeeded to the throne of his grandfather in 1727. During this brief reign he strengthened the institution of serfdom, but the real power behind the throne was Peter the Great's old friend Alexander Danilovich Menshikov, who had intended the young man to marry his daughter. This magnate was, in turn, succeeded by Vasily Dolgorukov, who then had the tsar betrothed to his own daughter Catherine. The coronation took place in Moscow in 1728 and the nuptials were set for January 30, 1730. However, a smallpox epidemic that had broken out in the old capital carried him off that very day and he was succeeded by his great-aunt Anna (1693–1740), daughter of Peter the Great's stepbrother and co-tsar Ivan V.

A strong-willed and autocratic empress, Anna attempted to avoid the hostile machinations of the old Russian boyars, or traditional nobility, preferring instead to favor the Baltic German aristocracy of the western provinces of the Russian Empire, today's Latvia, Lithuania, and Estonia, having been briefly married to the

Baltic German Friedrich Wilhelm, Duke of Courland. Rumor had it that her own romantic sentiments were directed toward a much later Duke of Courland, Ernst Johann von Biron. She appointed him to act as regent after her death during the minority of the infant Tsar Ivan IV (1740–64), but he enjoyed that role for only a few weeks. The throne was soon seized on behalf of the Empress Elizabeth (1709–62), the daughter of Peter the Great, and the baby tsar suffered an itinerant life, transferred from one fortress prison to another until his murder after the ascension of Catherine the Great.

Anna was a highly cultured person but one with a biting and vindictive sense of humor. A story is told that to better humiliate the elderly Prince Mikhail Golitsyn, who had incurred her displeasure, she had obliged him to marry in the winter of 1739–40 a similarly elderly lady, a member of the Mongol-related Kalmyk peoples of central Siberia. The couple were obliged to arrive at their forced wedding on an elephant, dressed as court jesters. The empress provided the marriage cortege with a fleet of carriages, each containing the subjects of a different ethnic minority within the empire and each pulled by a different animal. A specially constructed ice palace, 25 meters (80 feet) in length and nine meters (30 feet) high accommodated the "festivities," in particular the "consummation" of the marriage with the bride and groom stripped naked for the occasion, albeit in the vicinity of a considerably provided stove. All the classically inspired decorations were made of ice, including furniture and plants, at a cost of some 30,000 roubles.

The Empress Elizabeth, who succeeded Anna, was a committed autocrat and obviously allowed little room for dissent amongst her courtiers, but in this age of growing Enlightenment values she had her humane side too, and thanks to her, capital punishment was abolished for the first time in Russia in 1744. It was reintroduced again later in her reign in 1755.

Elizabeth was, in turn, succeeded by her nephew Tsar Peter III (1728–62), a grandson of Peter the Great. As with his grandson Tsar Paul, his pro-Prussian sympathies would prove his undoing and he was assassinated after reigning for only six months, to be succeeded by his German consort Catherine the Great, whom he had married in 1745. Catherine famously detested her husband and is thought to have been involved in bringing about his death.

Catherine (1729–96), a niece of the Tsarina Elizabeth for whom she felt little affection, acceded to the throne of Russia after the murder of her husband, with the assistance of her paramour Count Grigory Orlov, at the end of June 1762. His gift to the empress of the renowned Orlov diamond, weighing over 189 carats, now on view in the Kremlin, was an ultimately vain attempt at achieving a reconciliation after the commencement of her new relationship with her next lover Grigory Potemkin (1739–91), a minor aristocrat and military man whom she raised to the rank of prince.

The empress' relationship with Orlov produced a son, Count Aleksei Bobrinsky (1762–1813), whose descendants have since borne that title and surname. Historical anecdotes record that the baby was taken away from his imperial mother wrapped in beaver fur (*bobr* in Russian), from which his surname was derived, and the coat of arms she granted him as a count featured a beaver. As he approached maturity, the boy was given what is now known as the Bobrinsky Palace (situated on the Moika Canal and today a seat of the European University of St. Petersburg), which had been designed by the Italian Luigi Rusca. It remained in the family for a further six generations until it was confiscated after the Revolution.

When Catherine the Great assumed the throne her capital was on the threshold of its political and architectural heyday, but her government turned its back on those who had served the previous autocrats. Thus, Rastrelli, architect of the old regime, found his services in the new order no longer required and he was pensioned off, albeit generously. It was not merely a question that Rastrelli was tainted by close association with the late tsar but that, as the reign of Catherine progressed, the frivolity of the Baroque, and especially its Rococo variant was increasingly falling out of favor. Instead, the austerity and somber stoicism of the neoclassical came into fashion, much as it did in the rest of Europe, a design which correlated perfectly with the empress' highly secular philosophical and aesthetic ideals. Nonetheless, she carried on and strengthened the autocratic traditions of her predecessors and strove to discourage indiscipline among her subjects. In 1785 she issued strict regulations, for example, to craftsmen in which their formal obligations were laid down and strict prohibitions were made against drunkenness and waste.

Elite Culture

One of the greatest educational foundations in Russia was the Smolny Institute, and Catherine the Great was highly important in its foundation and development. Known as the Society for the Education of Noble Maidens, the establishment was set up in the central Smolny area by the Novodevichy Resurrection Convent in premises originally designed by Rastrelli. It was later endowed with a classical Ionic portico in Palladian-inspired work carried out in 1806–08 by Giacomo Quarenghi. Some 1,316 girls—a minority from the merchant class—passed through its portals between 1764 and 1796. The principal function of what was officially called the Catherine Institute, however, was the education of young noble ladies. Many of these were the children of impoverished minor aristocratic families with little or no financial means. Girls from earliest childhood up to the age of eighteen were accommodated.

Many of the Smolny alumnae helped to spread an extraordinarily high level of culture and manners throughout the empire when they married and returned to their rural estates. Some even played significant roles in the political life of the capital and Russia at the highest level. The most famous of these was Ekaterina Ivanovna Nelidova (1758–1839) who won the love and esteem of the Grand-Duke Paul, later Tsar Paul I, during the final years of the reign of Catherine the Great. She became indispensable in curbing the excesses of a deeply troubled monarch, subject to rages and violent mood swings, a fact even recognized by Paul's jealous German-born consort the Tsarina Maria Feodorovna.

The Pavlovsk Institute also catered for the nobility, in particular the orphans of military officers. It, too, had a section for non-aristocratic children whose fathers worked as doctors, artists, and actors. Yet it was the Smolny Institute which was most favored.

With its monumental portico it vied with the temple-like structure of the Academy of Sciences in terms of architectural dignity and the political power it represented.

Early in her reign in 1771 Catherine established a St. Petersburg branch of the House of Education, a foundation for boys which she had established in Moscow shortly before, endowing it with 20,000 roubles. However, it was specifically the boys of the nobility upon whom the greatest educational possibilities of the time were lavished: the students of the Noble Cadet Corps on Vasilyevsky Island. They memorably demonstrated their high cultural attainments in an entertainment put on to celebrate the Russian-Turkish Peace Treaty of July 1775. The future Second Lord (John) Hennike wrote in his diary, after visiting St. Petersburg:

> We were placed in an Amphitheater nearly semicircular, containing about seven hundred Persons; which turned upon an Axis. Near the Summit of this Axis was a Gallery of Music; and on the Top stood Peace with an olive branch in her Hand. The first performance was a Play in French; of which *l'amour de la patrie* was the subject. The Young Gentlemen of this Establishment were the only persons who exhibited throughout, and I must add, much to their own Credit, and our Satisfaction. At the conclusion of this Piece, a Ship was drawn on the Stage; from which the chief Characters descended; Waves were represented around it by Canvas; and Neptune with his subaltern deities attended… It was not Harlequin, who drove to Lilliput with his magic Wand; but in good Truth some strong capsterns that turned the whole Amphitheater round with its Company: first to a Scene of Sculpture, and then a second Time, to present us before a Carousel, richly illuminated.

Such highly sophisticated spectacles were just one product of Catherine's attempts to turn St. Petersburg into the Athens of the North. For her the real goal was to make her capital one of Europe's most luminous intellectual cities. To this end she invited the person who was without doubt one of Europe's most encyclopedic intellectuals, the Frenchman Denis Diderot. The harshness of the Russian winter climate notwithstanding, Diderot decided to accept the invitation and duly arrived in St. Petersburg, living at 9 St. Isaac's Square with the diplomat Aleksey Naryshkin. There he became an enthusiastic Russophile, learning first the language and then reading and collecting the best of contemporary Russian literature. Made a foreign member of the Imperial Academy of Arts, Diderot was as much charmed by the tsarina as she was by him. The fact that he spoke and wrote in French was no disadvantage as Russian was at this time a secondary language for many. Indeed, it was customary for many children of the Russian nobility to use Russian only with their nannies or otherwise on Sundays or Orthodox religious holidays, French being the main language, taught by their French governesses.

If Catherine the Great placed great emphasis on Enlightenment values as an expression of her autocracy, the symbolic value of the sculptures with which she adorned the city was also important. Étienne Falconet, recommended by Diderot, was unquestionably France's most important sculptor of the eighteenth century and his lengthy sojourn in St. Petersburg was to have significant consequences for the artistic life of the city and the power of the regime that it seemed to embody. His famous sculpture of Peter the Great, *The Bronze Horseman*, resting on its famous base, the *Thunder Rock*, is one of Europe's Baroque masterpieces. The sculptor lived in the city for twelve years from 1766 to 1778. It was only in 1782, however, that the completed sculpture was first revealed to public view and to great acclaim, the glory of Peter the Great reflected back on the Empress Catherine. In the early nineteenth century its fame was magnified yet further by the poem of Alexander Pushkin, "The Bronze Horseman." Pushkin's majestic imagery of Peter the Great was not appreciated by all of his contemporaries, in particular the Polish bard and nationalist Adam Mickiewicz, who also spent time in the capital. Rather than experiencing the emperor as a figure of victory, Mickiewicz projects him as a figure about to plunge into an abyss, bearing the Russian state with him.

In contrast with many other European countries of the period, some women exerted enormous influence on the political and cultural life of Russia during the reign of Catherine the Great. No one played a more significant role in this context than Princess Ekaterina Dashkova (1743–1810). Although she maintained that she had played an important role in the empress's coup d'état of 1762, Catherine herself denied this. Nonetheless, by all accounts she was a major figure at court and abroad, in particular in Paris, London, and Edinburgh. It was in Paris in 1781 that she met Benjamin Franklin and soon became the first woman to become a member of the American Philosophical Society (it would take another eighty years for another woman to join). Franklin, in turn, became the first American member of the Russian Academy of Arts and Sciences of which Dashkova had become director. Two years later she became an honorary member of the Swedish Academy of Sciences and in 1784 president of the Russian Academy. Her villa, Kiryanova, on the outskirts of St. Petersburg, was one of Russia's intellectual hubs during her lifetime.

Hero and Villain

When Tsar Paul I acceded to the throne after the death of his mother, Princess Dashkova was among the first to be exiled—fortunately not to Siberia, but to the province of Novgorod from where she was eventually allowed to live in Moscow. Paul's relationships were tortured and the empress had done everything to sideline him. She had had her reasons: Paul was highly cultured, having traveled to Italy as grand-duke in 1782, and a regatta was held in his honor in Venice (commemorated by the Italian painter Giovanni Antonio Guardi), but he was erratic, bad-tempered and notorious for his violent outbursts—courtiers were exiled to Siberia during his brief reign (1796–1801) for trivial misdemeanors. Worse, on a geopolitical level, he threatened the interests of Britain during the Napoleonic Wars by supporting Prussia, then allied to France, and so for these and other reasons he was murdered. To general relief at home and abroad, his son and Catherine the Great's favorite grandchild Alexander I succeeded him.

Tsar Alexander I proved during his reign (1801–25) to be one of Russia's most popular rulers both in Russia and abroad. Going on to help in the defeat of Napoleon on the side of Britain and her allies in 1814 (having formerly sided with Napoleon), his visit to London that same year saw him feted as Europe's most admired ruler of his time. Never again would a Russian leader achieve such popularity. At the Congress of Vienna, where he gained many advantages in the postwar settlement for Russia, he was also popular with the ladies. Anecdotes abounded. It was said that Alexander had asked of a married lady if he could be permitted to occupy her husband's place in his absence, for which he earned the coy rebuke, "Does Your Majesty consider me to be a province?"

At the conclusion of the Napoleonic Wars Alexander wished to erect an appropriately imposing structure in the tradition of ancient Roman emperors. He therefore appointed Quarenghi to design the neoclassical Narva Triumphal Gate, a wooden structure erected in 1814 to commemorate the return of Russia's victorious troops. It was rebuilt in stone between 1827 and 1834 and subsequently restored after the Second World War.

A far more ambitious commission handed to the Italian architect Carlo Rossi embodied the majesty of the Russian ruler in what is still one of St. Petersburg's most iconic landmarks: the General Staff Building, opposite the Winter Palace, built between 1820 and 1830. This monumental structure would witness almost a century later the massacre of the rebellious poor of St. Petersburg in what came to be known as the 1905 Revolution. Its principal facade is a superb example of Russian neoclassical architecture of its time, accentuated by the copperplated iron-framed sculpture which crowns it, namely a Winged Chariot of Victory with two warriors leading six horses, at which visitors heading for Nevsky Prospekt from the Hermitage can marvel from below. In front of it, right in the middle of Palace Square itself, stands the Alexander Monument, commemorating Russia's most popular ruler. As the Scottish author Leitch Ritchie wrote after it had been set up during the late summer of 1834:

The object has a truly noble and majestic appearance from which ever point of view it is beheld. The shaft is formed of a single block of marble brought from the quarries of Finland, and, exclusively of pedestal and capital, is eighty-four feet high. The pedestal is of granite, with allegorical bas-reliefs in bronze; and on the summit stands an angel, holding a cross with the left hand, and pointing to heaven with the right. The inscription, on the side of the pedestal next the palace, is nearly as simple as that of the monument of Peter the Great. It contains merely these words: *To Alexander I. grateful Russia.*

Nearby are the Senate and Seat of the Holy Synod, at that time administering the Russian Orthodox Church in submission to the tsar, which later, by those who disapproved of the power the tsar held over the Church, came to be known as the Babylonian Captivity. The buildings, connected to one to another by another majestic triumphal arch, were also built to the designs of Rossi from 1829 to 1832. Today the former accommodates the Russian Constitutional Court, only recently moved to St. Petersburg from Moscow. It is the Admiralty, however, which remains the greatest symbol of the reign of Alexander I, reflecting his desire to make Russia a great maritime nation, a goal for which Peter the Great had also striven.

Symptoms of Change

Tsar Nicholas I (reigning 1825–55) assumed the Russian throne upon the death of his brother Alexander I and after his elder brother, the more liberal Grand-Duke Constantine, had declined to accept it. This led to the uprising of the Decembrists, a liberal political movement which had sought to introduce Western European political values into the Russian autocracy, on December 26, 1825. The uprising occurred in reaction to what the Decembrists falsely perceived as the deliberate exclusion by Alexander of Constantine from the throne. It erupted at Senate Square (then known as Peter's Square) and involved some 3,000 mutinous soldiers and officers. Nicholas I himself confronted them and took the measure of having Count Mikhail Miloradovich, a popular military hero, speak to them. However, the rebel officer Pyotr Kakhovsky shot him dead while he was attempting to persuade the troops to lay down their arms and pandemonium broke out. The tsar ordered a cavalry charge and the rebels were quelled. Five of the Decembrists were hanged (the last official public execution in Russia) and many others were deported to Siberia. This action set the tone for Nicholas I's increasingly troubled reign, which ultimately led to the Crimean War, growing civil unrest and the rise of anarchism.

Despite the autocracy of the tsar the Russian nobility did have a significant political role to play, but outside of ministerial circles it was increasingly social rather than political. Its seat was the Assembly of the Nobility, designed by Rossi and situated opposite the Mikhailovsky Palace on the south-eastern corner of Mikhailovsky Square. Yet it was largely a social venue and in 1846 it began to be used for public concerts, especially at Lent, when public theaters were closed. Schumann, Liszt, and Berlioz were just some of the composers who appeared there during this period. On Mikhailovsky Street, opposite the Assembly of the Nobility, the La Russie Hotel opened its doors in 1824, accommodating such guests as Berlioz and Marius Petipa.

In 1848 the Assembly of the Nobility also rented the house of Count Orlov, chief of the gendarmerie, at what is today 39 Liteiny Prospekt. There the card game of *preferans* (preference) was introduced and it rapidly became the gambling rage of the capital. Orlov's home was just one of many social venues for elite society in St. Petersburg at this time. Others included the residence of Y. I. Golitizina at 30 Millionnaya Street, where a highly erudite circle gathered, and that of V. A. Zhykovsky, whose circle met on Saturdays in the 1830s. Erudition was a hallmark of elite society in St. Petersburg, and had its roots in Russia's highly developed educational system for the nobility and officer class.

Outside the court, military, and prosperous mercantile circles, however, the overwhelming majority of children, not only in St. Petersburg but in Russia as a whole, had no formal education. Those few individuals who did proceed through the established educational system, though, could achieve considerable prosperity and official status, even entering one of the fourteen ranks of the nobility. Along with the University of St. Petersburg, numerous academies also offered tuition, including the Imperial Academy of Art, founded in 1756, and the Academy of Medicine and Surgery, established in 1799, both achieving international renown. In 1829 the Main Pedagogical Institute of St. Petersburg opened to provide a steady and high-quality supply of teachers, drawing upon predominantly middle-class students. Nonetheless, as late as 1853 some 80 percent of pupils attending higher secondary schools, the so-called gymnasia, were still from noble families.

As for the children of serfs, who made up the bulk of the city's population, the opportunities for education were limited in the extreme. As late as 1804, statutes were introduced prohibiting children "in an un-free state" from entering a gymnasium, except with ministerial permission, although "lower" schools were open to them.

Despite the Emancipation of the Serfs, enacted by Tsar Alexander II in 1861, Russia as a country and St. Petersburg as its capital remained sharply socially stratified. In 1869, 14.2 percent of the city's entire population of 667,200 were nobles or of aristocratic background. Not surprisingly, court life dominated the capital, since 25 percent of the state budget went toward its maintenance, with three million roubles given over to its expenses in the middle of the century. (In Britain, by comparison, at this time court expenses were equivalent to 2.5 million roubles.)

The second of the social orders was composed of merchants, subdivided into those of the mercantile elite (*Kypzi*) who totaled some 22,333 or 3.3 percent of the whole, and merchants of more modest scope (*Meshane*), numbering 123,267, or 18.5 percent. The bulk of the city's population, however, was of peasant stock, 207,707, or 31 percent, many of whom had recently arrived in the city looking for work after emancipation. Many of these worked in domestic service, more than 60,000 in 1872.

Of course, in a highly militarized autocracy in which military service for all orders usually lasted for decades, the population of St. Petersburg in the navy or army was also high. Statistics gathered by the authorities record that over 132,000 people were members of the military or in families of members, that is 19.8 percent of the city's population, both noble and common.

It was against such a background of prosperity and deprivation that intellectual life in St. Petersburg flourished, not least in military circles. Once such example was Nicholas N. Raev, a hero of the Napoleonic Wars who married Sophia Alexeyevna, granddaughter of the famous scientist Lomonosov. Another was General Count Alexander Ivanovich Ostermann-Tolstoy, who had lost a leg in the Battle of Kulm in Bohemia before he retired in 1812. For him the relationship of a Russian to military service in his native country would always be different to that of foreigners in Russian military employ. As he put it to the Marchese Filippo Panlucci, an Italian serving in the Russian army, "You treat Russia like a uniform which you can put on and take off, as you like. For me, on the other hand, Russia is my skin."

Yet it was not only the military that the Russian autocracy depended upon but also its civil bureaucracy. As Nicholas I famously quipped, "Russia is ruled by its senior civil servants." During this tsar's reign imperial ideology was based on the concepts of "Orthodoxy, autocracy, and nationalism," ideas that have returned with a vengeance in our own time. The ideologue of this view was the minister of education and, after 1818, president of the Russian Academy of Sciences, Sergey Uvarov (1786–1855). Notorious among liberals and communists of later generations for his advocacy of the formulaic "Orthodoxy, autocracy, and nationalism," in his own time he had been considered a liberal by many and was by no means a national chauvinist. He was keen to propagate an interest in Oriental peoples, their languages and cultures. Others, like the historian Sergey Soloviev (1820–79), considered him the ultimate cynic and noted wryly that with respect to Uvarov's own convictions that he was an atheist, a liberal and, for all his Russianness, a man of letters who could only write in French and German.

In literary terms, it is still the great Russian author and playwright Nikolai Gogol (1809–52) who most skillfully captured the foibles of civil servants with his unforgettable portraits of their type, in such novels and plays as *Dead Souls* and *The Government Inspector.*

Rasputin

Without doubt, the most ominous figure in St. Petersburg in the years leading up to and during the First World War was the seductive—at least as far as the ladies of the court were concerned—Siberian pseudo-monk and mystic Grigori Rasputin (1869–1916). He lived at 64 Gorokhovaya Street, an address at which many finely dressed aristocratic ladies could be seen throughout the day. Yet his political machinations at court, in which he sought to dissuade the tsar from allying Russia with Britain and France against Germany, made him highly unpopular with pro-allied courtiers like Prince Felix Yusupov (1887–1967), who had studied at Oxford University before the war. He became Rasputin's assassin and later wrote in his memoirs of the scenario he set for the "holy man's" murder: "By eleven everything was ready in the basement on the Moika. The basement room, comfortably furnished… ceased to be a crypt. By the samovar boiling on the table were plates of Rasputin's favorite delicacies. It only remained to put the poison in the glasses." Rasputin's corpse ended up in the Malaya Nevka River.

On the surface, Yusupov might seem an unlikely assassin, unlike his brother Nikolai who was shot in a duel. A prominent aristocratic figure, he had married Irina, a niece of the tsar, and was famed for his role in masquerades and amateur dramatics, in which he often assumed the female roles. Yet he was passionately Anglophile and it is said that the murder was carried out in the presence of a British agent from the Secret Service. Yusupov eventually fled Petrograd in the wake of the Revolution, but did so three times, on each occasion removing some of his personal property in the process. Thus, with the help of a family retainer, he was able to extricate among other objects not only valuable jewels and a Stradivarius violin but two important paintings by Rembrandt, *Portrait of a Bearded Man in a Wide-Brimmed Hat* and *Portrait of a Young Woman with a Fan*, which are today on view in the National Gallery in Washington, DC.

The Lure of the Exotic

Autocracy in Russia has always needed an external enemy to con-
solidate internal consensus and the acceptance of a strong protec-
tive leader. In imperial days this leader was always the tsar and the
threats to Russia were real. The Ottoman Empire was frequently an
enemy of Russia, threatening the security of its southern borders, its
naval defense, its maritime trade and its expansionist desires. Yet at
the same time it was a source of fascination, social and cultural. In
St. Petersburg this was often expressed in architectural, pictorial and
literary terms throughout the nineteenth century. After the Great
Fire of 1837 the Russian architect Alexander Brullov had already
provided the tsar with the Moresque Bathroom in the restored
Winter Palace. Its famed bronze clock of unusual design, produced
by the Schreider Factory in the capital, is still on view there.

Other members of the imperial family were also enthralled
by Turkey. During the 1840s the Marble Palace was occupied by
the Grand-Duke Konstantin Nikolayevich (1827–92). His Turkish
Study, decorated with Arabic inscriptions and sumptuously decorated by the Russian artist Yakov Dodonov, was highly regarded
at the time. Of particular note is the study's gilt fireplace of yellow clay and the later porcelain fountain and marble basin, also
designed by Brullov. Konstantin's brother, the Grand-Duke Mikhail
Nikolayevich (1831–91), was a successful army commander during
the Russo-Turkish War of 1877–78, and the interiors of the New
Mikhailovsky Palace, at 18 Palace Embankment, 18—originally
designed by Andrei Stackenschneider—revealed this influence
when they were photographed in 1907 by the famed Karl Bulla. In
1949 the building was occupied by the Institute of Oriental Studies
and today belongs to the Institute of Oriental Manuscripts of the
Russian Academy of Sciences. Only the photographs remain of its
former exotic splendour.

In 1872 *Das Kapital* by Karl Marx first appeared in the
bookshops of St. Petersburg in Russian but made little impression on the political life of the capital at that time. Few of the
wider public noted its arrival and well into the early twentieth

century almost all of the peasants who dominated the city as never before—with 1,310,000 living there in 1910—were oblivious to it and not even remotely aware of the implications it contained for their future.

Not Marx, but Fabergé was the name which has come to serve as a byword for the final years of imperial autocracy. The headquarters of the jewellers Fabergé was built by the German architect Carl Schmidt in 1899. An eclectic mix of architectural elements, it has decorative features of both the Western European Gothic and Italian Renaissance in its facade and it still graces St. Petersburg today. The skills of craftsmanship which the House of Fabergé's *objets d'art* demonstrated in the final days of empire are legendary. Yet it had taken years of competition with other jewellery firms to achieve such recognition. Fabergé's most ancient competitor was the firm established by Carl Edvard Bolin as far back as 1796. Bolin's establishment was located at 10 Bolshaya Morskaya Street and so Peter Carl Fabergé (1846–1920), founder of the firm, decided to set himself up nearby at number 24, in the heart of the city off Nevsky Prospekt. Shortly before the Revolution Wilhelm Bolin astutely decided to open a shop in Stockholm and, appointed jeweller to the Swedish royal family, thrived in Sweden afterwards. By then, however, Fabergé had grabbed the limelight, putting not only Bohlin but other rivals in the shade when the firm was awarded the Grand Prix at the World's Fair, held in Paris in 1900, for an exquisite piece reproducing the imperial crown in a jewelled miniature. Tsar Nicholas II ordered a copy which he then exhibited in the Hermitage. With the advent of the Bolshevik Revolution it was none other than Leon Trotsky who was appointed director of the Commission for the Confiscation of Valuables, charged with selling seized valuables abroad for hard currency. With virtually no knowledge of the market himself, he was forced to make use of the services of those who had previously served the imperial court. Perhaps not surprisingly, he employed the gemologist Agathon Fabergé, Peter Carl's son, to value the confiscated

jewellery which was then collected and deposited at a reposi-
tory in the Kremlin. Agathon Fabergé, who had previously been
imprisoned by the Bolsheviks, did this work and, after having
much of his own personal property returned to him, transferred
many of his possessions to Finland where he ultimately fled.

5 | City of Blood
Revolution and War

With the assassination of Tsar Alexander II (see Chapter 9), the level to which anarchistic and communist values were threatening the integrity of the autocracy had become shockingly obvious. Yet under the consolidating, conservative reign of Tsar Alexander III a growing middle class and increasingly successful industrialization seemed to auger well for the future in this Russia's Silver Age, when a cultural blossoming seemed to go hand in hand with increased economic prosperity and industrial development.

The succession of his son and heir Nicholas II, however, boded less well for the future. Just under a million roubles were allocated for the coronation—a dramatic diminution on the almost three million-rouble bill for Alexander III's, thirteen years before. Free food was passed among the vast crowd, said to number up to half a million, who turned out to celebrate on May 18, 1896. But then a calamity ensued, which henceforth seemed to symbolize his ill-omened reign: well over 1,300 people were trampled to death during a stampede on the Khodynka Field where festivities were taking place. The tsar himself took responsibility for this "sin" which he felt weighed upon his soldiers, but it failed to make him cautious in affairs of state. Led on by some of his ministers, he engaged Japan, half way around the world, in a conflict which he could hardly have hoped to win, the Russo-Japanese War.

The war, which began in February 1904, had been intended to extend Russia's territorial and commercial interests at the expense of imperial Japan, recently modernized, but the country's ignominious defeat fatally undermined tsarist credibility. Brought to a disastrous conclusion in September that year, the war was the writing on the wall for Russian imperial system, though many failed to realize it at the time. The Grand Duchess Elizabeth Fedorovna, a near relation to Britain's heir to the throne, Prince Charles, showed her spiritual mettle after the assassination in February 1905 of her husband, the Grand Duke Sergei Alexandrovich, uncle of Nicholas II, by the Kremlin's St. Nicholas Gate. It had occurred not so much because of his role as governor general of Moscow but as a byproduct of popular dissatisfaction with the imperial system itself. His widow took an icon to the assassin, Ivan Kalyayev, in prison, with a message of reconciliation: "I have come to deliver to you the forgiveness of the Grand Duke, who himself was not vouchsafed the time to relay to you himself his forgiveness, as he did not have time to give it to you."

Terrorism remained rampant in St. Petersburg as in Moscow, with assassinations and bank robberies commonplace. Punishments were also severe: while only those over 21 could be executed, pregnant women convicted of capital crimes were only given a temporary reprieve of forty days after they gave birth until they were put to death.

A sense of malaise now hung over many in St. Petersburg. The author Dmitry Mereschkowski (1865–1941) wrote about his experience taking part in an obligatory "water assembly" in the presence of the imperial family in his historical novel *Peter the Great and his Son Alexei*:

> We were in a very sad mood. The unfriendly, pale blue river, with its low banks, the pale-blue sky, transparent as ice, the twinkling of the golden top of the wooden, yellow painted, marble-like steeple of the Peter and Paul Cathedral, its melancholic bell tower—all these increased our sense of misery, a misery the intensity of which I have only experienced in this city.

Yet not everybody shared this sense of foreboding. For example, the stage designer Alexandre Benois rejected the many negative impressions of St. Petersburg during these final years of the imperial system. On the contrary, for him, it remained a city of marvels, with an individuality and cultural *richesse* which was quite unparalleled.

Look at the old faces of St. Petersburg. It is hardly a typical European city. That said, it is also by no means a Russian city, but a completely unusual and doubtlessly grandiose and beautiful city. The style of the houses, the churches and the palaces, the size of the streets, the plan—all was of its own type. The components, of course, were borrowed: the columns, the ornamental gables, pilasters and later the classical bas reliefs, attics and vases were borrowed from France, Italy and Germany. Nonetheless, they were utilised in such an individualistic way that, ultimately, something magnificent and quite extraordinary was created.

With the eruption of the Revolution of 1905 in St. Petersburg, and the death of hundreds of protesters in front of the Winter Palace on Bloody Sunday, January 22, absolute power was swept away. In its wake, Nicholas II was obliged to accept not only a constitution, but the imposition of an elected national Duma or parliament. As the Frenchman Anatole Leroy-Beaulieu was said to have caustically commented to diplomats gathered around the Japanese Embassy in St. Petersburg, to which he was pointing: "There he is, the real liberator of Russia, he who has given her a constitution."

Yet matters remained edgy in the imperial capital and troops were a permanent presence, albeit less so than in the middle of the previous century, with one soldier for every 39 people in 1910. St Petersburg had by now become more a city of bureaucrats than soldiers, with 53,670 inhabitants in 1900 working in various levels of the government's administration and 69,576 by 1910.

It was also a city of politicians. Among them, Vladimir Dmitrievich Nabokov (1869–1922), father of the famous author, was a significant figure. The son of a minister of justice under Alexander II, he had trained as a lawyer before being elected to the country's first State Duma and becoming a leader of the Constitutional Democratic Party or "Cadets." In 1904 he had provided his house as the headquarters of the first All-Russian Zemtsvo Congress, which had encouraged the failed revolution of 1905. As a consequence of that debacle Nabokov had lost his position at the College of Jurisprudence. Yet after the establishment of the Duma his fortunes temporarily improved and with his assistance the Duma passed a vote of no confidence in the ministerial council which the tsar had appointed. This led within a couple of months to the dissolution of the Duma by the tsar, with criminal accusations brought against Nabokov. Found guilty, he, together with other deputies, was sent to the notorious Kresty Prison in 1908 for a three-month sentence, part of a trickle of political figures in these pre-revolutionary days that would become a flood after the success of the Bolsheviks. Yet Nabokov was hardly a radical since he by no means rejected the premises of constitutional monarchy. Moreover, his family was among the capital's wealthiest. Instead, he rejected autocracy in Russia as it had been exerted for centuries and looked to Britain for his model, political as well as cultural, and it is not surprising that the Nabokovs spoke English at home. They were just one of a number of prominent, and not so prominent, Anglophiles who envisioned a Russia more western in its values. As such, they could be seen within the context of a growing and assertive upper middle class which had confidence in the future. This was reflected in contemporary urban development. By 1913 highly innovative plans for the construction of middle-class housing were underway on Goloday Island, to the north of Vasilyevsky Island. The socially minded architect Ivan Fomin had intentions to create a model development which could serve as a template for the needs and lifestyle of the capital's newly prosperous professional, industrial and merchant classes.

The advent of the First World War put a brutal stop to such initiatives, which would only be revived eighty years later. In the meantime, St. Petersburg suffered a radical decline that lasted until the fall of Soviet Union in 1991. Rulers henceforth lived in Moscow, and its role as Russia's most powerful city had come to a conclusive end. Yet when the tercentenary celebrations of the Romanov dynasty were held in the winter of 1913 the streets of St. Petersburg were lit by over one and a half million light bulbs and special cinema projects cast brilliant images of the imperial family on the clouds above. Then few guessed amidst the joyous festivities what awaited not only the Romanovs and aristocracy but millions of Russians of all other classes as well.

Revolution

The First World War brought many changes to St. Petersburg on many levels, including mass mobilization of men. Both the Assembly of the Nobility and the Beloselsky-Belozersky Palace were turned into hospitals. A British doctor, Stephen Paget, left his recollections of the latter's transformation toward the end of 1916 into the Anglo-Russian Hospital:

> Our wards—three large and three less large—are the ballrooms and reception-rooms of the palace, all white and gold, lit with great chandeliers, and hundreds of lights on the walls. We are never tired of the magnificence of our wards. The ballrooms, which are the three large wards, open into each other by wide arches upheld by caryatides like those that guard the staircase. At the end of the largest of the wards there is an alcove, designed for an orchestra, but used now for the setting of an icon, and for a service every Saturday evening. The three reception-rooms likewise open into each other by double folding-doors, making a set of smaller wards, which are of the pleasantest size and very quiet. The six wards together take 190 patients. On the walls are carved and painted tablets, bearing the arms and the names of those [British] towns which have given one or more beds.

Virtually everyone in what was now Petrograd could now see that the end of the old Russian imperial regime was nigh. Vladimir Nabokov wrote in *Petrograd 1917*: "He who lived in the winters of 1915–16 and 1916–17 in St. Petersburg, remembers all too well, that there was a consciousness of catastrophe which deepened from day to day." The Austrian-Jewish novelist Joseph Roth (1894–1939) also visited Petrograd and wrote of Palace Square:

> An early winter evening brought fresh, soft snow, which fell together with the darkness, as if it were lighting it up. But so much snow fell that the square remained deep, and its level did not seem to change even by a centimeter. This square is too wide, I thought—too wide…

In that image a metaphor seems to have been made about Russia's politics, geography and society both before and after the Revolution, from which Russia has to this day not fully recovered.

In March 1917 members of the imperial family were arrested and kept under house arrest at their beloved Alexander Palace in the countryside to the south of Petrograd, remaining there until August of that year during which time Tsar Nicholas II was forced to abdicate. Later, Ellis Ashmead-Bartlett, Russian correspondent for the *Daily Telegraph* and no friend of Russian autocracy, wrote with nostalgia tinged with regret:

> I know nothing more calculated to give a pleasing picture of domestic bliss ruthlessly shattered than the Alexander Palace. The petty tyrant has already vanished into the dim pages of history, and only the memory of a devoted father surrounded by his happy family remains at Tsarskoe-Selo.

Soon violence erupted everywhere in the capital, not only in the working-class suburbs, where wartime conditions were harshest. The luxury Astoria Hotel came under attack in March during a serious confrontation between Russian military officers who, together with British counterparts (and their families), were being accommodated there and Bolshevik supporters on St. Isaac's Square. The British were eventually permitted to depart peacefully but fighting between the opposing Russian factions led to many deaths, the first of hundreds of thousand over the next few years. A new era of change had finally dawned in Russia as Lenin arrived at Petrograd's Finland Station on April 16, 1917, establishing himself at the mansion of the ballet dancer Matilda-Marie Kschessinskaya on the Petrograd Side of the city. This event inspired Vladimir Mayakovsky to write an ode to Lenin's arrival, an occasion which he saw as liberating for Russia at the time, but it would lead to the totalitarian regime which eventually forced the poet to put a bullet through his heart. Yet it was not Lenin's arrival but the blank shot fired from the cruiser *Aurora* which really started the violence of the October Revolution. On October 25, the ship's guns firing upon the Winter Palace were clearly audible in the House of the Nation Theater during the performance of *Don Carlos*, in which Feodor Chaliapin sang the role of Philip II. This was by no means the first time the ship had seen action: it participated in the Battle of Tsushima during the Russo-Japanese War in May 1905. Its captain, Mikhail Nikolay, had already been shot dead by the mutinous crew who supported the Bolsheviks and who started firing at the Winter Palace. Today, it is the oldest ship still commissioned by the Russian Navy and functions as a museum.

Velimir Khlebnikov (1885–1922, real name Viktor Vladimirovich Khlebnikov), a noted Futurist artist and member of the Hylaea group, which included Mayakovsky, described in his reminiscences *October on the Neva* this watershed which brought to an end the period of moderate provisional rule under Alexander Kerensky and opened that of the Bolsheviks, as Kerensky fled in disguise from the Winter Palace:

> The *Aurora* lay quiet on the Neva, opposite the palace, and the long roar of the pipe of its cannon which was directed toward it looked like an iron eye—the face of a sea monster.
>
> One said of Kerensky that he had fled in the clothes of a member of the Salvation Army and that the warrior maids of Petrograd, his final bodyguards, had bravely defended him.

The ensuing storming of the Winter Palace was a relatively tame affair, with little blood spilt in what was otherwise a notoriously bloody revolution. Only 3,000 soldiers were installed in the palace to defend it and many of these were cadets. The artillery for the assault had not been forthcoming and, in any case, the cadets largely disappeared by early evening, taking their weaponry with them. The remaining Cossack defenders departed a couple of hours later. It was then that an ultimatum was issued demanding the palace's surrender and by the early morning of October 26 the palace was occupied by the Bolsheviks with only a minimum of resistance. This was not the stuff of Soviet mythology, however, and so in order to glorify this event the communist authorities decided to create their own version of it.

In 1920 a mass theatrical spectacle was organized to commemorate the third anniversary of the "storming." The great director Nikolai Evreinov was brought in to orchestrate it, using stage sets designed by Yuri Annenkov. In the end, 125 ballet dancers were employed along with 100 circus entertainers and a total cast of over 2,000. When performed on outside the Winter Palace on November 7 that year, at least 100,000 spectators watched the event, without doubt the greatest theatrical happening of that troubled but exhilarating decade.

The rout of both the imperial regime and the February democratic revolution of 1917 was complete. The Christmas party held at the British Embassy, which had occupied the Saltykov Mansion (now the University of Culture) on the Palace Embankment just east of the Summer Garden since 1863, was the last of its kind ever held in imperial Russia. Meriel Buchanan (1886–1959), the only daughter of the last British Ambassador to the Imperial Russian Court left reminiscences of the glittering occasion:

> On Christmas night we invited the members of the Chancery and of the various Naval and Military Missions, as well as some of our Russian friends who had not yet left, for a party that was to prove itself, I think, the last party ever given in the British Embassy. Luckily it was an evening when the electricity was not cut off, so the great glass chandeliers blazed with light, the big rooms were crowded and filled with laughter, and though every officer present had a loaded revolver in his pocket, though there were rifles and cartridge cases hidden in the Chancery, for the moment we tried to forget the ever-present lurking danger, the sadness of approaching good-byes, the desolation and want hidden behind the heavy red brocade curtains which were drawn across the windows... British Naval Attaché Captain F.N.A. Cromie... Dennis Garstin, these were never to reach England alive. They were murdered by Red Guardsmen. The Russian officer who sat next to me at supper was imprisoned by the Bolsheviks scarcely a month later and was tortured to death. The husband of the friend with whom I stayed in the country was murdered by the peasants on his estate. Princess Soltikoff with

her white hair and beautiful tragic eyes, was to die of want and starvation within the year. Even the Embassy was not to escape the relentless fury of the Red Terror; sweating, expectorating soldiers were to invade the big rooms, silence and decay were to follow, mildew rotting the heavy brocade curtains, dust griming the windows, burst pipes spoiling the silk covered walls.

Yet for all this violence, in the aftermath of the Revolution about 1,000 British subjects remained in Petrograd. Some, it is true, were in prison, including the chaplain of the Anglican church, Bousfield Lombard, and after a couple of years only about 200 remained in the city, the lowest level since the early eighteenth century. Some had fled, of whom many were assisted by Violet Froom, matron of the Anglo-Russian hospital during the First World War. Many others were trapped, like one British musician who had successfully hidden his Stradivarius violin in the organ pipes of the Anglican church—the one brought out by Prince Yusupov and secretly and successfully expatriated back to the owner's family—although the musician perished in Soviet captivity.

It was the First World War which had created the backdrop to the Revolution and civil war, without which neither would have happened as they did, setting the murderous tone of the era: between one and a half and two million men are said to have fallen in Russia during the course of the war between 1914 and 1917. Yet bad as that period was, much worse was to follow, with between nine and thirteen million people dying during the Revolution and civil war, many through violence but others through the famine which struck in 1917, disease, especially influenza in 1918–20, and the brutal elements. Fuel was scarce, especially after 1918, and the bitter cold of winter killed the inhabitants in their hundreds of thousands almost as steadily as would be the case later during the Blockade of Leningrad in the Second World War. Mortality rose from 23.4 per thousand in 1917 to 70.5 per thousand in 1919. The population of Petrograd diminished by almost two-thirds. The Jewish writer Isaak Babel (1894–1940), originally from Odesssa, focused in his St. Petersburg report of 1918 upon the grotesque commonplaces of everyday life, with drunks, invalids, and prostitutes jostling with one another on Nevsky Prospekt as if in a painting by Georg Grosz. Industry and trade were also in freefall, with the former dropping to less than one-fifth of its pre-war value by 1920.

All this was the product not merely of the Revolution but of Russia's role in the First World War. Imperial Germany had deliberately provoked a war against Russia in the knowledge that within a few years the country would have proven an even more formidable enemy, taking into account Russia's economic and industrial growth before the conflict. Yet the war had not proceeded as Germany anticipated and the Kaiser's war cabinet had seen fit to support Lenin, who, with his fellow Bolsheviks, had promised an immediate withdrawal of Russia from the war. It is said that Lenin, unable to obtain an American visa from the embassy in Bern, Switzerland, where he was in exile, went to the German Embassy, where he received one instead. This permitted him to cross wartime Germany and eventually make his way back to St. Petersburg, where he served German purposes in pulling Russia out of the war. This occurred after the Bolsheviks seized control, by the Treat of Brest-Litovsk, signed on March 3, 1918, ending Russia's participation in the First World War.

The bloodbath that followed in the immediate wake of the Revolution has gone down in history as among most brutal of such events. Among the first to suffer were members of the imperial family who were imprisoned and then executed by the Bolsheviks in the Peter and Paul Fortress. Then the wider population fell victim to mob violence. Maxim Gorky wrote about lynch justice in St. Petersburg during the Revolution in the newspaper *New Life*, tracing back its pent-up violence to pre-revolutionary times:

> The Honorable People's Commissars have abolished the old courts of justice and, in its place, instituted 'lynch justice,' the bestial law of the street, which has been elevated to the law. Yet even earlier, before the Revolution, our streets delighted in violence... Nowhere does a man love to beat another, with such frequency, with such keenness, with such joy as with us in Russia.

Gorky saw this terrible trait as rooted in past exploitation:

> These people, who have been brought up with abuse, have now
> seized what they consider to be their right to, in turn, torture oth-
> ers without hindrance. They take what is their 'right' and, entering
> into this lust of violence without reserve, with unfathomable grue-
> someness... This blood sullies the flag of the proletariat, tarnishes
> its honor and smothers its social idealism.

On March 12, 1918 the capital was officially moved back
to Moscow, some three centuries after it had been transferred to
St Petersburg. Famine threatened the ravished city and its sharply
reduced population. In January 1918 the bread ration stood at
200 grams; by April it was reduced to 50 grams, as massive movements of migration took place with a recorded 179,000 men returning from the front. The English novelist Hugh Walpole, arriving
shortly afterwards, focused in his novel *The Secret City* (1919) on
Sennaya Square, famous from the novels of Fyodor Dostoyevsky:

> Monstrous groups of flats towered above us, and in the gather-
> ing dusk the figures that slipped in and out of doors were furtive
> shadows and ghosts. No one seemed to speak; you could see no
> faces under the spare-pale-flamed lamps, only hear whispers and
> smell rotten stinks and feel the snow, foul and soiled under one's
> feet... It was a city ruined, like an old dowager whose glory days
> were long past... Away from the splendour it stretched, dirty and
> decrepit and untended, here piles of evil flats, there old wooden
> buildings with cobbled courts, and the canals twisting and creep-
> ing up and down through it all. It was all bathed, as I looked down
> upon it, in colored mist. The air was purple and gold and light blue,
> fading into the snow and ice and transforming it. Everywhere
> there were the masts of ships and the smell of the sea and rough
> deserted places—and shadows moved behind the shadows, and
> yet more shadows behind them, so that it was all uncertain and
> unstable, and only the river knew what it was about.

War and Blockade

During the interwar years and up to the verge of the Second World War the inhabitants of St. Petersburg suffered the fate of those of the rest of the Soviet Union, with tens of thousands purged—often from the older Bolshevik cadres—and hundreds of thousands sent to the Gulag, the brutal political prison camps scattered throughout the country from the Arctic to the Pacific. Joseph Stalin had by now consolidated his power over the whole of the Soviet state, first seized in the mid-1920s after the death of Lenin, sending not only those perceived to be hostile to the Soviet state in general and himself in particular to their deaths or the Gulag camps but even, during the purges of the 1930s, many of the old Bolsheviks who had brought him to power.

Even so, some members of the old aristocracy would occasionally visit Leningrad and marvel at the Soviet "improvements in the life of the common man" with which the authorities regaled them. One such was Sofia Bobrinskaya (descendant of an illegitimate son of the Empress Catherine the Great), the so-called "Red Princess" who had been born on the English Embankment (known as the Red Fleet Embankment at the height of the Soviet period). Her mother had been quite an imposing figure on the pre-revolutionary social scene and when the war broke out she and her family took an active role. Others, however, who remained were not taken in by the Soviet propaganda. These included the Tatar aristocrat and poet Anna Akhmatova, who wrote of her experience of a "Night of stone, whose bright enormous star stares me straight in the eyes, promising death, ah, soon!" in her renowned "Requiem" of the summer of 1939.

All these sufferings would be eclipsed by the torments the country experienced during the course of the Second World War. The Soviet Union suffered more than any other country, with some 20 million of the 34.5 million who had been mobilized killed, wounded or captured from 1939 to 1945. Even then, it was civilians who suffered most: up to eleven million soldiers died in the war, but some fifteen million civilians perished as well, over a million in Leningrad alone.

That the city survived at all was to many a miracle. After all, Hitler's plans for Leningrad were clear-cut. As the *Oberkommando* of the German Wehrmacht put it in a secret protocol of September 23, 1941:

> The Führer has decided to wipe St. Petersburg off the face of the earth. There is no desire whatsoever to allow this urban center to continue in existence… In this existential war, we see no point in allowing even a part of its urban population to survive.

To achieve this complete annihilation Hitler implemented the notorious blockade. Thus, of all Russia's cities including Stalingrad, Leningrad suffered the most, with a death toll ten times greater than Hiroshima. By the end of September 1941 the city was almost completely surrounded. For almost 900 days it suffered catastrophic isolation and deprivation. As the "Red Princess" later wrote of this period about which she heard from friends and relatives:

> By December, people were chewing leather to relieve the pangs of hunger and corpses sat or lay, frozen, in the streets. There were no electricity, no newspapers, no contact with the outside world except for loudspeakers all round town which broadcast news bulletins, music and poetry. And when the people manning the radio became too weak to keep up a continuous service, they set up a metronome beside the microphone. By its regular heartbeat it told the people that their city was still alive.

Countless historic buildings were destroyed or badly damaged, among them the Hermitage Museum which suffered the devastating effects of artillery shells and two aerial bombs during the blockade. It is said that when packers arrived to evacuate art treasures from the Hermitage they found more than a hundred bodies of its staff in the basement. Cannibalism also occasionally occurred. Yet despite all such horrors major epidemics were largely avoided because of the strict sanitary measures introduced by the city's administration. Food became an ever more desperately sought after commodity, with bread rations reduced to a daily 125 grams per non-working person at the height of the blockade, a desperately low figure but still more than double that during the worst of the revolutionary period a generation earlier. The literary critic Lydia Ginzburg (1902–90) wrote in her *Notes on the Blockade*:

> A single overwhelming passion overwhelmed people in the winter, when they got to a shop counter. They hardly spoke a word; they just stared at the bread with manic impatience over the shoulder of the person in front... The neck grew longer. The muscles of the face tightened. The buyer and seller came into contact with one another. Both fought wordlessly for every single gramme.

An unspoken taboo, however, prevented anyone from eating right away, there in front of everyone, when at any moment a hand might reach out to grab at the bread.

Many of the blockade's victims are buried at the Piskarevskoe Memorial Cemetery just outside the city. The poet Olga Bergholz (1910–75) provided a memorable inscription for the memorial sculpture there, which remains embedded in the Russian psyche: "No one is forgotten, nothing is forgotten."

Despite the siege and blockade concerts continued to be held in Leningrad with extraordinary fortitude. The core of the city's Radio Orchestra remained, fourteen musicians under the conductor Karl Eliasberg (1907–78), assisted by a variety of other musicians. The rehearsals began on March 30, 1942, and their performance on August 9 of Shostakovich's new Seventh Symphony remains one of the most impressive cultural events ever to have occurred in a war-time situation and was broadcast throughout the country—arguably one of the greatest morale boosters of this period when the very survival of the Soviet Union and its people was at stake.

At first, leading literary figures like Akhmatova remained in Leningrad, where her early experience of the war enabled her to begin work on her "Poems without a Hero," begun in 1940. With the advent of the catastrophic blockade, however, Akhmatova was evacuated from Leningrad in September 1941. First, she was taken to Moscow and then to the less threatened central Asian city of Tashkent, where she remained until May 1944.

The blockade was eventually broken—with British aid—in January 1944, but it continued to inspire for decades artists and literary figures throughout the world. Some sixty years later the British author Helen Dunmore published her novel, *The Siege* (2001), to considerable acclaim, making it, like the Holocaust, an event of such horror and magnitude that the human mind struggles still to comprehend it.

Crime and Punishment

The end of the Second World War did not mean that the years of killing had come to an end. On the contrary, the so-called Leningrad Affair (1949–52) proved that threats, perceived or real, were also within. Stalin's mortality, in tandem with the virtually unlimited power he held, meant that a jockeying for position would ensue at the highest levels. In Leningrad the local Communist Party elite felt themselves strong enough to challenge their Moscow rivals. In this, however, they were mistaken. With the Moscow communist leadership victorious, the former mayor Aleksey Kuznetsov, the acting mayor Pyotr Popkov and all their deputies were arrested. Twenty-three received the death penalty, and a further 181 prison sentences or exile. More than 2,000 officials lost their jobs and membership of the party. The misery did not end here as their families also suffered the inevitable consequences of being exiled to Siberia or elsewhere, their livelihoods removed. Only during the so-called Khrushchev Thaw, in which some of the excesses of the Stalinist period were mitigated and brought to public attention, were some of those convicted rehabilitated.

During the final decades of the Soviet Union the crime rate was low compared to imperial days, even despite economic decline. Yet after the fall of communism, during the chaotic years of the 1990s, murder and violent crimes reached levels in St. Petersburg unheard of since the early 1920s. Criminal gangs collected a tax on many legitimate businesses, undermining the city's developing economy, and both big and small companies were targeted. After President Putin took power, however, a dramatic reduction in crime occurred, which has persisted to this day, and for many this is reason enough to support him as president. By the early 2000s many of the criminal who had sapped the economic blood of St. Petersburg were dead, in prison or had gone straight, consolidating their ill-gotten gains in legitimate businesses. Corruption on various levels remained a major problem, but a growing middle class was emerging in which the young were the principal participants. St. Petersburg, it seemed, was truly becoming a successful European city.

Yet the advent of Islamist extremism, which led to outrages in New York, London and elsewhere, eventually made itself felt in St Petersburg too. The bombing on November 27, 2009, of the Nevsky Express, a high speed rail service linking Moscow to St. Petersburg, killed 28 passengers and injured a further 96 near the town of Bologoye in Tver Province. The Moscow metro system had suffered a number of bombings which killed many people, but St. Petersburg seemed spared, that is until April 3, 2017. A bomb detonated in a carriage traveling between Sennaya Square Tekhnologichesky stations left fourteen people dead in the country's second city, with dozens more injured. Two days later, in an act of solidarity with the victims, St. Petersburg's famed football team Zenit laid flowers at the scene.

6 | The City Imagined
Literature and Theater

Virtually from its foundation St. Petersburg attracted literary intellectuals not only from Russia but elsewhere in Europe. One early organization that provided a hub for such *literati* in the early days was the Society of Learned Friends. A key member was Prince Antioch Kantemir (1708–44), who had migrated to Russia from Moldova in 1711. He entered the service of Peter the Great, and his residence, built by Rastrelli, was located on land granted by the tsar at 8 Palace Embankment, adjacent to that of St. Petersburg's first archbishop, Feofan Prokopovich. The Pachtuv Palace now stands on the site of the former three-story house.

Kantemir was a keen man of letters and wrote a variety of lyrical verse on St. Petersburg, showing his wit as a man of the Enlightenment. He reserved his most pointed barbs, in the service of the tsar, for those who did their best to thwart Peter the Great's reforms, both religious and secular. His wry expression, "with a smile through the tears," still lives on in Russian colloquial speech. Active in the diplomatic service of Peter's successor, the Empress Anna, he died while on a mission to England and France in 1732.

Kantemir, as well as his neighbor Prokopovich (discussed in Chapter 9), were typical of the supporters who bolstered Peter the Great's autocratic reforms and who came from outside the old aristocratic Russian circle of boyars. Many of the tsar's keenest and most intimate backers were Ukrainian or Polish by birth, from ethnic backgrounds which historically straddled both East and West. The importance the tsar gave to academic pursuits helped to create a body of thinkers whose collective wisdom serviced both autocrat and state.

Along with Mikhail Lomonosov, a number of other prominent men of science and the arts were members of this circle. In the world of literature Vasily Trediakovsky was of note as the first Russian poet to use classical forms and metric verse. Alexander Symarokov (1717–77) later joined this circle during the middle years of the eighteenth century during the reign of the Empress Elizabeth. His greatest importance to the cultural life of St. Petersburg was the role he played in the development of the dramatic arts. For this reason he was labelled the Father of Russian Theater by Russia's greatest literary critic Vissarion Belinsky (1881–48).

Early Theater

As early as the reign of the Empress Anna, members of the imperial court and the world of culture had recognized the need to bring the dramatic arts to the new capital, and so the country's only theatrical troupe, based at Yaroslavl under the direction of Fyodor Volkov, was imported to St. Petersburg. In the socially stratified and highly status-conscious city, however, the actors' living arrangements created practical problems. Strict governmental regulations forbade their accommodation in noble residences such as the spacious Menshikov Palace because of their rank as commoners, and so they were housed in the more limited confines of the Golovkinsky House next door.

Court balls were a highly valued form of entertainment, with musical and literary pretensions. The Empress Anna was fond of them, as well as of other less lofty forms of social entertainment and took a keen interest in the construction of suitable venues for them, some of a highly eccentric nature. The venue built in 1739 was perhaps the most striking: it was a palace of ice constructed next to the Winter Palace itself. Not only balls but the weddings of her court jesters took place there and on one notorious occasion it was used for the court wedding of the disgraced Prince Mikhail Golitsyn and his Kalmyk bride Anna Buzheninova, whom she intended to ridicule publicly. Although much of the palace had already melted away by April 1740, a certain English visitor, Dr. John Cook, was still able to marvel at its ruins in July of that year:

> The walls were of ice; the bed-stead, and all pieces of household furniture were made of ice; they fired out of ice cannons: But for what? To do honor, or, which is the truth, to ridicule the Russ nobility in the person of a poor foolish pair, taken from the best family in Russia.

The Empress Elizabeth also adored theater and in 1755 had a portable one installed near her own palace apartments. The acting standards did not bear comparison with international theatrical troupes and so it became her priority to import actors and actresses from abroad. As a result, Russia's first permanent theater company was established in St. Petersburg in 1756, with the finest performers she could obtain. Again because of restrictions that sought to restrict financial extravagance and inordinate displays of luxury their productions were held in the two-story theater built within the Golovkinsky House, where Symarokov, its first director, had established his residence. In 1756 Elizabeth also ordered the formal establishment of a Russian Tragedy and Comedy Theater, in the Summer Garden, thereby putting the capital's theatrical life on a more stable footing. It was built the following year by Rastrelli and was connected to the Summer Palace by a series of staircases and covered passage ways. Although it was to remain the main theatrical venue only until 1761, the performances of the empress' own Italian company were long remembered, along with French and German ones as well. Yet it is the Hermitage Theater (1783–87), by Giacomo Quarenghi, which was an especially impressive gem, his chef d'oeuvre set within the walls of the Winter Palace in the neo-Palladian style popular throughout European courts at the time. Its external facade was erected in 1802 and it was later connected by an arch, with gallery space above, to the Old Hermitage to the north, according to the designs of Leon Benois, a son of court architect Nicholas Benois, who created a foyer to the theater there in 1902. The world famous interior amphitheater is adorned by a Corinthian colonnade and statues of figures from Greek mythology as well as bas reliefs of literary figures such as the Frenchmen Molière and Racine, the Italians Pietro Metastasio and Baldassare Galuppi and the Russian Alexander Sumarokov. Ballets are still held there today.

The St. Petersburg Imperial Kamenny (Stone) Theater was originally built in 1783 in a neoclassical style by the Italian Antonio Rinaldi, and achieved considerable acclaim at its opening with Giovanni Paisiello's opera *Il mondo della luna*. Then, in 1802, it was renovated by Thomas de Thomon to accommodate an audience of 1,500 and was renamed the Bolshoi (Big). On New Year's Day 1811 it caught fire and was badly damaged, requiring a major reconstruction. During the following seven years, performances were held at the German Theater, which had recently opened on Palace Square. Fully restored, the Bolshoi reopened on February 3, 1818, with the ballet *Flore et Zéphire* by the Frenchman Charles-Louis Didelot (1767–1837). This theater played a central role in the literary life of the capital not only for its famed productions, both musical and dramatic, but because of the prominence it was given in Russian literature, not least in Alexander Pushkin's verse novel *Eugene Onegin*, in which the principal character's presence at the theater is of considerable importance for the plot.

The theater survived for over a century but, judged unsound, finally closed as a venue for the performance of opera and ballet in 1886, after which only concerts were held there. In 1896 it was given over to the St. Petersburg Conservatory of Music and was largely demolished. By then, however, the famed Alexandrinsky Theater (1828–32), embellished by majestic Corinthian loggias which still grace its facades and with a commanding statue of Empress Catherine the Great in front, had assumed the role of St. Petersburg's principal dramatic theater.

The city's theaters attracted some of the most famous actors and actresses of the European stage. Many of them were promoted by the noted and powerful Russian author and critic Alexander Radishev (1728–1806). The French actress Mademoiselle Georges (real name Marguerite Joséphine Weimer) was one of the most popular of those performing during this period. Beautiful and charming in her youth, it was said that in his consular days Napoleon had been her lover. In the Russian capital, however, Count Alexander von Benckendorff, the Baltic German nobleman who was head of the secret police during the reign of Tsar Nicholas I, patronized her and she settled at 59 Moika Embankment. Her first performance in Russia was the tragedy *Phèdre* by Racine, which took place at the Imperial Bolshoi Theater on July 13, 1808, to a full house. As the reactionary French philosopher Count Joseph-Marie de Maistre,

The frozen River Neva and the Hermitage (Eugene Slobodin/Wikimedia Commons)

Nevsky Prospekt, 1799, by Benjamin Patersen (Hermitage Museum/Wikimedia Commons)

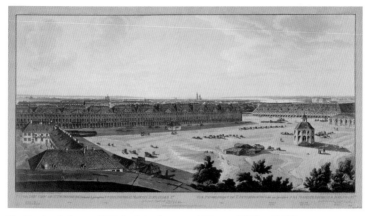

The Twelve Colleges, 1802, by John Augustus Atkinson (1775-c. 1833)
(Hermitage Museum/Library of Congress, Washington DC)

The monumental Great Arch of the New Holland naval complex
(Evgeny Gerashchenko/Wikimedia Commons)

The ornate Avtoto metro station (Alex "Florstein" Fedorov/Wikimedia Commons)

The Vorontsov Palace in winter (Heidas/Wikimedia Commons)

The Admiralty spire (Alex "Florstein" Fedorov/Wikimedia Commons)

Peter the Great's *Kunstkammer*, with its astronomical observatory
(Alf van Beem/Wikimedia Commons)

The Marble Palace, on Palace Embankment, now part of the Russian State Museum
(@ A. Savin/Wikimedia Commons)

Fire in the Winter Palace 17 December 1837, 1838, by Boris Green
(Hermitage Museum/Wikimedia Commons)

The Annunciation Bridge with St Isaac's Cathedral behind
(Mike1979Russia/Wikimedia Commons)

The art nouveau Singer House or House of Books
(Alex "Florstein" Fedorov/Wikimedia Commons)

The storming of Nöteborg (Oreshek), 1702, by Alexander von Kotzebue. Peter the Great is in the center of the painting (Wikimedia Commons)

Aerial view of The Peter and Paul Fortress and Cathedral
(Andrew Shiva/Wikipedia/CC BY-SA 4.0)

Étienne Falconet's *The Bronze Horseman* in Senate Square, homage to Peter the Great (Florstein/Wikimedia Commons)

Empress Catherine the Great, 1763, by Fyodor Rokotov
(Tretyakov Gallery, Moscow/Wikimedia Commons)

The General Staff Building seen from Palace Square
(Wolfgang Moroder/Wikimedia Commons)

Photograph of Rasputin and two high-ranking officers, 1907, by Karl Bulla
(Wikimedia Commons)

The cruiser *Aurora* (Otto Jula/Wikimedia Commons)

One of the last photographs of Tsar Nicholas II, showing him at Tsarskoye Selo after his abdication in March 1917 (Library of Congress, Washington DC)

Alexander Pushkin, 1827, by Orest Adamovich Kiprensky
(Tretyakov Gallery, Moscow/Wikimedia Commons)

Portrait of the Writer Fyodor Dosteyevsky, 1872, by Vasily Perov
(Tretyakov Gallery, Moscow/Wikimedia Commons)

The route to exile: *The Vladimirka Road*, 1892, by Isaak Levitan
(Tretyakov Gallery, Moscow/Wikimedia Commons)

The Hermitage Museum by the frozen River Neva
(Eugene Slobodin/Wikimedia Commons)

Portrait of an Unknown Peasant, 1784, by Ivan Argunov
(Tretyakov Gallery, Moscow/
Wikimedia Commons)

The Merchant's Wife at Tea, 1918, by Boris Kustodiev
(State Russian Museum/Wikimedia Commons)

The Bay tree egg by Fabergé, owned by Viktor Vekselberg
(Testus/Wikimedia Commons)

Smolny Cathedral   (Florstein/Wikimedia Commons)

Church of St John the Baptist at Chesme Palace   (@ A. Savin/Wikimedia Commons)

The Kazan Cathedral   (Dennis Jarvis/Wikimedia Commons)

The glittering Great Hall at the Catherine Palace (Dennis Jarvis/Wikimedia Commons)

The Kushelev-Bezborodko Dacha (Januarius-zick/Wikimedia Commons)

Ambassador of Sardinia to Russia, was said to have put it, "I found the tone of her declamation did not ring true, turgid like everything which emanates from Paris." Yet, whatever criticism there might have been about her highly intellectual, rather than emotionally expressive performance, he was thoroughly convinced that

"With respect to her appearance, there is no doubt about it— she is beautiful!"

Her rival was the Russian Ekaterina Semionova, famed for her performance as Aménaïde in Voltaire's *Tancrède* and whose highly emotive style contrasted with the intellectual approach of Weimer, with committed partisans on both sides. The actresses nonetheless maintained a publicly cordial relationship, although sometimes laced with malice. Tongues wagged on one occasion, according to Alla Beliakova, after Georges sent Semionova 30 roubles for a ticket in a third-circle box, the latter returning the "compliment" by sending 200 roubles to Georges for the same seat. Georges was said to have replied with French irony,

> Gracious madam! If you have sent me your 200 roubles as a judgement on my talents, words fail me as to how I should thank you, and to this I will supplement another 250 to give to the poor. However, if you are merely sending me a gift, please be advised that in Paris I have a fortune of some 200,000 francs.

When very young, Georges had already come to the attention of Tsar Alexander I, who rapidly succumbed to her charms. During the Napoleonic Wars, witty repartee between them became the talk of the capital. When she requested permission to return home before the invasion of Russia, the emperor was said to have replied to her in this exchange:

> "I am willing to go to war with Napoleon if it allows me to keep you in Russia."
>
> "But, Sire, my place can only be now in France, not here," she retorted.

"Well then," the tsar quipped back, "I shall send my army before you, so that I can take you there myself. Allow my army to go ahead of you and I shall take you there myself." (From Alla Beliakova "Violets for Bonaparte," *Taleon Magazine*, May 2004)

Georges was to have the last word: "Do not trouble yourself, sire. I am quite happy to await the arrival of the French in Moscow, which will happen sooner!"

Together with her father and sister, she did finally return home from Russia in that fateful year 1812. She left a gap in the theatrical world of the capital which no one could fill for years to come.

Soirées

Theater was important in the cultural life of St. Petersburg, but society hostesses also played a significant part, with soirées and other such events central to the imagination of the city. Noble palaces and other residences formed the principal venues. The French architect Thomas de Thomon was tasked with rebuilding the eighteenth-century Laval House at the English Embankment as the home of the society hostess Countess Alexandra Laval. There the famed architect Alexander Brullov lived in a separate apartment. Visitors to her soirées included such literary luminaries as Pushkin, Lermontov, Alexander Griboyedov and the Lithuanian-Pole Adam Mickiewicz, the latter living at 39 Kazanskaya Street. Mickiewicz wrote his famous *Crimean Sonnets* there, which achieved as much renown in Russia as in his native Poland. Laval's daughter Ekaterina was an important cultural figure of feminine virtue, having gone down in history as a symbol of conjugal fidelity and self-sacrifice: she had married the Decembrist conspirator Prince Sergei Trubetskoy, who after his conviction was condemned to decades-long exile and penal labor in Siberia, a fate that she shared with her husband until their rehabilitation. Many other Decembrists would end up in Shlisselburg Fortress on the shores of Lake Ladoga.

Another prominent property situated at 12 Nevsky Prospekt belonged to Count Mikhail Miloradovich, descendant of an aristocratic family of Serbian origin and a military hero who was appointed governor of St. Petersburg in 1818. According to the historian Alexander Mikhailovsky-Danilevsky who visited Milora-dovich, his apartment resembled a

> furniture shop or fine art dealer's for the great quantity of diverse object and items it contained... Almost every room had its own kind of lighting: in one light was provided by wax candles, in an-other by alabaster lamps; in a third the candles were placed in such a manner that you could not see them and they lit the paintings alone. One room was fully lined with mirrors: not just the walls, but the ceiling too was made of mirrors. Another room was fur-nished with divans in the Turkish manner and the most salacious paintings hung there. In the middle of the library was an aviary... "Where is your bedroom," I asked him. "I don't have a bedroom," he replied. "I spend the night where I feel like."

Miloradovich was eventually to move to a state apartment on Bolshaya Morskaya Street in 1822. There he continued his eccen-tric bachelor lifestyle. Unfortunately, he was shot on Senate Square by the Decembrist conspirator Pyotr Kakhovsky. According to S.S. Shults Jr in "A Russian Bayard" (*Taleon Magazine*), "Right before his death he dictated his will. Among other thing it stated, 'I request the Emperor, if it be possible, to grant freedom to all my men and peasants.' Not one of the Decembrists did anything similar before the reforms of 1861!"

Alexander Pushkin

Another Decembrist sympathizer was Russia's greatest poet, Alex-ander Pushkin (1799–1837). The great-grandson of Hannibal, an African slave who had been given to Tsar Peter the Great, emanci-pated as a boy, elevated to the nobility and then trained as a military officer in France, Pushkin enjoyed all the benefits which aristocratic life afforded in Russia at this time. He finished his schooling at the Tsarskoe Selo Lyceum, Russia's finest educational establishment for the boys of the nobility, during a period in which he and his family had moved to St. Petersburg from Moscow in 1814. Here they came to live a peripatetic existence, moving from one part of the city to another. In 1818 they settled at 185 Fontanka Embankment, where the poet completed his epic poem "Ruslan and Ludmila," only to move again, in 1820, into a rather typical wooden house of few architectural pretensions at the Griboyedov Canal Embankment in the Kolomna neighborhood. Here he completed his "Ode to Liberty," which took many of the values of the French Revolution as inspiration. Yet it is the poem "The Little House at Kolomna" which bests captures his everyday impressions of that relatively new part of St. Petersburg in which he lived.

Pushkin then established his own domestic independence, frequently staying during the later 1820s at the Hotel Demuth at 40 Moika, where he wrote his poem "Poltava" about the famous battle in which Tsar Peter the Great defeated the warrior King Karl XII of Sweden in 1709. Fellow poet and dramatist Alexander Griboyedov (1795–1829) also stayed there in 1828, and the two frequently met, sometimes with Adam Mickiewicz, who often dined with them there. Griboyedov, best known for his play *Woe from Wit*, was inspired by the English poet Thomas Gray's comment that it was a "folly to be wise." He would meet his death as a diplomat in the Persian capital, Tehran, where he was torn apart in the Russian Embassy by an anti-Russian mob in 1829, an act for which the Shah of Persia's son would eventually be forced to apologize on a later visit to St. Petersburg.

Literary societies played an important role in St. Petersburg's cultural life, and as a young man Pushkin joined the society known as the Green Lamp, led by Nikita Vsevolozhsky, with whom he played cards. The society's name subversively suggested hope and light, while its members wore red caps, a symbol at the time of their free-thinking and anti-autocratic political convictions.

Some of the figures Pushkin encountered later figured prominently in his poems and stories. For example, the character of the elderly countess in the 1834 short story *The Queen of Spades* was based on Princess Natalya Petrovna Golitsyn (1741–1827), who lived on Gorokhovaya Street in a late eighteenth-century three-story house which still exists today. A society beauty who had lived in England as a child and later in Paris at the French court, she was maid of honor to Catherine the Great. Apparently notorious for her miserliness, Natalya, who died at the age of 97, was also known behind her back in later years as *la Princesse Moustache* because of her conspicuous facial hair.

Her grandson, Prince Sergei Golitsyn, first told Pushkin a fascinating anecdote about her, one that the poet would use to great effect in his writing: Golitsyn had requested from his grandmother some ready money to pay for his gambling habit, but rather than giving him the cash she had told him which cards to play. This she did using the inside knowledge of cards which she had acquired while a young lady in France at the court of Louis XVI. Then a gentleman said to be the Comte de Saint-Germain had provided her with the appropriate information relating to three cards, and this she divulged to her grandson, who duly won. This was the kernel of the famous story which Pushkin—and later Tchaikovsky in his famous opera of the same name—was to develop so successfully.

Yet it was another of her relations, Princess Evdokiya Golitsyna (1780–1850), known as "la princesse nocturne" and "la princesse minuit," who exerted an even more profound influence on Pushkin's piece: an anecdote circulated that a gypsy had once prophesied that the princess would die at night, which so terrified her that she decided to turn her days into nights, and her nights into days. Evdokiya had married Prince Golitsyn, a man of great means but infamous for his lack of physical and social charms. She more than made up for his failings by her own social skills. Her evening salon was so highly prized that visitors included not only Pushkin but older notables such as the historian Nikolai Karamzin and poet Piotr Viazemsky.

A lady of considerable education, the princess was interested in chemistry and physics. She was also very eccentric and became convinced—erroneously—of the deleterious effects of the potato, only recently introduced into Russia. Yet she was interested in mathematics and made her own most noted contribution written in French, "De l'analyse de la force." Pushkin first encountered her at a soirée at the Karamzins' home toward the end of 1817 when she was a generation older than him. Nonetheless, as Karamzin confided to Viazemsky, "Pushkin is terribly in love with Pythia Golitsyna and spends his evenings with her at her home.

Pushkin was not only enamored of the princess. When he wrote of St. Petersburg's most famous ballet master of the period Charles-Louis Didelot, "the ballets of Didelot are performed with liveliness and are full of unusual elements," it was less the ballet master than one of his most famous pupils, the ballerina A.I. Istomina (1799–1848), who really entranced Pushkin—a figure who graces such poems as "The Prisoner of the Caucasus" and "Ruslan and Ludmila."

Istomina was merely a foretaste of the romantic infatuations and loves in which Pushkin was to be involved. A frequent visitor to the Fontanka Embankment, the venue for many soirées, he was the guest of the artist, historian and archaeologist Aleksey Olenin, president of the Imperial Academy of Arts from 1817 and one of its most prominent members. Pushkin's recollections from these gatherings were eventually compiled by him in lines for which Mikhail Glinka eventually wrote music, reflecting the poet's romantic feelings for society beauty Ekaterina Ermolovna. Yet more dramatic was one of Pushkin's tempestuous affairs, this time with Agrafena Zakrevsky, a society beauty of the time notorious for her seductive powers. Her husband had become minister of the interior in 1828, when they moved from Helsinki, capital of Russian Finland, to St. Petersburg. Her fascinating notoriety had traveled with her, since in Helsinki Agrafena had been the scandalous talk of the town because of her penchant for infidelity and subsequent cruelty toward lovers. Pushkin, unaware of her reputation, failed to heed advice from her victims and was left distraught.

Not one to remain disconsolate for long, he was soon to find the love of his life in Natalia Goncharova, the great society beauty. They married and Pushkin moved from Moscow and came to stay in 1831 at the Kitaev Dacha, near the Catherine Palace at Tsarskoe Selo, now a museum. The following year, they moved to 53 Galernaya Street in the center of St. Petersburg, where they remained from the autumn until May 1832. They then settled first at 20 Fyrstatskoy Street (in a building which has since been demolished) before moving once again in the winter of 1832–33 to 26 Bolshaya Morskaya Street and then to 5 Panteleamonskoy Street (today's Pestelya Street). This was a particularly attractive locale since the Summer Garden was nearby across the River Fontanka. Pushkin often walked there, writing, "the Summer Garden is my kitchen garden. I wake up and go there in my dressing gown and slippers. I am at home there." Even so, the family once again moved in August 1834, to 32 Palace Embankment, where they stayed until May 1836 before moving to Pushkin's final home, at 12 Moika Embankment. There he was working on a history of Peter the Great, a figure whom, together with Voltaire, he greatly admired, when he met his premature death. Today it is the site of the Pushkin Apartment Museum and offers a rare and fascinating insight into his life both personal and literary.

Pushkin's death was not from natural causes—he was fatally wounded in a duel with Georges-Charles de Heeckeren D'Anthès, an Alsatian military aristocrat resident in the city who was openly pursuing his wife Natalia. The duel took place on January 27, 1834, and Pushkin was wounded by a bullet in the stomach, which led to his death two days later. Today a memorial obelisk marks the site where the deadly duel took place at Novaya Derevnaya, near the Pushkinskaya metro station, where a small sculpture of the poet preparing for his duel by Mikhail Anikushin commemorates the event. Although originally planned to be held at St. Isaac's Cathedral, his funeral was secretly moved by the authorities, fearful of a political demonstration, to the smaller church of the Imperial Stables, built by Vasily Stasov between 1817 and 1823. His body was then removed to the Svyatogorsky Monastery in the province of Pskov, not far from his beloved country estate Michaelovsky, today a museum to his memory. In St. Petersburg, it is his monumental statue by the twentieth-century sculptor Mikhail Anikushin in the center of Arts Square which is his most visible memorial.

Duels, though officially illegal, were a hazard of the time for the aristocracy and intelligentsia, and fellow literary luminary Mikhail Lermontov (1814–41) was another victim. Lermontov was a frequent visitor to the city and was best known for his novel *A Hero of*

Our Time (1840), with its Romantic hero estranged from the society in which he lived, and his play *Masquerade*, written in 1836 but first published in 1842. Lermontov shared Pushkin's hot temper and was quick to turn to the duel in matters of honor. On February 18, 1840, he dueled with Ernest Barante, son of the French Ambassador, at a site not far from where Pushkin was shot. On this occasion, however, the conclusion was happier. After duelling with rapiers, they took up pistols; Barante fired and missed, while Lermontov deliberately shot to the side away from his opponent.

Lermontov left St. Petersburg for the last time in February 1841, exiled by Tsar Nicholas I for his subversive views. He was not so lucky in his second duel: he was killed at Pyatigorsk in the Caucasus on July 27 that year after his teasing of an old school friend, Nikolay Martinov, overstepped the mark and led to the deadly duel. "A dog's death for the dog," the tsar is reputed to have commented. Today Lermontov is immortalized by a bust in the Alexandrinsky Gardens by V.P. Kreitan (1896) and a monument on Lermontovsky Avenue by B.M. Mikeshin (1916).

Gogol, Turgenev, and Dostoyevsky

The greatest literary figure to rival Pushkin at this time, was Nikolai Gogol (1809–52). He led a highly peripatetic life in the capital, first staying in the spring of 1829 at the inexpensive Hotel Naples on the corner of the Ekaterininsky (now Griboyedov) Canal and Voznesensky Prospekt. Later he moved to 42 Gorokhovaya Street, taking up residence on the fourth floor in what was then a poor quarter of the city, but as his finances improved so did his accommodation. In late 1829 he established himself on the more fashionable Ekaterininky Canal, taking rooms with friends on the fifth floor of the residence of a prosperous merchant, I.D. Zverkov, from which he left a fascinating record of his time in his short story *Diary of a Madman*, published in 1834. By the year before, however, the eccentric author had already moved once again to Malaya Morskaya Street, where he was to remain until 1836. By now his writings were bringing him success and in 1834 he was appointed assistant professor at the University of St. Petersburg. He also took up studies at the

Imperial Academy of Arts. This was a highly fruitful literary period in Gogol's life, a time when he wrote one of his most popular short stories, the surreal *The Nose* (1836), which later became the subject of Dmitri Shostakovich's ballet of the same name (1930).

Gogol also lived for a while in what was then an outlying suburb of St. Petersburg, Kolomna. Like Pushkin before him, Gogol left his impressions, declaring that "Here it is neither the capital, nor the province," but rather a no man's land which provided its own peculiar inspiration. As Vladimir Dmitrievich Nabokov would later write with respect to Gogol in *Petrograd 1917*:

> It was no wonder, that the city of St. Petersburg revealed wonders, as Russia's most extraordinary Russian went down its streets. For St. Petersburg was just that: a reflection in a tarnished looking glass, a gruesome confusion of objects, of which improper use has been made. Things which went backwards, the more they ran forwards, bright gray nights instead of the usual black and black days—the "black day" of a shabby office clerk.

For Nabokov, Gogol's weird visions of a pig that lived in a house or a nose that rode in a coach were only to be expected of a city like St. Petersburg. And the city which Gogol admired was a cosmopolitan place, its main thoroughfare Nevsky Prospekt an avenue in which all types of humanity from countless countries were to be found, a fact also mirrored in its architecture. He wrote a panegyric on the subject, *On Architecture in the Present Times*, praising the city's modern and eclectic architecture:

> A city should be composed of a variety of masses, so to speak, which together give pleasure to the eye. The greater diversity of styles the better. There should be one building sombre and Gothic, as well as one eastern, smothered in ornament, one Egyptian, monumental in style, and one Greek, evincing its delicate proportions, all on the same street.

This is an effect still apparent in St. Petersburg today, almost two centuries after Gogol walked its streets. Not inappropriately, the author is commemorated today in the pedestrian zone of Malaya Konyushennaya Street by a modern full-size statue by M.V. Belov, A.A. Ananyev and C.B. Astapov. Here the author is depicted as both contemplative and melancholic, characteristics which together left him spiritually agonized but immensely productive.

Another author who took inspiration from the classic imagery of St. Petersburg, albeit in a grim and rather begrudging way, was Ivan Turgenev (1818–83). More generally known for his tales of rural life—he lived at the estate of Spasskoye-Lutovinovo near Oryol in south-western Russia—Turgenev wrote in *Visions: A Phantasy* (1868):

> Pale Nordic Night! Is it then really a night at all? Is it not rather a pale ill day? I have never liked the nights of St. Petersburg… our Nordic Palmyra. Everything is bright, everything is obvious and clear in a sinister way, while everything sleeps a sad sleep… The evening redness—a consumptive redness—has not departed yet and will not leave the white starless sky until the morning. Its reflection lies upon the silky shimmering surface of the Neva, which hardly moves and lightly murmurs, as its cold, blue flow rolls onwards.

It was in St. Petersburg that he both enjoyed and was tortured by his volatile relationship with Pauline Viardot, a famous French singer, but a modern sculpture of him situated on Manezhnaya Square, in the heart of the city by Valentin Sveshnikov and Yan Neyman gives no hint of this. Rather, he appears here as the philosopher Vasily Rozanov once put it: "Turgenev is so great in stature that he seems to be more solid furniture than a living person."

It was in contrast to Gogol, and more in the vein of Turgenev, that Russia's greatest author of the third quarter of the nineteenth century, Fyodor Dostoyevsky (1821–81), found his own inspiration in St. Petersburg. As a child Dostoyevsky was plagued by illness. In particular, he suffered acutely from epilepsy, the experience of which enabled him to describe the illness later in life with extraordinary precision in his late novel *The Brothers Karamazov* (1879–80). At the age of fifteen he had moved from Moscow to St. Petersburg, where he enrolled at the Engineers' College, established in 1819 at the notorious Mikhailovsky Castle, where Tsar Paul I had been murdered by courtiers in 1801. His curriculum included not only engineering, but Russian, French and history, including that of architecture. With his fondness for the night, it was then that he did most of his creative writings. Certainly, his life was haunted even at an early age by ghosts, even before he had taken up residence at the castle. His family background left its own indelible mark: his father had died young, officially of a stroke, but more probably—as his family believed—strangled by a disaffected serf on their estate near Moscow.

Upon leaving college, Dostoyevsky lived at 11 Vladimirskaya Prospekt from 1842 to 1845. It was just one of the twenty apartments which he occupied in the capital during the rest of his life—his lengthy Siberian imprisonment and exile excluded. However, in the spring of 1847 he moved to the corner of Voznesensky Prospekt and Malaya Morskaya Street, where a highly creative period began; at this time he wrote some of his most admired short stories including *White Nights*, full of a hauntingly beautiful atmosphere. There is also an ominous element in these stories that would soon overshadow Dostoyevsky's own life in a way which almost led to the firing squad. A nearly fatal venue meeting was to take place at one of St. Petersburg's most fashionable cafés.

For Dostoyevsky, the allure of the pastries and cakes of Wolff and Beranget, a haunt of Pushkin—where he drank his last coffee before his duel—was to have almost dire consequences: there he became acquainted with the radical Mikhail Petrashevsky and joined the so-called Petrashevsky Circle, an anti-tsarist discussion group. As a result, on April 23, 1849, the young author was arrested and his apartment searched. Incriminating subversive evidence was found and, along with 21 other suspects, he was sent to court, tried and convicted. Condemned to death—the execution by firing squad was to take place on December 22 in Semyonov Square (now

Pioneersky Square), adjacent to where the Semyonovsky Guards Regiment was stationed—he was reprieved by the tsar at the eleventh hour, even as he waited at the square for his sentence to be carried out. Dostoyevsky later incorporated his experiences in another of his great novels, *The Idiot*, written when he lived abroad.

Spared death by order of Tsar Nicholas himself, his sentence was commuted to four years' hard labor imprisonment in Siberia, a confinement followed by further years of compulsory military service. Bowing to the inevitable and transferred from the Peter and Paul Fortress where he had been held with the other radicals, he left the capital on December 25, 1849, finally arriving at Omsk where he spent his captivity. A famous painting, *The Vladimirka Road to Siberia* (Tretyakov Museum, Moscow) by Isaak Levitan (1860–1900), a Jewish artist who himself had suffered banishment from Moscow, captured in a compelling image the road taken by these convicts into eastern exile.

Once there Dostoyevsky found life almost unbearable. As he wrote at the time:

> In summer, intolerable closeness; in winter, unendurable cold. All the floors were rotten. Filth on the floors an inch thick; one could slip and fall... We were packed like herrings in a barrel... There was no room to turn around. From dusk to dawn it was impossible not to behave like pigs... Fleas, lice, and black beetles by the bushel...

Finally released, he was inducted into military service at Semipalatinsk, where the famous archaeologist A.E. Wrangel was also based. He assisted Dostoyevsky not only in rehabilitating himself, but in acquiring a minor military promotion. He also married there before finally, in March 1859, being demobilized from the army and permitted to return to St. Petersburg. Sadly, only five years later, in 1864, both the author's wife and his brother Mikhail died. Yet not all was doom and gloom: on February 15, 1867, his indispensable stenographer Anna Snitkina became his second wife.

It is still said in St. Petersburg today that the house in which Raskolnikov, the idealistic murderer of *Crime and Punishment*

(1866), was said to have lived was based on what is today 19 Grazhdanskaya Street. (It was near here that the author of this book was robbed in the unsettled days of the early 2000s when St. Petersburg was still subject to a degree of lawlessness.) The home of the old woman pawnbroker, Raskolnikov's victim, was modeled on 104 Griboyedov Canal and remains a somewhat forbidding apartment block with its seemingly endless spiral staircase. That on which Sonya Marmeladova's apartment was based is still to be found at 73 Griboyedov Canal, making this part of St. Petersburg truly Dostoyevsky territory. Many of the buildings mentioned in his works have deep, well-like internal courtyards, with passageways from one to another, so that even now it is said that anyone wishing to move in anonymity from one part of the city to another can still do so through these darkened courtyards. Conversely, central to the setting and atmosphere of this and other novels by Dostoyevsky is Sennaya Square, with its crowds, as lively today as it was in his day.

In 1873 Dostoyevsky's professional life, like his private life, had many facets. He became editor of the journal *Grazhdanin* (The Citizen) at offices situated at 77 Nevsky Prospekt. His focus was broad and he had strong opinions on all aspects of the modern world. For example, the architectural eclecticism of the age was abhorrent. As he wrote in his *Diary of a Writer* (1873), ."..it is not possible really to define the architecture of today. It is a disordered confusion, yet one completely appropriate to that of our times." It was in this journal that his extraordinarily powerful diaries came to be published before Dostoyevsky moved to 6 5th Sovitskaya Street (formerly Rozhdestvenskie Street), where he rapidly completed his novel, *The Adolescent*. After the death of his three-year-old son Alesha, he and his family moved to what is now 5 Dostoevskogo Street. This building now houses the Dostoyevsky Museum and some of his novels and short stories are performed there as plays. There they lived for six years until his death on February 9, 1881. Despite his explicit wish to be buried at the Novodevichy Convent in Moscow, he was interred at the Alexander Nevsky Monastery cemetery in St. Petersburg: the price for a plot at the former had proved to be prohibitively high.

Somerset Maugham, visiting the cemetery in the following century, described the author's funerary bust in words which could be said to have succinctly summed up the man:

> It is a face devastated by passion. The dome of the head is stupendous and evokes irresistibly the thought of a world great enough to contain the terrible throng of his creatures... There is agony in that face, something terrible that makes you want to turn away and that yet holds you fascinated. His aspect is more terrifying than all his works. He has the look of a man who has been in hell and seen there, not a hopeless suffering, but meanness and frippery.

Anton Chekhov

The final great star in the late nineteenth-century literary firmament of St. Petersburg was, of course, Anton Chekhov (1860–1904), even if he is primarily known for depicting the life of rural Russia. He lived primarily as a child in Taganrog, Moscow and at his beloved White House by Yalta, in Crimea. Internationally renowned for plays like *Uncle Vanya* and *The Cherry Orchard*, which explore the problems and nuances of life in the remote Russian countryside in the post-Emancipation period, he also brilliantly captures the gaiety and excess of the pre-Lenten festivities of Maslenitsa, the annual Eastern Slavic religious and folk holiday, in the capital in *The Stupid Frenchman*:

> Pourquoi looked around and was taken quite aback. The waiters, pushing and jostling with one another, were carrying veritable mountains of pancakes... People sat at tables, eating mountains of pancakes and salmon caviar... with the same appetite and daring as the fine-looking gentleman... "What an amazing thing," Pourquoi thought as he left the restaurant. "If the climate is extraordinary here, stomachs are even greater marvels! What an incredible country!"

Maxim Gorky

The Silver Age of Russian literature was now dawning in St. Petersburg and its leading figure was Maxim Gorky (real name Alexei

Maximovich Peshkov, 1868–1936). He first arrived in the capital from the south of Russia in September 1899, but it was not an auspicious experience as reimagined in his novel series *The Life of Klim Samgin*, which only came to be published decades later in 1927–36. As he put it, "Sorrowful was the suppressed noise of the strange city and humiliating the petty gray people in their masses of great houses, while everything together created a frightening and depressing sensation of one's own existence."

Once established, however, life improved after he took a position at the socialist-leaning journal *Zhizn* (Life), edited by V.A. Posse, which came out in the years 1897 to 1901. His writings were already inflammatory and ominous in tone, warning of the approach of a "Storm! And soon the storm will break!" Gorky stayed with Posse for three weeks at Nadezhdinsky Street, now Mayakovskaya Street, in the heart of the city. Not long after he left the capital but returned for a second time to Posse in February 1901. Although the magazine was soon shut down by the tsarist government and Posse went abroad, Gorky stayed on, moving in with yet another publisher, Konstantin Pyatnitsky, at Nikolaevsky Street, now Marata Street, conveniently located across the street from Pyatnitsky's Znanie (Knowledge) publishing house.

Then, the following year, Gorky's first play, *The Philistines*, was performed at the Panayevsky Theater, situated at 4 Admiralty Embankment, having previously premiered in Moscow. Konstantin Stanislavski (1863–1938), the world renowned theater director, drama theorist and actor who had included the play in the repertoire of his famous Moscow Arts Theater, left a memorable impression of the occasion:

> At the dress rehearsal at the Panayevksy Theater all the "government types" of St. Petersburg were crawling about... Even in the theater itself and all around it there were a multitude of policemen; on the square in front of the theater the horses of the gendarmes passed to and fro: one had the impression that it wasn't a dress rehearsal which was taking place, but preparations for a battle.

The actress and theater owner Vera Komissarzhevskaya (1864–1910), who lived at 27 Anglisky Prospekt (English Prospect), played a key role in furthering Gorky's reputation. On November 10, 1904, she staged the premier of his play, *Summer Folk*, at her theater, still functioning today at 19 Italianskaya Street. Yet in spite of or because of his success and in the wake of his anti-governmental writings, Gorky was briefly imprisoned in the Peter and Paul Fortress in early 1905—giving him a halo of martyrdom which never left him. In view of these recent events and after his rapid release, Gorky went abroad in 1906, only returning in 1913 when amnestied. The following year, he rented a flat on the sixth floor of an apartment block at 23 Kronverksky Prospekt. This remained his cherished urban pied-à-terre when he came to the city from his dacha situated on the Karelian Isthmus, in what was then a part of Finland.

During the war years Gorky kept very busy, working on his own political-literary journal *Letopis* (Chronicle) from 1915–17. It attracted the literary stars of the period, including the novelist Ivan Bunin, famous for his evocations of life in the aristocrat Russian country houses of the late nineteenth century. Bunin fled after the Revolution to Paris, however, and in 1933 won the Nobel Prize for Literature. Much of his writing casts a nostalgic look at a bygone era; as he himself put it, "A passion for cemeteries is a very Russian characteristic." As for Gorky, he embraced radicalism and was involved with the anti-war and revolutionary publishing house Parus, the offices of which were located at 18 Bolshaya Monetnaya Street. Despite its political stance it was particularly noted for its children's books, which drew upon such notables from the world of art as the theater decorator Alexandre Benois, who contributed illustrations.

With the advent of the Revolution and until the autumn of 1921 Gorky made his apartment in town his principal home. This enabled him to devote more time to establishing the socialist and pro-revolutionary journal *Novaya Zhizn* (New Life), based at 64 Nevsky Prospekt. Not long afterwards, during these heady revolutionary days, together with Benois, the opera singer Feodor Chaliapin and painter Yevgeny Lansere, he joined the commission established to oversee the preservation and encouragement of

Russian art. Then, in September 1918, Gorky founded a new publishing house, Vsemirnaya Literatura (World Literature), located at 36 Mochov Street, which was speedily integrated into the newly established communist system of ownership and administration. He also became involved in a number of other ventures. Of particular note was the establishment of the so-called House of Arts in part of the old Yeliseyev Mansion at 15 Nevksy Prospekt. It functioned from November 20, 1919, until 1923, financially supported to a large degree by the Petrograd Soviet under Lenin. Its activities were multifaceted and the poet Nikolai Gumilev (1886–1921) was for a period put in charge of the study of poetry there; his works often focused on Petrograd in rich urban imagery, especially in his poem "The Confused Street-car," in which he considered life, politics and the catastrophe which had befallen Russia and which would soon lead to his own death and, a generation later, to the lengthy imprisonment of his son. Many international notables came to visit the House of Art, including H.G. Wells. Sharing radical views, Wells and Gorky became friends, and Wells went to stay with Gorky.

During the early revolutionary days Gorky assumed an important role in the new state, in particular as director of the Expertise Commission, set up in the former British Embassy. He himself recorded:

> The palace that once sheltered the British Embassy is now like some congested second-hand art shop in the Brompton Road. We went through room after room piled with the beautiful lumber of the former Russian social system. There are big rooms crammed with statuary; never have I seen so many white marble Venuses and sylphs together, not even in the Naples Museum. There are stacks of pictures of every sort, passages choked with inlaid cabinets piled up to the ceiling; a room full of cases of old lace, piles of magnificent furniture.

For many intellectuals of that period, however, his reputation now became tarnished. As the poet and writer Zinaida Gippius (1869–1945) wrote disparagingly in her diary: "Gorki greedily buys up all types of vases and enamelware from the detested 'bourgeois' who are starving to death… Gorky's apartment resembles a museum or a Chinese junk."

During the civil war Gorky's health deteriorated and in an attempt to cure his tuberculosis he went abroad in November 1921, living mostly in Sorrento. This departure was in reality exile, since he had fallen out with Lenin and the Bolsheviks over their brutal repression of dissent, especially after his close friend Nikolai Gumilev was executed by the Cheka, the Soviet state security organization, on trumped up charges of monarchist conspiracy. When Gorky finally returned to Russia in 1928, having been personally invited by Stalin himself, he lived in Moscow, but visited St. Petersburg twice in 1929 and 1931, when he stayed at the Europa Hotel. Baroness Moura Budberg, who later became a mistress of H.G. Wells, was deeply taken by Gorky and recalled how he had experienced in his youth a "toothache in the heart" which had led him later in life to adopt the pen name *Gorki*, a word which means bitter in Russian. She herself became a figure of increasing interest, if not notoriety, not least because of her affair with R.H. Bruce Lockhart, the British Consul and secret agent in Russia during the Revolution, and, in 1934 she became a principal character in the book and film, *British Agent*, which focuses on Bruce Lockhart, his machinations and those turbulent times.

Today a statue dedicated to Gorky's memory is located outside the Gorkovskaya metro station, near where he lived on the city's Petrograd Side.

From Silver Age to Soviet Rule

During the late nineteenth and early twentieth centuries the tradition of society hostesses and intellectuals holding salons continued unabated. Among the most noted literary salons were those held by the Symbolist poet Zinaida Gippius and her husband Dmitry Merezhkovsky. They lived at the house of Prince A.D. Myryz at 24 Liteiny Prospekt, and these occasions became emblematic of high culture in the Silver Age. This building had been built in 1874–85 in a rather eclectic Moorish cum Turkish style, which suited the theatrical tastes of Merezhkovsky and his guests, and it enjoyed impressive view over the Transfiguration Cathedral. The guests included people from the overlapping worlds of the theater, art and politics, including such diverse individuals as Benois, the ballet impresario

Sergei Diaghilev, the portrait painter Valentin Serov and the political who would later be minister-chairman of the Russian Provisional Revolutionary Government, Alexander Kerensky.

Another important salon was hosted by the writer Lydia Zinovieva-Hannibal with her husband, the theoretician of Russian Symbolism, Vyacheslav Ivanov, who lived at 35 Tavricheskaya Street. Alexander Blok, Mikhail Kuzmin, the theater director Vsevolod Meyerhold and the artist Konstantin Somov often came to visit and there Blok gave a first reading of the poem "The Unknown Lady":

> And every evening (or am I imagining?)
> Exactly at the appointed time
> A girl's slim figure, silk raimented,
> Glides past the misted window grime.
>
> And slowly, passing through the revelers,
> Unaccompanied, always alone,
> Exuding mists and secret fragrances,
> She sits at the table that is her own.

Kornei Chukovsky, most famous for his children's poetry, recalled the occasion:

> I remember that night, just before dawn, when he read, for the first time, 'The Unknown One'—it seems, just after it was written... There was a way out from the tower into the attic and the roof, and in the white Petersburg night, we, painters, poets, artists... went out under the whitish heavens, and Blok, sluggish, outwardly serene, young, tanned (he was already tanned by early spring), climbed out onto the large iron framework, to which the telephone wires were connected, and in response to our persistent entreaties already for the third and fourth time, recited his eternal ballads in his restrained, smouldering, unwilling, tragic voice ... then when he'd finished, suddenly from below, there emanated from the Tavrichesky Gardens, the songs of many nightingales which rushed like a wave upon us.

Thus, on the verge of the First World War St. Petersburg was a truly imposing city. As the author Andrei Bely (Boris Nikolaevich Bugaev, 1880–1934) put it in his Symbolist novel *Petersburg* (1913) with perhaps a touch of hyperbole: "The other Russian cities are just heaps of wooden houses."

Another figure important in the new generation was the Futurist Vladimir Mayakovsky (1893–1930). He arrived in St. Petersburg in 1912 and on November 17 made his first public performance on stage at the Stray Dog café's basement. Radical and provocative, he signed the Futurists' manifesto, *A Slap in the Face of Public Taste*, the following month; it advocated "throwing Pushkin, Dostoyevsky, Tolstoy, etc, etc off the steamboat of modernity." The Stray Dog, a cellar meeting place for avant-garde intellectuals and artists lasted from 1911 to 1915 until the First World War and a ban on the sale of alcohol made it unviable. Open once again since 2012 with performances of theater, music and dance, it is still located at Arts Square. Today it attracts a mix of tourists and those curious about the Silver Age and its bizarre name. It was apparently Tolstoy who came up with the name, according to its owner: "One day, when we were searching for a cellar that was vacant… A.N. Tolstoy unexpectedly said, 'Are we not like stray dogs searching for shelter?'"

After, the Revolution Mayakovsky moved permanently back to Moscow in March 1919, although he frequently visited St. Petersburg afterwards. Tormented by his complex relationship with the Soviet state and its repression as well as by his own troubled personality, he committed suicide there in April 1930.

One of the most important members of the literary circle that was prominent at the Stray Dog was the poet Anna Akhmatova (real name, Anna Gorenko; 1889–1966). If in Soviet times the city was to take on a gray and bleak appearance, in these late imperial days St. Petersburg was a colorful place and few were more colorful than her. As she later wrote, "the houses were predominantly painted red (like the Winter Palace), purple, rose and nothing like the beige and gray, which now bears up so poorly in the winter mists and the Leningrad evening twilight." She was a luminary in the flourishing literary world of the Silver Age, her strikingly unconventional beauty reputedly due to being descended from the Tatar Khan Akhmat (hence her pen name). Her marriage, moreover, made her one half of the celebrity couple of the time, for at the age of twenty she married the ill-fated poet Nikolai Gumilev, who had previously become a leading member of the so-called Acmeist group. The tempestuous marriage was not to survive for long, but their shared vision of St. Petersburg as a cultural hub of vibrancy and color lasted much longer.

Not all of her contemporaries, in particular some foreign poets, shared her love of the city. The German Rainer Maria Rilke (1875–1926), though intrigued by the urban ambiance, felt that it stunned rather than quickened his senses, finding a hallucinatory quality in its streets, parks, and courtyards. As he put it in his poem "Night Drive" which considers St. Petersburg, and in particular the Neva Embankment and Summer Garden, after dark, "the night in its wakefulness had neither heaven, nor hell in it… The granite—feels itself falling, from the empty wobbling brain, until one does not see it anymore." Osip Mandelstam (1891–1938) saw a more sinister side to the city, especially along its river banks: "There is the Fontanka already—this Undine of tramps and hungry students with their long greasy mess of hair, this Lorelei of boiled crabs, which make their music on boats with broken teeth—the protecting river of the unnoticeable Little Theater, with its hard, bald, witch-like, after Patschuli smelling Melpomene." It was precisely the bowels of the city, with all their dangers, which most fascinated him. He warned,

> One only needs to dissolve the thin skin of the Petersburg air in order to see the layer hidden beneath. Under the Swan and … down by the Gagarin Quay, under the dusty cloud of the Gutschkow Lane, under the French tasty morsels of the dying Embankment, under the mirror eyes of the apartments of noble lackeys lurks something unexpected.
>
> Yet the Feather, which this skin has dissolved, is like the spoon of a doctor which has become infected by diphtheria. One touches it at one's own peril.

After another short-lived marriage Akhmatova lived with the art historian and critic Nikolai Nikolaevich Punin (1888–1953) at Fontanka Embankment. On the surface it was a recipe for trouble: Punin's ex-wife and children also lived there. Political difficulties also complicated the situation. Punin and Akhmatova's son, Lev Gumilev (1912–92), were both arrested in 1935. Akhmatova's relationship with Punin suffered and collapsed but she continued to live at the same address, even after Punin's new bride moved in as well in what she described as "a stratification of wives" which accumulated over the years. The former site of such complicated domestic arrangements now houses the Akhmatova Museum, dedicated to her memory, which opened on the centenary of her birth in 1989.

Returning once again to Leningrad in May 1944 after her evacuation during the Nazi blockade, she found it "a terrible ghost that pretended to be my city." Worse, in August 1946, she endured a concerted attack on the very essence of her literary oeuvre when she was accused of propagating a "bourgeois-aristocratic aesthetic and delicate sensibility—'art for art's sake'—which was out of step with the needs of the people." Andrei Zhdanov, the director of Soviet cultural policy and reputedly a possible heir to Stalin himself, invidiously wrote that she was "a nun or a whore, or rather, a nun and a whore, who combines harlotry with prayer. Akhmatova's poetry is utterly remote from the people." Punin also suffered political persecution and in 1949 was again arrested for activities against the Soviet people. This time his fate was sealed and he was sent to a Gulag camp in the Russian Arctic. Like countless others he never returned. Her last years were spent in a flat at 34 Lenin Street together with Punin's family, in an apartment block in which many figures from the world of culture lived after political pressures were eased.

Despite all the hardships he endured because of political persecution and imprisonment under Stalin, Akhmatova's son Lev Gumilev became a noted historian and ethnographer. It was his ordeal which served to inspire one of her most famous and tragic poems, "Requiem." As she wrote, referring to Kresty Prison:

In those terrible years of the iron rod, I spent seventeen months in the queue outside the prison in Leningrad. One day I "identified" myself. A woman standing by me with lips that were blue from the cold, who, of course, hadn't the faintest idea who I was, regaining her consciousness from her numbed state, whispered into my ear (here everyone spoke in a whisper):

> And are you allowed to write?
> I answered, Yes.

Then something not unlike a smile slipped onto her face, which had never been there before.

During the mid-1920s disenchantment with the Soviet regime had already come to permeate the literary intelligentsia as a premonition of what was to come. Konstantin Vaginov (1899–1934), a member of Nikolai Gumilev's Acmeist group, wrote *Kozlinaya pesn'* ("Goat Song," 1925–27):

> Now there is no Petersburg. There is a Leningrad; yet what has Leningrad to do with us—the author is a coffin maker by trade, not a carpenter of cradles. If he is given a coffin to examine, he knocks at it and quickly gleans which was the master craftsman who made it and, indeed, he can remember who the parents of the deceased were. Just at this moment he is making a coffin for his own twenty-seven years. That is a terrible amount of work to complete…

Aleksey Tolstoy

A spectacular growth in literacy was one of the principal goals of the Soviet regime and it was achieved. To this end, the artist Vladimir Lebedev (1891–1967) redeveloped the iconic Singer House into the Petrograd State Publishing House in 1919 (from 1938, the House of Books) which remains the city's leading bookstore. One of the few prominent writers who always remained in favor with the Soviets in general, and Stalin in particular, was Aleksey Nikolayevich Tolstoy.

His mother Alexandra Turgenev was a relation of Ivan Turgenev but had married into the family of Count Nikolay Tolstoy and the child had been born against the tumultuous background of adultery and an ensuing attempted murder. In consequence, the child grew up in an isolated and atheistic milieu, ostracized by much of society. During the Revolution he first sided with the White Army against the Bolsheviks and then fled abroad after their defeat. In 1923, however, Tolstoy returned from exile in Paris, publicly criticizing "the lamentable nature of the White emigration" while praising the Bolsheviks as "unifiers of the Russian land." He took up residence at Zhanovskaya Embankment, where he wrote the science fiction novel *Aelita* that same year. Like Turgenev and Dostoyevsky, he was hypnotized by the city's luminous skies. He wrote in *Peter the First* (1929–45) in words as true in his own times as in that of Russia's Westernizing tsar:

> Petersburg lived its cold-bubbling, excessive, night-drenched life. Phosphorescent summer nights, splendid, voluptuous, sleepless nights in winter, green tables and glimmering gold, music, rotating couples behind the windows, splendid troikas, gypsies, duels in the gray light of dawn, by the howl of the icy winds and the piercing shrillness of flutes—troop parades before the terror filled view of the Byzantine eyes of the Tsar. That was the way the city lived.

Tolstoy's accommodation with the totalitarian rule of the new government proved to be far more successful than that of most of his literary colleagues. He unquestioningly agreed to provide propaganda for the Bolshevik regime. As he candidly put it to the émigré artist Yury Annenkov whom he encountered in Paris in the 1930s,

> I am just an ordinary human being who wants to live, live well, in the moment. As for my literary creativity, who gives a damn? If they want propaganda plays, why should I care? I'll give them what they want!

Postwar Years

The postwar years after the death of Stalin in 1953 brought a new generation of artists to the fore, of whom the most internationally renowned was the essayist and poet Joseph Brodsky. He was born into a Jewish family at the height of the Second World War in 1940. He first came into close contact with Akhmatova in 1962, and the following year he was arrested for "living as a parasite on the fatherland" and sent to Arkhangelsk Province. Only in 1972 was he allowed to migrate to America and, once there, he became internationally famous, his work so praised in the West that in 1987 he won the Nobel Prize for Literature.

In "A Guide to a Renamed City" from his collection *Flight from Byzantium*, Brodsky praised the statue of Lenin standing in front of the remodeled Finland Station for the simple reason that, he argued, the revolutionary's decision to make Moscow the Soviet capital in 1918 saved St. Petersburg from major demolition and redevelopment: instead, the curse fell upon Moscow. For him, the history and character of Leningrad prevented any such development, since

> Petersburg was never, not even in the reactionary times of Nicholas I, a center of power. Every monarchy is founded on the feudal principal of voluntary or involuntary subjugation to the rule of one person, whom the church supports. At the end of the day, each form of subjugation is an act of the will, just like a voting form. The basis of Lenin's ideal, however, was to manipulate the human will itself, to control reason, and that was something new for St. Petersburg.

In the tradition of so many literary figures of the city—whether St. Petersburg, Petrograd, or Leningrad—the white nights of summer cast a lyrical spell. In a veritable rhapsody Brodsky exclaims,

> at 2 o'clock in the morning you can read and write without a lamp; the towering houses, without shadows, with gold embellished roofs, seem like delicate porcelain images. It is so still, that you can almost hear the clatter of a spoon which is falling down in

Finland. The glass-like rose color of the sky is so bright, that the bright blue watercolor surface of the river can hardly find its reflection... On such nights one finds it difficult to fall asleep, it is too bright and no dream can approach this reality. This reality, in which man casts no shadow—like water.

This yearning for the old St. Petersburg, rather than drawing further opprobrium upon the poet for his anti-Soviet stance, actually won some approval. Interestingly, as many historical buildings in and around St. Petersburg were wiped out, a new nostalgia appeared, fostered by the state as means of promoting solidarity. This took a variety of forms. The Soviet-named 25 October Avenue was given once again its pre-revolutionary name of Nevsky Prospekt, and Volodarsky Avenue became Liteiny Prospekt, all by official decree in January 1944.

The British author J. B. Priestley was among the first foreigners to visit Leningrad in the autumn of 1945 but he left few impressions of the battered city. Rather it was Isaiah Berlin, who arrived in November 1945, who left the most striking impressions of its literary revival:

> Gennady Moiseevich Rachlin is a small, thin, gay, baldish, red-haired Jew, noisy, shrewd, immensely and demonstratively affable, and probably the best-informed, best-read and most enterprising bookseller in the Soviet Union... Having certain vaguely romantic literary ambitions, founded on the memory of the famous booksellers of the nineteenth century who acted at once as the publishers, distributors and patrons of literature—his own site is on the site of Smirdin's famous establishment, he has converted one of his rooms in his bookshop into a kind of club for writers and other favored visitors, and in this room, which Miss Tripp (the British Council representative in Russia) and I were kindly invited to frequent, I was enabled not only to purchase books with a degree of comfort unknown in Moscow, but to make the acquaintance of several well-known literary persons, such as Zoshchenko, Akhmatova, Orlov, Dudin.

According to Anthony Cross in *St. Petersburg and the British*,

> It was precisely Akhmatova and Mikhail Zoshchenko, whom Berlin had met at the end of 1945, who were attacked and abused less than a year later by A. A. Zhdanov, the former First Secretary of the Leningrad Communist Party and later, as Secretary of the Central Committee in Moscow, responsible for ideology. The notorious "Leningrad Affair" followed in 1949–52, when, at the instigation of Stalin and Beria, cases were fabricated against almost all the leading political figures from the Second World War, leading to imprisonment and execution.

Immediately, after the collapse of the Soviet Union, Russian literature entered a difficult period, but some authors like the controversial Mikhail Shishkin and dissident Vasily Aksyonov came to the fore, based mostly in Moscow. Tatyana Tolstaya (born 1951), the granddaughter of Aleksey Tolstoy, did, however, grow up in Leningrad before moving to Moscow in the 1980s and then to the United States. New Realist author Alexander Karasyov (born 1971) continues to live in St. Petersburg. Predominantly a tragic-comic short-story writer, he has written about life in the Russian Army during the Second Chechen War based on his own experiences in such works as *The Chechen Stories* and *Traitor*, and not about St. Petersburg as such. It remains to be seen, however, whether the heady days of the Silver Age of the pre-First World War period in St. Petersburg can ever be revived.

7 | Visualizing the City
Canvas and Screen

At the founding of St. Petersburg the relationship of the new capital to art was an essential component of imperial plans. As Russia's maritime gateway to Europe, it was essential that the visual arts, like architecture, should serve the tsar and the needs of the state. In this respect, the first generation of local artists played an important role, in particular Andrei Matveyev (1701–39) and Ivan Nikitin (1690–1741). Matveyev enjoyed the patronage of Tsar Peter the Great and was sent by him in 1716 to the Low Countries. He was apprenticed to the Dutch painter Carel de Moor before attending the Royal Academy of Fine Arts in Antwerp from 1723 to 1727, the first Russian artist to be trained abroad. Upon his return in 1727 he was appointed court artist and worked on a variety of decorative projects including a triumphal arch for the Empress Anna. He also worked at the Peter and Paul Fortress. He is most famous for the self-portrait he created with his wife, now in the State Russian Museum.

Nikitin, by contrast, began his studies with a Dutch artist in the Kremlin, but later moved to St. Petersburg with the court before traveling on to Venice and Florence for further studies. Upon his return he worked again at court on various portraits, many of which are also now in the State Russian Museum, but soon fell foul of Metropolitan Feofan Prokopovich, the Westernizing head of the Russian Orthodox Church in St. Petersburg, against whom Nikitin was found to have agitated. The Empress Anna eventually granted him an amnesty, but not before he was tortured, imprisoned and exiled to Tobolsk in Siberia.

Matveyev and Nikitin were followed in the next generation by Ivan Argunov (1729–1802), Dmitry Levitsky (1735–1822), Fedor Rokotov (1736–1808), and Vladimir Borovikovsky. Argunov, a serf of the highly cultured Count Sheremetev and his majordomo in

St. Petersburg, had shown artistic talent and so was permitted to study with the German painter Georg Grooth in St. Petersburg. His most famous work is *Portrait of an Unknown Peasant* (1784), now in the State Tretyakov Gallery in Moscow and depicting a beautiful serf girl in colorful regalia. Levitsky, by contrast, is most famous for his portrait of the Empress Catherine the Great. Of Jewish background and a native of Kiev, then under Russian sovereignty, he also painted numerous portraits of young ladies who attended the famed Smolny Society for the Education of Noble Maidens. Rokotov was another artist of serf background but was emancipated and became a student at the newly founded Imperial Russian Academy of Arts in St. Petersburg, later becoming a professor there. He then devoted himself to paintings of fashionable ladies at court, of which his *Lady in a Pink Dress* (1770s) is the most famous, now in the State Tretyakov Gallery. Borovikovsky, from a Cossack family, worked in a similar genre but also devoted himself to icon painting. He painted various icons for the Kazan Cathedral, but despite the Church's prohibition he became a freemason of the Dying Sphinx Lodge in 1819. This fortunately does not appear to have affected his religious commissions.

The Imperial Academy of Arts

Primary to the artistic needs of the state in particular and society more generally was the establishment in 1757 of the Imperial Academy of Arts, still flourishing today as the St. Petersburg State Academy Institute of Painting, Sculpture, and Architecture, dedicated to the memory of the artist Ilya Repin. The initiative for this endeavor was that of the learned scientist Mikhail Lomonosov and Count Ivan Ivanovich Shuvalov, a favorite of the Empress Elizabeth. Its foundation was a key event in the cultural life not only of St. Petersburg but of Russia in general, as it became the single most important educational establishment with respect to the arts up to our own time. When it first opened it was located in the Shuvalov Palace on what is now Italianskaya Street, but not long after its establishment it was moved to its present site on the shores of the Neva, at the University Embankment.

In 1764, not long after Catherine came to the throne, construction of a new palatial edifice to house the academy was commenced. The Russian architect Ivan Betskoi masterminded the project. The Frenchman Jean-Baptiste Vallin de la Mothe and Professor Alexander Kokorinov (1726–72), who had contributed much to the interior of the Shuvalov Palace, carried out the designs. Construction continued for 25 years from 1765–89. It was Prince Dmitry Golitsyn, the Russian Ambassador to Paris, who saw to it that French rather than Italian elements dominated. It is a three-story neoclassical brick palace-like building, the front and back facades of which boast majestic tetra-style Tuscan porticoes resting on a rusticated base. Highly innovative, its classical entablature is the first of its type in Russia. Covered in painted stucco, its crowning dome is surmounted by a statue of Catherine the Great as muse, a modern sculptural rendition which replaces the original long gone since the nineteenth century. A highly "rational" building, expressing Enlightenment architectural values, there are four symmetrical courtyards along the periphery with a large circular one at the center. Its central courtyard contains a sculpture of Shuvalov and there is also a museum which contains not only important pictures and sculptures but extraordinary models of some of the city's most significant buildings. Its entrance is framed on the banks of the Neva by the two monumental sphinxes brought from Egypt in this period.

The Rumyantsev Mansion

The Rumyantsev Mansion (also known as the Kochubey or Leuchtenberg Mansion because of other previous owners), located at 44 English Embankment, was originally built for Mikhail Golitsyn in the 1740s, but eventually passed into the hands of Prince Nikolai Rumyantsev—his mother was Ekaterina Golitsyna—in the early nineteenth century and eventually to Lev Kochubey and his wife Daria de Beauharnais, a granddaughter of Tsar Nicholas I who would be murdered by the Soviet authorities in 1937. It was a byword for magnificence in St. Petersburg at the time. As John Quincy Adams, Minister to Russia between 1809 and 1814 and later president of the United States, noted at the time of his visit to the palace:

> There was a gallery of pictures, many of them by great masters, and nearly equal to that of Count Strogonoff; antique busts and statues… Japan porcelain, very rare; a splendid dining-hall, with tables laid… for about two hundred persons… a hall where part of the company were seated at cards, hung round with the finest Gobeline tapestry… Sevres porcelain coffee-services and vases; bronzes of the most exquisite workmanship… a toilet service of solid gold; and last, but chiefest to my value, a miniature picture of Peter the Great, painted from the life, when he was in France…

It underwent various renovations and its current facade dates from 1835 by Vladimir Glinka. It is now the Museum of the History of St. Petersburg, with an important permanent exhibition of the Blockade of St. Petersburg in the Second World War.

The Hermitage

With respect to the visual arts, the establishment of the world-famous Hermitage Collections by the Empress Catherine the Great in 1764 was of the highest importance. The main Winter Palace itself, discussed previously, was renovated in 1764, when 225 Dutch and Flemish paintings were added to the collection. This collection had originally been intended for King Frederick the Great of Prussia but was purchased by the empress from the Berlin art dealer Johann Ernst Gotzkowsky. The principal building to house the artworks, which later came to be known—somewhat confusingly today—as the Old Hermitage was constructed in 1771–87 by Yury Felten. The Hermitage Museum now consists of five linked buildings on the Palace Embankment: the Winter Palace, the Small Hermitage, the Old Hermitage, the New Hermitage (1839–52), and the State Hermitage Theater.

Its collection of paintings and other works of art (over three million, of which only a fraction are on view) ranks alongside the world's greatest, on a par with the National Gallery in London, the

Louvre in Paris and the Metropolitan Museum of Art in New York. Among its most glittering treasures are Scythian gold jewelry, without doubt the most important collection of its kind in the world. It includes a unique golden necklace of Greek design (fourth century BC) stemming from the Caucasus, with ornate filigree workmanship. Egyptian, Etruscan, Hellenistic, and other Middle Eastern examples of jewelry and sculpture figure prominently. Oriental art from China and Southeast Asia is also exhibited, including vases, porcelain, and textiles, some of which are almost two millennia old. There is also an extensive collection of arms, armor, and military medals from around the world.

Other artifacts of more recent vintage include the extraordinary Peacock Clock, which formerly belonged to the notorious Elizabeth, Duchess of Kingston-upon-Hull, who had fled to Russia in 1777, having been convicted of bigamy in her home country shortly before. It is a musical clock, the dial of which is hidden in an artificial mushroom, composed of three life-size mechanical birds including a peacock, an owl, and a rooster which flap their wings, raise their gilded heads and tails and twist about, with all such movements accompanied by chimes, mimicking the sounds of the birds. It attracted the attention of Grigory Potemkin and through him of Catherine the Great, who, when she had had enough of the duchess, notorious for her licentiousness, forced her to leave St. Petersburg while leaving her clock behind. Another decorative item of great note is the immense malachite Medici Vase (1839–42) with gilded bronze handles, made at Yekaterinburg on the edge of the Ural Mountains to the design of Ivan Hallberg. The brilliant green mosaic-like pieces which compose its surface required some 256 kilograms of stone.

For all the magnificence of these and other works of art, it is really its collection of paintings which has brought the Hermitage international fame. Celebrated works from the Renaissance include two paintings by Leonardo da Vinci, *Madonna and Child with Flowers* (1478–80) and the *Madonna Litta* (c. 1490–91). In the former, the viewer sees a rare example of da Vinci's early work, which was sold to the museum by the Benois family in 1914. The latter, purchased from Count Litta in Milan in 1865, is, on the other hand, a

later work and an early example of *contrapposto*, a pictorial arrangement of the Christ Child's figure with hands and arms counterposed
against legs and feet, a style popular in the High Renaissance. Other
important works of the Renaissance include Raphael's *Conestabile
Madonna* (c. 1504) and *Madonna with the Beardless Joseph (Holy
Family)* (c. 1506). From the Mannerist period of the late Renaissance there is Titian's *Saint Sebastian* (1570s) and Caravaggio's *The
Lute Player* (c. 1596), originally from the Giustiniani Collection in
Rome. The sheet of music which the musician is following has been
confirmed as a composition by Caravaggio's Franco-Flemish contemporary Jacques Arcadelt.

Dutch Masters also form an important focus of the Hermitage Collection. Chief among these are Rembrandt's masterpiece *The
Descent from the Cross* (1634) and *Sacrifice of Isaac* (1635), both powerful works in which the use of *chiaroscuro*, the painterly contrast of
light and shade, heightens the drama. There are also Baroque works
by Rubens, including *Landscape with Stone Carriers* (1620) and
Bacchus (1636–40), whose voluptuous figure borders on the obscene.

The majority of important European artists from other centuries are also represented in the collection, including the eighteenth-
century Venetian Canaletto and the British Sir Joshua Reynolds.
From the early nineteenth century are major works by Caspar David
Friedrich, including *On Board a Sailing Ship* (1818–20) and *Night in
a Harbor* (c. 1818–20), both so expressive of the mystical spirituality
of German Romanticism which he embodied in his painting.

Nonetheless, it is in works from the Impressionist period of
the late nineteenth century that the Hermitage excels, with many
purchased by Russian collectors at the beginning of the twentieth
century. These include works by Vincent Van Gogh (*Thatched Cot-
tages and Houses*, 1890), Paul Gauguin (*Pastorales Tahitiennes*, 1892),
Henri Rousseau (*In a Tropical Forest. Struggle between Tiger and
Bull*, 1909) and Henri Matisse (*Dance*, 1910).

World of Art

The Russian collectors were characteristic of the years before the
First World War when St. Petersburg, as well as Moscow, enjoyed

an awakening of the study of art and architectural history, just before conflict and revolution swept so many away. Among the leading personalities who assisted in this process was Count Valentin Zubov (1884–1969), curator of the Gatchina Palace and founder of the country's first Russian Institute of Art History, where the highest level of academic research is still carried out to this day, supported by the Ministry of Culture of the Russian Federation. Through his largesse it opened in March 1892 in Zubov's splendid mansion to the west of St. Issac's Cathedral at 5 St. Isaac's Square.

Another cultured aristocrat, society hostess, Princess Maria Klavdievna Tenisheva (1858–1928), made possible one of the most important artistic movements in late nineteenth-century St. Petersburg. This was the so-called World of Art movement which tried to turn its back on modern industrialized society, preferring instead to focus upon "aesthetic values" and the national romantic in art, in particular folk art. The first issue of the *Mir iskusstva* (World of Art) magazine was edited by Sergei Diaghilev, and patron of the arts Savva Mamontov also provided considerable assistance. Among the key figures who were its proponents were Nicholas Benois and his sons, Leon and Alexandre, the latter especially noted for his famous theater designs of the early years of the twentieth century and post-revolutionary period while in exile in Paris. Nicholas Benois' younger daughter Ekaterina (1850–1933) was also involved in the movement and went on to marry the sculptor and painter Yevgeny Lansere. She spent considerable time in Vienna and Venice during the early twentieth century but returned to live to the old capital in 1920 and remained there for the rest of her life.

During the late nineteenth century and into the early years of the twentieth, portrait painting thrived in St. Petersburg as never before, creating a golden age for the genre. One of its leading figures was the history and portrait painter Ilya Repin (1844–1930), a native of eastern Ukraine who lived in his country house Penaty at Kuokkala (now Repino) by the Gulf of Finland just to the north of St. Petersburg. It is now a museum of art dedicated to his memory, rich in memorabilia from his time there. Many of his works, however, are accessible in the heart of St. Petersburg at the State Russian

Museum, founded in 1895 by Tsar Nicholas II to commemorate his late father Tsar Alexander III. These include *Barge Haulers on the Volga* (1870–73), a powerful image of Russia's toiling population, *Portrait of the Composer Modest Mussorgsky* (1881), one of Russia's leading composers of that time, and *Ivan the Terrible and His Son Ivan* (1885), a dramatic representation of the country's brutal sixteenth-century tsar, who killed his eldest son in a rage. The Repin St. Petersburg State Academy Institute of Painting, Sculpture, and Architecture today carries his name.

Boris Kustodiev (1878–1927), another member of the *Mir iskusstva* circle, was also influential in the pre-war years and was elected to the Imperial Academy of Arts in 1909. His greatest fame came after the Revolution, however, when he was hailed as one of the greatest Russian artists of his generation, specializing in provincial scenes depicted in bright colors. One of his most successful works is *Maslenitsa* (1919), today in the Isaak Brodsky Museum in St. Petersburg, which focuses upon the peculiarly Russian folk delights of this pre-Lenten celebration. His fame was enhanced by an exhibition of his works in May 1920 at the House of the Arts, even though it was the only exhibition of his works held during his lifetime. One of his most famous works is *The Merchant's Wife Taking Tea* (1918), an iconic image of a lady from the Russian merchant milieu—a segment of society on the verge of extinction—in the State Russian Museum. It was not only his subject matter which appealed, but his expressive and exuberant use of paint, which created, as Alexandre Benois put it, a "barbaric fight of colors." Strangely for an artist who gained prominence after the Revolution, most of his works before that time have Russian Orthodox references; as the artist himself said, "The church in my painting is my signature." He was also an influential book illustrator, producing a total of 41 volumes in 1925, an impressive output bearing in mind that he had been confined to a wheelchair because of spinal tuberculosis since 1916.

Kazimir Malevich (1879–1935), a Russian of Polish ethnicity, was another leading artist of the 1910s, quite different from Kustodiev and others because of his abstract Modernist approach.

His experimental exploration in his paintings later helped create the avant-garde genre known as Suprematism, a word derived from Latin which signifies the highest form. For him, it was the zenith of artistic evolution in which artistic forms are simplified and abstracted into basic geometrical shapes. Malevich was also very active in the design of porcelain at the former Lomonosov Imperial Porcelain Factory, renamed the State Porcelain Factory in the post-revolutionary period. It was Nikolai Nikolaevich Punin (1888–1953), its new director, art scholar, and later husband of Anna Akhmatova (discussed in Chapter 6), who first asked the painter, along with fellow Suprematists Nikolai Suetin and Ilya Chashnik, to provide the new designs for it.

During the early Soviet period Malevich achieved his greatest fame as an exponent of geometric abstract art from his groundbreaking manifesto, *From Cubism to Suprematism*, first published in 1915. Supportive of the Revolution, he became director of the Petrograd State Institute of Artistic Culture in 1923. Yet he soon faced the disapproval of Stalin and his apparatchiks, not least for the deep Christian spirituality which informed much of his work, as well as for his "bourgeois" abstractions. In 1926, the Institute was shut down and the authorities attempted to coerce him to adopt the tenets of Socialist Realism, an artistic trend admired by Stalin and the Communist Party which utilized an idealized form of everyday realism to celebrate socialist values and the new leading role of the proletariat in the Soviet Union. Malevich's international fame helped to protect him and he kept a relatively low profile, dying a natural death of cancer—unlike many of his contemporaries as the notorious purges were getting underway. Many of his works are to be found in the Benois Wing of the State Russian Museum, often with themes of peasants and workers, as well as others depicting geometric abstractions, the human form often just recognizable within these formal structures.

Alexander Korovin (1870–1922) is also of significance in pre-war St. Petersburg arts. From a highly prosperous mercantile background—his father was proprietor of a major fabric shop in the Apraxin Court—his home at Nikolayev Street (now Marat Street) housed a collection of modern Russian paintings. These included Leon Bakst's *Dinner* from 1902, in which an alluring lady brazenly stares into the eyes of the viewer, Alexandre Benois' *Commedia dell'arte* (1906) and Konstantin Somov's *Skating Rink in Winter* (1915), all now in the State Russian Museum. Had the Revolution not intervened, Korovin had planned to establish his own museum on Vasilyevsky Island to accommodate his collection of 238 paintings, porcelain and other works of art. However, the State Russian Museum, like the Hermitage, benefited from the confiscation of paintings and other works of art inherited or collected over the centuries by aristocrats, industrialists, and even the artists themselves. Today it includes in its collections a vast collection of Russian paintings and other objects from the Russian Middle Ages to the avant-garde. The Symbolist art of Mikhail Vrubel (1856–1910), the elegant society portraits of Valentin Serov (1865–1911) and the Byzantine-influenced works of Kuzma Petrov-Vodkin (1878–1939) contrast with the analytical realism of Pavel Filonov (1883–1941) and the abstract art of Wassily Kandinsky (1866–1944), making the museum a veritable microcosm of Russian art, politics, history, and culture. Its collection of Kandinsky's paintings includes such early works as *Lake* (1910) and the wartime *Dusk* (1917), powerfully expressionist in their almost lurid use of color and pointing to his relation to the German Expressionist *Blauer Reiter* group. Although he moved back to Russia from Germany from 1914 to 1921 he eventually returned there, connecting himself to the Bauhaus of Walter Gropius at Weimar, rather than facing the increasing hostility of the authorities to his "bourgeois" and "overly individualistic" art. With the seizure of power by the Nazis in 1933, he moved to Paris, where he died in 1944, one of the greatest Russian figures of twentieth-century art. But for Stalin, it was Alexander Gerasimov (1881–1963) who most embodied the aesthetic ideals of Soviet Socialist Realism, and it was he who was the favorite portrait painter of Stalin himself. He was appointed director of the Union of Artists of the USSR, as well as of the Soviet Academy of Arts, and saw it as his duty to suppress "cosmopolitanism" and "formalism," both anathema to the party leadership. His ultimate posthumous accolade was the issue of a stamp with his image commemorating the centenary of his birth in 1981.

The End of Private Ownership

The overthrow of the tsarist government and the imposition of the Bolshevik regime in St. Petersburg had immense repercussions for the visual arts in the old Russian capital. In August 1918 private ownership of real estate was abolished and all property of any note, including works of art, was confiscated into the public domain. This affected many buildings, but in particular the great palaces of the recently murdered tsar and his family, as well as countless monasteries and churches. As the German author Stefan Zweig wrote in *Travels to Russia*, during the interwar years:

> The Hermitage, even before the war, was a great museum, as large as the Louvre, or that of London and Berlin. That said, however, it, has evolved and expanded through the expropriation of Russia's art to an extraordinary degree. One can compare it to having the works from the Viennese, Happ, Liechtenstein, Harrach, and Czernin galleries, all private Viennese collections, as well as exquisite objects and works of art individually requisitioned from thousands of churches and monasteries of old Austria, collected together and incorporated into a single collection, in order to get a vague impression of the fantastic extent to which the Hermitage expanded as a result of the Communist privatisation of art.

Yet in these early years the preservation of the Hermitage Collections was largely due to the efforts of the artist and critic Alexandre Benois, who served as Keeper of Pictures from 1918 to 1926, and stressed the immense importance of the Hermitage's treasures to the cultural life of the Soviet Union. Nonetheless, after his departure and exile abroad many works were sold off by the Soviet state—in desperate need of hard currency—depleting the collection of more than two thousand works during the years 1930–34. These included masterpieces by Jan van Eyck, Titian, Rembrandt, Rubens, and Raphael, unhesitatingly purchased by western collectors. The most important of these was the American Andrew Mellon, scion of the famous banking family, who donated 21 paintings from the Hermitage to the United States government. They form the core collection of the National Gallery of Art in Washington, DC, which he founded in 1937. Other museums in the United States also benefited, including the Metropolitan Museum of Art in New York to which the Armenian oil magnate Calouste Gulbenkian donated Watteau's *Mezzetin* in 1934.

The mansions of the wealthy bourgeoisie were also confiscated in the wake of the Revolution in Leningrad together with their art collections and given over to uses deemed useful to the new regime. This was the case with the Yeliseyev family. The famous Yeliseyev Mansion, situated on the left side of the Moika by the old iron Police Bridge with its lavish *nouveau riche* decoration, became the House of the Arts, abbreviated to DISK, in late 1919, though at one time it also provided premises for the Institute for Marxism and Leninism.

Maxim Gorky and children's poet Kornei Chukovsky were the organizers of the House of Arts, which became a communal block of apartments and a meeting place for artists and writers. Georges Annenkoff remembered in his memoir: "The House of Arts had a very cheap and, in certain cases, free canteen for artists. The literary and artistic gatherings, debates, discussions and arguments continued without let. The literary studio produced many important works… Every morning, the rubbish bin in the courtyard would be filled with the torn manuscripts and scribblings of the inhabitants and guests of the House of Art." Nina Berberova, a young poet at the time who was in regular attendance there, recalled how the old servants of the Yeliseyev brothers continued to remain there after the Revolution as if confiscated themselves, serving tea and biscuits from the silver trays of their former masters. Two grand pianos provided music from the previous century such as Strauss waltzes, while eminent Silver Age poets like Nikolai Gumilev, Akhmatova's first husband, and Andrei Bely continued, at least in the short term, to recite. Foreign literary visitors were welcomed there, not least English visitors like the author, H. G. Wells, who attended a lavish dinner given in his honor.

Later, in 1923, a cinema was opened in the building, renamed Barrikada in 1931. It remained open throughout the siege and blockade of Leningrad, finally closing in a state of decline in the 1980s. The reconstruction of the new Taleon Imperial Hotel, with its rooftop spa, spelled the end of the old building in its previous form but continued its long cultural history into the twenty-first century.

New money in the post-Soviet era has generated a new breed of private art collectors such as Viktor Vekselberg, reputedly the fourth richest man in Russia, whose collection of fifteen Fabergé jeweled eggs takes pride of place in the Shuvalov Palace. An attempt to buy a painting by Boris Kustodiev at auction at Christie's was less successful, however, as specialists later cast doubt on the painting's authenticity and the auction house was forced to refund him.

Cinema

With the advent of moving pictures, a new cultural medium of expression had arrived in which Russians would rapidly excel to a degree only equaled in Hollywood (and, some might say, not even there). The Russian cinema began almost immediately after the first foreign films were introduced. On May 4, 1896, at the Aquarium, a variety theater situated at 10 Kamennostrovsky Prospekt, a first viewing took place of a filmed production of the operetta *Alfred Pasha in Paris*. The projectionist on this notable occasion was none other than Francis Doublier, the operator for the Lumière brothers.

During the following decade the cinema world of St. Petersburg expanded dramatically with up to 250 film theaters—far greater in number than those in Moscow despite the fact that most films were produced there—although many of these ultimately folded. The first purpose-built "cinema-theater" was the Pikadilly, which opened in 1913. Later, under the Soviets, in 1932, it was renamed Aurora.

Another important cinema in St. Petersburg is Dom Kino, located at 12 Karavannaya Street, near Nevsky Prospekt, architecturally prominent for its monumental colonnade of eight columns surmounted by lavish Corinthian capitals. Popular with students who frequent its café (there is also a restaurant), it is a principal venue for art films shown in their original languages, as well as for cartoons and novelty films.

Today St. Petersburg boasts a large number of cinemas, among the most recent of which is the Angleterre Cinema Lounge, a single-screen venue in the historic Hotel Angleterre at 24 Malaya Morskaya Street, just off St. Isaac's Square, which shows six to seven movies a day in their original languages.

Numerous companies have worked in St. Petersburg producing films throughout the last century and into the new millennium. Of these, the St. Petersburg Documentary Film Studio is worthy of mention, having produced and distributed such films since 1932, making it the oldest such company still in business, albeit privatized in the post-Soviet period.

There were also magazines dedicated to the cinema, of which the most famous was *Petersburg Cinematograph*. Today, as then, Nevsky Prospekt is the main district for cinemas, with those such as Cinema Aurora at number 60 now showing films both foreign and Russian.

None other than the renowned filmmaker Sergei Eisenstein (1898–1948) had studied architecture and engineering at the Petrograd Institute of Civil Engineering before joining the Red Army during the civil war. Later he would produce his two masterpieces, *Battleship Potemkin* (1925) and *Alexander Nevsky* (1938), the latter with the music of Sergei Prokofiev. With respect to Leningrad, however, it is his film *Ten Days that Shook the World* (1928), which is most pertinent, based as it is on the American John Reed's dramatic reportage which focuses on the October Revolution in what was then Petrograd. Scenes include the arrival of Lenin at the Finland Station, the *Aurora's* shelling of the Winter Palace and the ensuing insurrection.

In the early years Cinema Aurora showed silent films, accompanied by live music, as well as popular concerts in their own right. The renowned classical composer Dmitri Shostakovich (1906–75) played the piano there, while the jazz and popular singer Klavdiya Shulzhenko (1906–84) also performed at the Aurora. She was most noted during the 1930s for singing the Spanish Basque Sebástian

Yradier's *La Paloma*. In 1945 she was awarded the Order of the Red Star, and in 1971 she became People's Artist of the USSR. By that stage, though, she had turned her attention to Russian folk music. The Aurora underwent major renovations in 1998 and now not only shows the latest films but hosts concerts and theatrical events in its two auditoriums.

VISUALIZING THE CITY

8 | Stage Life
Music and Theater

From its foundation music was not neglected in the new Russian metropolis. On May 16, 1703, St. Petersburg's first formal musical event occurred, a performance by the Court Choir of Moscow, in which some thirty singers took part. Tsar Peter the Great was no fan of Italian opera but he saw the importance of its introduction as one more means to westernize Russian society and culture. Moreover, he did like singing: he sometimes sang himself as a bass in his own court choir. He also very much admired gypsy choirs and many of his courtiers followed suit in this taste, also taking part in a wide range of other musical activities. His favorite, Alexander Menshikov, established his own orchestra with a choir of twelve singers.

Yet it was Peter the Great's sister, Natalia Alexeyevna (1673–1716), who established the city's first musical theater opposite her palace at what is now the crossing of Tchaikovsky Street and Chernyshevskaya Prospekt. She composed some musical pieces for the productions and employed sixteen musicians as well as a choir. Unsurprisingly, it became an important venue for the tsar and court.

The Empress Anna, meanwhile, established a foundation for the education of the sons of young noblemen in 1731, in which music and dancing were important subjects. It was established in the Menshikov Palace after the owner's arrest and imprisonment made its spacious rooms available. The theater which was rapidly established there became a significant part of the cultural life of the nobility and visiting guests of St. Petersburg. Its first theatrical director was Alexander Sumarokov (1717–77), Russia's first if one excepts Fyodor Volkov (1729–63), who established the country's earliest public theater at Yaroslavl at about the same time. Sumarokov was an actor, playwright, and poet, and together with his partner Yakov Shumsky was interested in all aspects of theatrical production and administration.

In contrast to Peter the Great, Anna adored Italian music, particularly opera, facilitating the arrival of Italian opera singers to the country, the first of whom arrived in 1731. In 1732–35 she ordered the building of a new theater for the Winter Palace by Rastrelli. In the summer months a more intimate venue was provided in Peter the Great's own Summer Garden. The Italian Francesco Araja (1709–75), a former student of the Royal Conservatory at Naples who had begun composing operas in 1729, was hired to provide the music. He did this for a wide range of events beyond the remit of opera: court ceremonial, balls, and *bel canto*. Many of the decorative effects were provided by the Italian theatrical designer Giorgio Bona. Among his most noted designs were those used in Araja's first opera in St. Petersburg, *La forza dell'amore e dell'odio* (The Power of Love and Hatred), a work rich in military themes put on in honor of the empress' birthday on November 29, 1736. On this occasion, grandiose gardens, castellated towers, and majestic fountains provided the most striking elements of the stage scenery. However, it was Araja's production of *Seleuco* which made the most powerful impression. The empress attended the dress rehearsal on April 26, 1744, and saw in it highly important political references; it was composed to mark the peace treaty concluded with Sweden in 1744. A journalist wrote in the *Sankt-Peterburgskie Vedomosti*, Russia's first newspaper:

Araja's music deserves all the praise it receives; the performances of the finest actors… were highly accomplished and natural. The orchestral music was very fine… The decorations of the theater, the depictions of perspective and the machines invented by Signor Valeriani are all magnificent… At the end of the opera Her Imperial Majesty was pleased to show her delight by applauding … the honorable ministers of the diplomatic corps confirmed that never before had such a perfect and splendid opera been seen, not least in respect to the theatrical decoration and related machinery.

Due to this official esteem, Araja was awarded the position of Master of the Imperial Choir and, except for a visit to his native Italy in 1741–42, he remained in Russia until 1762, staging fourteen operas. One of these, *Cephalus and Prokris*, was staged in 1755, the first opera to be sung in Russian with its text provided by Alexander Sumarokov and based on a story from Ovid's *Metamorphoses*. Unusually for the time, the roles of *castrati* were taken by child singers.

Araja also involved other Italians in his musical projects, among them the Florentine poet Giuseppe Bonecchi, the Roman stage painter and landscapist Giuseppe Valeriani, his assistant Antonio Peresinotti and, most importantly, the *castrato* Lorenzo Saletti from Florence. So highly was the latter valued that he was paid as much as the court conductor himself, around two thousand roubles. He went on to perform major roles in such operas as *Eudossa incoronata, o sia Teodosio II* and *Alessandro nell'Indie*, before leaving Russia for good in 1758. The libretto for the former was Bonecchi's final work, and the Empress Elizabeth herself took the role of the main heroine. L. Belyakaeva-Kazanskaya recalls Saletti's sycophancy in *Silhouettes of Musical Petersburg*:

> "I must admit," the Florentine wrote in somewhat fawning terms, "that I covertly show my esteem in the name of Eudossa. My verses signify something splendid. When I portray her immortal glory, her heroic virtues which embellish her throne, I have the name Eudossa on my lips, but Elizabeth in my heart."

Native Russian opera composers now entered the stage, among the first of whom was Yevstigney Fomin (1761–1800). He studied music in Bologna but after his return produced numerous operas including the melodramatic *Orfey i Evridika* (*Orpheus and Eurydice*, 1792), the comic opera *The Americans* and *The Golden Apple*, first performed after his death. In 1756 the empress also established a new theater company in St. Petersburg, formed around that established by Volkov in Yaroslavl. Sumarokov was appointed its director and the first performances, dance and music as well as dramatic theater, were staged on Vasilyevsky Island.

With the Empress Elizabeth's death in December 1761 an era drew to a close—the so-called "age of gilded poverty." She had successfully established such cultural institutions as the Imperial Academy of Arts and the University of Moscow, but it had been a time when the empress, like so many at her court in the years to come, had lived beyond her means (in just one example, her personal estate comprised 15,000 dresses as well as a vast hoard of silk stockings). Her son Tsar Peter III reacted to this profligacy with one of many draconian commands which horrified his court: he immediately ordered the Italian Opera Company disbanded. The tsar himself left the old wooden Winter Palace and moved into the new unfinished stone replacement still in progress. Rapidly falling into disrepair, the old residence was demolished in 1767. Nonetheless, that same year the commission for a new purpose-built Opera House was given and the leading French sculptor Étienne Maurice Falconet was asked to contribute to it. Initially it was given over to Shrovetide entertainments, but then Falconet used it not as an opera venue but as a studio in which to create what was to become his most famous Russian sculpture, *The Bronze Horseman* (discussed in Chapter 4). Peter III was thus by no means a philistine; he loved music and was an accomplished violinist. The future composer Maxim Berezovsky sang in his choir and the violinist Ivan Khandoshkin played in his orchestra at the little opera house and theater he had built at his palace of Oranienbaum, formerly the country house of Menshikov.

Horn orchestras were popular at this time. The court orchestra established under Jan Maresh for the Empress Elizabeth started the fashion in St. Petersburg, playing a significant part not only in hunting expeditions from the capital but also on other occasions. As a result, the most prominent members of the nobility, including intimates of the empress Grigory Orlov and Kyril Rasumovsky, rapidly acquired their own horn orchestras. Most famous, though, was that of Prince Grigory Potemkin, her most important field marshal and, most probably, morganatic second husband. Composed of two hundred musicians, it performed at the Tauride Palace the empress had constructed for him. The fashion for horn orchestras continued throughout the rest of the century: the coronation of Nicholas II was especially memorable in this respect. With the end of the imperial order, however, these magnificent sounds were finally extinguished. Some examples of these brass instruments can still be seen at the Museum of Music at the Sheremetev Palace on the Fontanka.

Organ music also became fashionable despite the fact that the instrument was prohibited in Orthodox religious services. The first organs arrived in St. Petersburg in the early eighteenth century soon after its foundation, and both Menshikov and Natalia Alexeyevna owned and enjoyed hearing performances on them. Interestingly, concerts on the ancient organ of the Menshikov Palace are still held to this day on many Sundays at midday, just as they have been for centuries. The organ would long remain a sought-after instrument; later in the century each of Potemkin's palaces was equipped with one. By the nineteenth century, the organ had become an ever more popular musical instrument, by which time the Protestant and Catholic churches of the city were all suitably equipped.

As the Russian opera culture took shape, so too did that of ballet, which would become the country's most accomplished musical genre. In 1738 the Empress Anna founded the Russian Ballet Company, the country's first and ancestor of today's Mariinsky Theater. The Italian ballet master Antonio Rinaldi (1715–59) was instrumental in its artistic development, but it was the Frenchman Jean-Baptiste Lande, based at the College of the Nobility, who took the initiative of opening a school to train native Russian dancers.

Aristocrats and Serfs

Catherine the Great was certainly one of Russia's most cultured and civilized rulers. Yet she was not fascinated by music and she candidly admitted that "ultimately, music is rarely more than noise in my ears." Even so, she knew its political significance in a wider context and invited famous Italian composers to St. Petersburg, among them Domenico Cimarosa (1749–1801), one of the most important of his generation. One exception to her lack of musical interest was her fondness for *opera buffa*. The Italian troupe specializing in this comic genre led by G. Loccatelli had arrived in Russia in 1757 and was immediately received with critical acclaim. The empress was also by no means untutored in operatic production, writing librettos for five operas on generally military themes to music written by various composers.

Apart from the small imperial theater adjacent to the Summer Garden on the Field of Mars, there was Rinaldi's Imperial Kamenny Theater (later Bolshoi), a monumental stone structure completed in 1783 on a site where the Rimsky-Korsakov Conservatory now stands. Its main facade was decorated with statues, including one of Minerva, the Roman goddess of wisdom and the arts, made out of Carrara marble. Sir John Carr has left us a description, not only of its architecture but of the society who patronized it and their servants. He wrote:

> At four angles in this spacious area, are four pavilions of iron, supported by pillars of the same metal, within which, in winter, large fir fires are constructed, the wind being kept off by vast circular moveable shutters or iron, for warming and screening the servants of those who visit the theater in the winter. Previous to the erection of these sheds, many of those unfortunate persons were frozen to death. The government, attentive to the lives of the people, has interdicted performances at the opera, when the frost is unusually severe.

The Bolshoi Theater remained the city's most important theatrical venue, hosting both the Imperial Ballet Company and Imperial Opera Company until 1886 when the deteriorating fabric of the building required its demolition and the companies moved to the Mariinsky Theater.

Foreigners during the reign of Catherine the Great, like Count Esterhazy, Ambassador from the Hapsburg Empire, were especially impressed by operas with Russian themes such as those by V. Pashkevich, in which the exotic dances and songs of Siberia featured, sometimes with as many as 500 performers at on stage at one time.

During the reign of Tsar Paul I productions continued to be staged at the Hermitage, but others, of high quality, were now performed elsewhere in the capital in private houses and theaters, as an ever widening interest in music spread beyond court circles. It was about this time that the first public concert hall in Russia opened at 30 Nevsky Prospekt toward the end of the eighteenth century, but during Lent theatrical and other productions were prohibited, a tradition which continued until the end of imperial times.

Serfs played an important role in virtually all aspects of the city's life but nowhere more so than in its aristocratic inhabitants' domestic entertainment. In their St. Petersburg mansions, Count Razumovsky had as many as a thousand serfs and Count Stroganov six hundred, but it was Count Peter Sheremetev's retinue which had the greatest impact on the musical world, since they included artists of considerable fame. This allowed Sheremetev's son Nikolai (1752–1803) to play a major part in the city's music and theater. With over 210,000 serfs under his ownership throughout the Russian Empire, he could pick and choose whom he liked for his performances. He had become a highly skilled violoncellist during his time in Paris before he returned to St. Petersburg, in 1775. Soon the private theaters he directed in Russia became famous for the quality of productions performed by highly trained serfs. In particular, he collaborated with the Italian composer Giuseppe Sarti (1729–1802) on eight operas. Catherine the Great wrote the libretto for the opera *The Novgorod Hero Boyeslayevich*, with music composed by Yevstigney Fomin. In 1795 St. Petersburg became the focus of most of Sheremetev's productions and many serf performers were transferred there from his estates near Moscow. Not only his performers but also his craftsmen earned fame, not least the violin maker Ivan Batov, the quality of whose violins and violoncellos earned him the sobriquet the Stradivarius of Russia.

Sheremetev was closely involved in the artistic world of his serfs, but also on occasion in a more intimate sphere. He became romantically attached to a former serf, the highly talented, though not especially beautiful, singer and actress Praskovia Kovalyova (1768–1803), who had first appeared on his stage at the age of eleven. She was emancipated in 1798 and three years later she married Sheremetev, with the full approval of Tsar Alexander I, only to die tragically a short time later of consumption after the birth of her son Dmitri (1803–71). The poet Anna Akhmatova, a resident of the Sheremetyev Palace well over a century later, commemorated her in "Poem without a Hero," lamenting her tragic fate.

By 1861, on the eve of emancipation by Tsar Alexander II, the Sheremetevs possessed around 300,000 serfs throughout the country, and some of these were sent to Dmitry's palace in St. Petersburg. The large servants' quarters which he added in 1867 were designed by court architect Nicholas Benois. Even before then, though, by the early 1850s the Sheremetyev chapel choir had some ninety singers. After the death of Dmitri Sheremetev it ceased to function, but another small choir of fifteen singers was established under the direction of his son Alexander, attracting such guests as Tsar Alexander II to intimate concerts held in the palace's Etruscan Room. Strange to say, along with his keen musical interests, Count Alexander Sheremetev was a devoted fire-fighter. In 1879 he founded the Russian Fire-Fighting Society, establishing two units of firemen for the city and laying down the first fire-fighting regulations in Russia. His relative and neighbor, Nikolai Volkov-Muromtsev, left a jocular account of him:

> Uncle Sasha, who owned a number of excellent estates across the breadth of Russia... for some reason liked Vysokoye the most. There he built a splendid hospital with 35 beds and a fire station with a watchtower. This was his main preoccupation and for that reason he was well-known as the 'the Fire Chief Count'... Whenever he attended a reception or ball at the Winter Palace and news of a fire became known anywhere in the city, he was immediately informed of the fact. Immediately, he would drop everything and rush to put on his fire-fighting gear and hasten to the scene of the blaze, either by carriage or by motor car. Even when he came to visit us on our estate, he always brought with him his helmet, uniform, hooks and axes. Then my father would tease him: "But Sasha, you've forgotten your fire engine and ladder at home!"

Meanwhile, the Museum of Music in the Sheremetev Palace was established. The initiative for the museum came, not from the Sheremetev family, but from Baron Konstantin Stackelberg (1848–1925), who had established the Imperial Court Orchestra in 1882. The museum opened in 1900 with an exhibition of 300 instruments and a rich collection of manuscripts. It was augmented in 1907 with a major donation by the Dowager Empress Maria Feodorovna, widow of Tsar Alexander III. After the outbreak of the Revolution, Alexander Sheremetev fled abroad in 1918, after which his palace was confiscated and became the headquarters of various literary organizations. His museum was then reorganized into a museum of Russian nobility before reverting to the Museum of Music in the 1980s.

The Imperial Capella

In 1763 the court choir was re-established as the Imperial Court Choral Capella by the Empress Catherine the Great, its new Italian title a sign of growing Western influences to be found in the musical life of St. Petersburg. The first performance in Russia of Giovanni Battista Pergolesi's *Stabat Mater* was in March 1774, just one of many such innovative events over the following decades.

The first director of the Capella was Mark Fedorovich Poltoratsky (1729–95), followed by Dmitry Bortniansky (1751–1825), who ran the Capella from 1796 until his death. Bortniansky had spent much time in Italy, studying not only music but art and architecture and had been made an honorary member of the Imperial Academy of Arts. He also composed comic operas in French and church choral music. Tsar Alexander I was so pleased with his work that in 1816 he put him in charge of all ecclesiastical musical performances in the city. Under his directorship, the singer and composer Alexander Varlamov (1801–48) took an active role in the Capella, becoming one of the most important musical figures in St. Petersburg at this time.

Fyodor Petrovich Lvov, author of *On Singing in Russia* (1834), was its director from 1826–36, succeeded by his son, the talented violinist Aleksey (1798–1861), who composed the old imperial anthem, *God Save the Tsar*.

Robert Schumann wrote in 1844: "The Capella is the most splendid choir which I have ever had the pleasure to listen to; the basses at times remind one of the deep sounds of an organ, while the trebles resound with magic, better than the most splendid female voices."

The Capella moved from the old Winter Palace to an eighteenth-century house nearby on the Moika Embankment, near so-called Singers' Bridge. The house and concert hall were rebuilt in the 1880s and the Capella became the secular Leningrad Academic Glinka Capella. In 1920 females joined the choir, while boys' voices were phased out. Later, a separate boys' choir was established but from the 1950s the two frequently sang together. Later, after the Revolution, in French exile, the author Ivan Bunin wrote nostalgically of the musical joys he remembered:

Indeed, at the time, when the choir softly sang
O "Soft light"—with tender emotion
I forgot my discomfiture
and my heart glowed with joy...

The Capella was severely damaged in the Second World War, but was then fully reconstructed.

Dancing

Throughout this period the court remained the focus of social life and dance, but events in private mansions and elsewhere were much enjoyed by the aristocracy and wealthier bourgeoisie. During the Napoleonic Wars the advent in 1810 of the mazurka—later made famous by Chopin—created a popular trend, even if it arrived not from Warsaw but from Paris. Any excuse for a ball was appreciated, but it was the carnival period of Maslenitsa week, just before Lent, which was the busiest time, with balls held at the Winter Palace, in the Assembly of the Nobility and at the merchant-oriented Burghers' Club. The waltz was the most popular of dances, despite its initially perceived loucheness.

During the 1840s the polka became the rage among all segments of the population. Originally a Czech dance from Bohemia like the mazurka several decades before, it had become highly popular in Paris before being introduced by Russians who had first experienced it in the French capital. Unlike the mazurka, however, some among the nobility condemned its vulgarity and it was never introduced at court.

The Mikhailovsky and Mariinsky Theaters

One of the great opera and ballet houses in the first half of the nineteenth century was the Mikhailovsky Theater, built on the square of the same name (now Arts Square) in 1833 by Alexander Brullov but based on Rossi's plans. The theater had no resident company but rather hosted performances by foreign companies or by artists from the Mariinsky Theater. The famous Italian ballerina Maria Taglioni (1804–84), who revolutionized dancing *en pointe*, performed in numerous roles there from 1837 to 1842. In Leo Tolstoy's epic novel *Anna Karenina*, the Mikhailovsky Theater, with its French productions, provides the backdrop for various intrigues. Operas were also performed, including the first staging of Jacques Offenbach's *Orpheus in the Underworld* in 1859. German productions, too, came to the theater once or twice a week, catering for the city's 80,000 German residents. Many of these productions were scrutinized before the public by critics, the most famous of whom was Vladimir Stasov (1824–1906), famous for his sharp tongue. Among the most memorable performances was the operetta *The Gypsy Baron*, staged on April 23, 1886, with Johann Strauss II himself conducting.

The arrival of the renowned American dancer Isadora Duncan (1877–1927) in 1904 was a major sensation, one which she repeated during her brief life, tragically cut short in a motorcar accident. Diaghilev observed that her St. Petersburg debut administered to Russian ballet "a shock from which it could never recover." And if St. Petersburg had fallen in love with her, she had fallen in love with St. Petersburg. As she wrote in a letter to the editor, published in the magazine *Ogonek* in 1908:

Petersburg!
Life!
Enthusiasm!
Action!
Here all is new in spirit. Primitive
Strong
Great spaces -
Great lines -
Great flowing Neva.
Inspiration!
Opportunity!
The future all here -
Great country
I greet thee
I dance here with you.

After the Revolution, impressed by the Soviet system, she made an extended visit to the new communist state, eventually meeting and marrying the poet Sergei Yesenin, eighteen years her junior, in 1922. He left her the following year and later committed suicide, but she proudly kept the Soviet citizenship she had recently acquired throughout her life.

Meanwhile, by 1920 the Mikhailovsky Theater reopened as the State Academic Comic Opera Theater, one of several changes of name. After it was re-baptized the Maly Opera Theater in 1926, it focused predominantly on experimental music, Shostakovich making his debut there in 1930 with *Nos* (The Nose). Recently renovated, it has recovered its original name and still flourishes today.

It is the Mariinsky Theater, however, which is most renowned in the wider world, home for over a century and a half to the world's greatest opera and ballet. Named in honor of the Empress Maria Alexandrovna, consort of Tsar Alexander II, it was designed in 1859–60 by the architect Alberto Kavos on the site of a former equestrian circus that had burned down, but Nicholas Benois (1813–98) took an active role in its construction. The Mariinsky

Theater opened with great fanfare on October 2, 1860, with Glinka's *A Life for the Tsar*. Later, Mussorgsky, Rimsky-Korsakov, and Tchaikovsky would all have their opera and ballet premieres there, giving it a worldwide reputation for the highest quality of performance.

In 1883–86 the architect Viktor Shreter undertook major renovations at the Mariinsky Theater, with many internal wood constructions removed and replaced by metal ones so as to minimize the risk of fire. Various decorative features were also altered, giving the theater a new eclectic look. The Imperial Opera and Ballet were relocated to the Mariinsky Theater in 1886 because the Bolshoi Kamenny Theater was viewed as structurally unsafe. The celebrated choreographer Marius Petipa staged many of his best-known works in the 1890s there, including the ballet classics *The Sleeping Beauty* (1890), *The Nutcracker* (1892), *Raymonda* (1898) and the revival of *Swan Lake* (1895).

After the upheavals of the Revolution, the Mariinsky was renamed the State Academic Theater for Opera and Ballet, and in 1935 the Kirov, in memory of Lenin's murdered Bolshevik colleague. The Kirov Theater then reverted to its pre-revolutionary name in 1992, the same year that Valery Gergiev became its principal conductor, remaining there to this day as arguably Russia's most admired director/conductor. In 1968–70 the theater underwent a major refurbishment with a variety of technological improvements. Yet the greatest redevelopment occurred from January 2006 when another major renovation took place, including the construction of a new stage across the Kryukov Canal and an associated concert hall in Dekabristov Street.

Musical Avant-Garde

If St. Petersburg is a city whose music preserves the best of the nineteenth-century classical tradition, it also became noted for its avant-garde music. In the early twentieth century ballets such as *The Seasons* by Alexander Glazunov (1865–1936), with songs written by the Grand-Duke Constantine Constantinovich Romanov, featuring prominently. Glazunov, for many years professor at the Conservatory, was an avant-garde figure in the sense that he integrated both traditional Russian and modern European elements in his work. However, the late Romantic elements, which showed the influence of both Rimsky-Korsakov and Alexander Borodin, continued to dominate much of his music in the post-revolutionary period, dismaying the Soviet authorities, whom he had at first supported. Unable to cope with their increasing demands to compose music to suit their ideology, he went into exile in 1928.

Famous artistes included Feodor Chaliapin (1873–1938). Arguably the greatest opera singer in this period, Chaliapin appeared for the first time at the Mariinsky on April 5, 1895, in the role of Mephistopheles in Gounod's *Faust*. His deep bass voice and his innovative naturalistic style of acting made him a legend in his own time. Striking contemporary stage designs often formed a backdrop to his singing and frequently reflected the radical values of the World of Art movement (discussed in Chapter 7). Other major innovating figures were active in St. Petersburg, including the locally born choreographer and dancer Mikhail Fokin, who made his debut at the age of eight under the direction of Marius Petipa. The German composer Arnold Schönberg was hosted in the city in 1912 by the Futurist polymath Nikolai Kulbin, and conducted his symphonic poem *Pelleas und Melisande*. But perhaps the swan song of the old regime was the world's first Futurist opera, *Victory over the Sun* by the composer Mikhail Matyushin and the librettist Aleksei Kruchenykh, who used an experimental, and incomprehensible, language known as *zaum*. Its premiere, held on December 3, 1913, was predictably condemned in the press as "wild, boring, indecent and senseless." Even *The Rite of Spring* by Igor Stravinsky (1882–1971), born in the suburb of Oranienbaum, the discordant premiere of which seven months earlier in Paris had caused a riot, seemed conventional in comparison.

Other innovative composers also visited and conducted in St. Petersburg, among them Richard Wagner, who first came in 1863, and Gustav Mahler, in 1887, 1902, and 1907. The first two visits were as a conductor, but in 1907 he conducted his Fifth Symphony, watched by Stravinsky. The venue at which both performed was the famed Assembly of the Nobility, a center then as now of orchestral music. One of Russia's greatest composers, Peter Tchaikovsky gave his last public performance there on October 16, 1893, conducting his Sixth Symphony shortly before his death from cholera. Tchaikovsky lived as a child at Sergeivskaya Street (now Tchaikovsky Street), later occupying various addresses and finally 13 Malaya Morskaya Street together with his brother, where he died. His funeral procession on October 23, 1893, was immense. It was also the first time that a full orchestra joined a funeral cortege, an innovation which in the revolutionary period became customary for important political and cultural figures.

Many performers at the Assembly of the Nobility were put up at the Hotel La Russie opposite. After major renovations and enlargement through the acquisition of neighboring houses it reopened as the luxurious Grand Hotel Europa, a name it still retains: Tchaikovsky, Richard Strauss, Claude Debussy, Sergei Prokofiev, and Stravinsky all stayed at one time or another. The hotel underwent a major restoration in 1991 and still caters for some of the musical world's leading figures. Its art nouveau decoration is still one of the best examples in the city.

In 1921 the building which housed the Assembly of the Nobility had become known as the St. Petersburg Philharmonia. The first performance on June 12 that year was Tchaikovsky's Sixth Symphony, Concerto for Violins and Orchestra and his musical fantasy *Francesca da Rimini*. Later, on May 12, 1926, Shostakovich's First Symphony was performed, conducted by Evgeny Mravinsky. Shostakovich lived first on Bolshaya Morskaya Street and then at 2 Podolskaya Street. Later, during the blockade of Leningrad during the Second World War, Shostakovich performed his famed Seventh "Leningrad" Symphony, first in the city on July 19, 1942. "Neither savage raids, German planes, nor the grim atmosphere of the beleaguered city could hinder the flow," he recalled of the composing process. "I worked with an inhuman intensity I have never before reached."

Jazz and Pop Music in Leningrad/St. Petersburg

During the heady post-revolutionary days of the 1920s, before Stalinism had taken a reactionary grip on the music world of

Leningrad, jazz became highly popular. The Soviet Union's first jazz band was founded there under the leadership of Leonid Utyosov (1895–1982), a noted Jewish singer and comic actor from Odessa who collaborated with the musical conductor and film composer Isaak Dunayevsky (1900–55). Utyosov was the first popular singer to be made a People's Artist of the USSR, in 1965. During the 1950s the city's first jazz club Kvadrat opened and in the following years the popular band Druzhba (Friendship) was established, under the leadership of Dr. Aleksan Bronevitsky and Edita Piekha.

During the 1960s jazz increasingly gave way to underground rock emanating from the United States and Britain. Rock groups like Argonavty and Kochevniki became highly popular among student groups at concerts and festivals. Then, in the early 1970s, new bands such as Aquarium appeared, benefiting from a greater tolerance toward this sort of music by the authorities. The new Leningrad Rock Club, formed in 1981, offered a venue to bands like DTT, Kino, Zoopark, and Secret. The fad for "happenings," which had crossed the Atlantic, also took hold in Leningrad. *Pop Mekhanika* was one such inspired event in the 1980s, directed by Sergey Kuryokhin and involving more than three hundred people together with animals on stage. He would later be honored by having the annual International Music Festival in the city named after him, as well as the Kuryokhin Center, a venue for cutting-edge music.

Modern Revival

It was for its classical music that Leningrad was most renowned, and the Great Philharmonic Hall and other venues in Leningrad enjoyed a resurgence of activity after the Second World War. Restoration and renewal were the order of the day in the city's concert halls. In 1949 concerts were once again held at the Engelhardt House at 30 Nevsky Prospekt after a major renovation. This venue is today known as the Small Philharmonic Hall.

Despite the collapse of the Soviet Union, classical musical in St. Petersburg has continued to thrive. Today the Great Hall of the St. Petersburg Philharmonia is dedicated to the memory of Shostakovich and accommodates an audience of over 1,500. More recent renovations of the hall have followed, the latest in 2006–07. The Philharmonia currently encompasses two world-class orchestras: the St. Petersburg Philharmonic, dating back to 1882, and the St. Petersburg Academic Symphony Orchestra, founded in 1931. Yuri Temirkanov has been the former's principal conductor since 1988, and Alexander Sergeyevich Dmitriyev in charge of the latter since 1977.

In 1995–97 the former Imperial Capella underwent a major restoration. Alexander Chernushenko, a People's Artist of Russia and son of Vladislav Chernushenko, the previous conductor, carries on there in this capacity. The latest restoration of the concert hall was completed by the beginning of the new millennium, and since then it has hosted a wide variety of musical events from concerts of Spanish religious music to a performance of Korean classical and traditional music in November 2006, to celebrate the appointment of a Korean consul general to St. Petersburg.

New venues have also been established, including the Chamber Music Theater, which opened in a nineteenth-century mansion on Galernaya Street in 1987 under the direction of Yuri Alexandrov. It is home to the St. Petersburg Chamber Opera Company, which has already won a world-class reputation for its orchestra and soloists. The experimental Zazerkalye ("Beyond the Looking Glass") Children's Musical Theater opened in the same year at Rubinstein Street under the direction of Alexander Petrov and the conductor Pavel Bubelnikov. It produces musical drama for children and adults, with a repertoire ranging from Bach to Stravinsky. Modern music has also not been forgotten in St. Petersburg, and such popular musicals as Roman Ignatyev's *Monte Cristo* draw large audiences, as do countless jazz, *Russian chanson*, and pop venues. The splendid Russian tradition of music thus carries on through the third millennium.

Performances are held throughout the year, but it is during the annual White Nights Festival, which takes place from late May to July, that the zenith of the musical season in St. Petersburg is reached. It is also during this period that the Stars of the White Nights festivities are held at the Mariinsky Theater as well as at some outdoor venues, a tradition which goes back to 1993. This is when some of the world's leading classical (and pop) performers will come to St. Petersburg, attracting vast audiences, as when the Rolling Stones played in front of 50,000 fans in Palace Square in July 2007. The Chinese-American cellist Yo-Yo Ma has also been a sell-out performer at his concerts, usually held at the Rimsky-Korsokov Conservatory, as was the late Portuguese *morna* singer Cesária Évora, the "barefoot diva" from the Cape Verde Islands.

For all the focus in St. Petersburg on traditional classical music, there is also a thriving serious contemporary music scene. For example, the St. Petersburg Contemporary Music Center organizes international new music festivals, the latest of which was held in the city in late May 2016. Venues for the festival included the leading concert halls: the Mariinsky Theater Concert Hall, the Great Philharmonic, the Jaani Kirik Concert Hall, and the Rimsky-Korsakov Conservatory, hosting a wide spectrum of contemporary and often experimental music.

Local talent is not lacking and includes Boris Filanovsky (born 1968), founder in 2000 of eNsemble, St. Petersburg's first and only ensemble of contemporary music, of which is currently director. His musical compositions suggest the influence of such postmodern and conceptualist authors as Vladimir Sorokin and Lev Rubinstein. He is also a member of the Structuralist Resistance Group, which brings together other innovative composers of contemporary music in Russia.

9 | Faith in the City
The Role of Religion

W hen Tsar Peter the Great became autocrat of all Russia the stage was set for a radical change in the Orthodox Church, the established church of the state, of which he declared himself emperor in 1721. Upon the death of Patriarch Adrian in 1700, he introduced an Erastian system of Church leadership and administration, entailing the abolition of the office of patriarch, the highest in the Russian Orthodox Church, and its substitution with a Holy Synod, under the control of tsar himself. It would be based for much of the pre-revolutionary period in a grand neoclassical building constructed from 1829 by the Italian architect Carlo Rossi, who had previously built the Senate. This arrangement continued for over three centuries until a patriarchate was re-established in 1917 just after the February Revolution, when St. Tikhon, Metropolitan of Moscow, was instated (he would be "deposed" by the Soviet authorities in 1923). Although he died in hospital two years later, he was declared "glorified," canonized by the Russian Orthodox Church in 1981 as one of "the new martyrs and confessors of the Soviet Yoke"; his body, concealed in the Donskoy Monastery in Moscow, was only rediscovered in 1992.

The Peter and Paul Cathedral

One of the first and most important of St. Petersburg's churches, or more accurately temples (known as *kram* in Russian), was that at the Peter and Paul Fortress. Even today this splendid Baroque monument, dedicated to St. Peter and St. Paul, is both architecturally and historically significant since it is the final resting place of all the Tsars of Russia who have been buried since the time of Peter the Great. The church that towers above the fortress today is the replacement of an earlier wooden version, the building of which had commenced in 1703, the year of the city's foundation. That structure had been laid out in the form of a cross surmounted by three spires, with walls painted to imitate stone and brick. As late as September 2006, the Dowager Empress Maria Feodorovna, mother of the last tsar Nicholas II and sister of Britain's Queen Alexandra, was interred here, over seventy years after her death and her first burial in Roskilde Cathedral in Denmark, where her brother reigned as King Christian X. Rising to a height of 122 meters (400 feet), it is one of the city's most prominent landmarks, built by Domenico Trezzini from 1712–33. Its geometrical regularity and large windows, admitting light to illuminate the interior, are highly atypical of traditional Russian ecclesiastical architecture. Rather they draw on Western tradition, incorporating the Enlightenment architectural values which were gaining currency in Sweden and England, while reflecting Trezzini's own education in Rome. Its tower was the one of the last parts completed and its carillon clock was imported from Holland. Corinthian capitals over fauxmarble piers grace the interior, which is composed of three principal aisles. All of these elements unite to create an imposing picture, but its gilded iconostasis by Ivan Zarudnyi is its most impressive internal feature, the individual icons of which are said to be by the Moscow artist Andrei Pospelov. A lightning strike damaged the cathedral in 1756, but it was eventually restored by another famous Italian architect Francesco Bartolomeo Rastrelli, son of the Florentine architect and sculptor Carlo Bartolomeo Rastrelli (c. 1675–1744), who had been invited to Russia by Peter the Great, impressed by his work at the Palace of Versailles. Later restorations were carried out in 1896–1908 by three other architects—D. I. Grimm, A. O. Tomishko, and Leon Benois. Further restorations would follow, the most recent of which has only just been completed.

The Alexander Nevsky Monastery

Trezzini also carried out other ecclesiastical projects during this period. The most important of these, from 1710, was the construction of the Monastery of the Holy Trinity and St. Alexander Nevsky, the thirteenth-century Russian warrior-saint who, with the assistance of the Mongols, defended Russia against both the Catholic Swedes and Teutonic Knights in 1240. This victory has led him to be seen as the spiritual protector not only of St. Petersburg, but of Russia itself. It is not surprising therefore that the city's main thoroughfare was almost immediately named after him and the monastery itself was constructed at its far end, at the confluence of the Neva and Chernaya rivers. As with the Peter and Paul Cathedral, traditional Russian models for the new monastery and church were rejected. Instead, a Western European symmetrical, rectangular plan was adopted in 1715, which was to incorporate a tower and spire similar to that at the fortress church. Consecrated in 1724, the Church of the Annunciation and of St. Alexander Nevsky took many years to complete and, though Trezzini's designs were followed, it was actually completed much later by the Bavarian architect Theodor Schwertfeger (c.1680–c.1739). Unfortunately, much of his work had to be pulled down later in the century because of structural flaws and so the monastery as we know it came to be built by the Russian Ivan Starov from 1776–90. In its final form it is a highly innovative building, featuring an imposing Baroque eastern entrance but also with many neoclassical features evident in its extensive use of pilasters.

Archbishop Feofan Prokopovich

Peter the Great may have looked westwards for his technological and bureaucratic models, but he was thoroughly Eastern in his autocratic approach to political rule. In both Church and state he carefully chose those in positions of authority who would bolster his own. When then the need arose to select a metropolitan for the See of St. Petersburg, Feofan Prokopovich (1681–1736) suited him down to the ground. A highly "westernized" cleric, he had been a student at the Kiev Academy in his native city, after which he had moved to Rome. There he converted to Roman Catholicism before returning to Kiev in 1704 and to Russian Orthodoxy. Yet many of the Western European values with which he had been inculcated in Italy continued to motivate him.

It is said that Prokopovich came to the attention of the tsar during a thanksgiving service in 1709 in Kiev for the latter's victory at Poltava, a battle which helped to destroy Swedish hegemony in northern Europe. So impressed was Peter with Prokopovich's oratory that he enlisted his assistance forthwith. The metropolitan supported Peter in his suppression of the patriarchate in favor of the Holy Synod's domination of the Church (and hence tsar's domination of the Synod) in his eloquent Spiritual Regulation:

> ...he has to justify the unlimited power of the autocrat with nationalistic arguments, Feofan's treatises A Word on the Power and Honor of the Tsar and The Truth of the Monarch's Will justified the autocrat's God given powers for both religious and state reasons.

Thus it was God himself who had given the tsar to the Russian state, and his failure to exert his authority with respect to both Church and state would itself be a moral lapse. When in October 1721 Peter accepted the title of emperor in the Senate, after a service of thanksgiving in the long since demolished wooden Holy Trinity Cathedral (the oldest church in St. Petersburg, first consecrated in 1703), the ceremony clearly expressed for all to witness what both Peter and Feofan wished to achieve, namely the outward confirmation of this new autocratic order.

With such credentials it is not surprising that Feofan became the tsar's most important spiritual adviser—to the horror of those Orthodox prelates who looked upon Prokopovich as a crypto-Catholic and a westernizer. Yet if the metropolitan outraged many old-fashioned clergymen, Western visitors were often enchanted by him. A Danish guest in the city in 1736 left this favorable impression of the archbishop:

> This honorable man assisted Peter the Great in carrying out his reforms of the Church... As a young man, he had traveled extensively in Europe and Asia. In every manner of scholarship few could boast of his learning, in particular, amongst the clergy of Russia. Along with history, theology and philosophy, he was exceptionably knowledgeable in mathematics, a subject in which he was deeply interested. He was fluent in many European languages, both in terms of comprehension and speech, a facility he nurtured diligently into old age.

Even the metropolitan's official seat reflected his Western neo-classical values, for Karpovka, where Prokopovich lived, was a Palladian mansion situated on the left bank of the Neva with a classical facade of eight pilasters. As if to confirm the union of Church and science in this dawning age of Enlightenment, the scientist and educational reformer Mikhail Lomonosov resided nearby. With such a neighbor it is not surprising that the archbishop also took a keen interest in popular education and founded a school for poor children, which functioned for fifteen years. Russia's first medical university, with a hospital, now occupies the site, dedicated to the memory of the Nobel Prize–winning experimental psychologist and behaviorist Ivan Pavlov (1849–1936).

Prokopovich's knowledge was broad, and as a gifted author his writings focused on secular as well as religious themes. He wrote not only sermons and philosophical treatises, but poems, plays, and essays. As such, he considered himself a man of progress—just like the tsar—and truly lamented his passing in the famed funeral oration which he held for Peter in 1725:

> What are we doing now? We are burying Peter the Great! Is it not a dream? Not a vision of the night? Oh, what a real sorrow! Oh, what certain bitter reality! Contrary to all expectations and hopes he has ended his life who has been the cause of our innumerable benefactions and joys, who has resuscitated Russia as if from the dead, and has raised it to great power and glory...

Prokopovich also enjoyed wide support at court. Count Piotr Tolstoy, the head of the Secret Chancellery, a body set up by Peter the Great to investigate suspicious political activity and crimes, and Andrei Ushakov who succeeded him, both admired him for his enlightened learning and innovative ecclesiastical practices. Yet for all his progressive values, he remained a man of his time. He had no qualms, for example, about torture, and religious toleration remained alien to him: he zealously persecuted Old Believers, who refused to accept the reforms of the seventeenth-century Patriarch Nikon because of the threats they posed to the order of the state, as much as to the Church. Nonetheless, his tragi-comedy *Vladimir* (1705) reflects many of the values of this increasingly rational age, and he was a founding member of the city's first literary society, which included numerous other intellectuals of the time.

In 2003 a memorial chapel was built to commemorate the tercentenary of St. Petersburg, which commemorates Feofan's old Holy Trinity Cathedral on Trinity Square, a building which has disappeared after various fires and final demolition in 1933.

Religious Monuments

Although Peter the Great devoted the bulk of his energies to worldly power and glory, he by no means neglected to embellish his new capital with costly religious monuments. It is interesting that the tsar, in the interests of aesthetics, had for a time considered the Swedish court architect, Nicodemus Tessin the Younger, employed by the tsar's long time enemy King Karl XII, for the construction of a new cathedral on Vasilyevsky Island, which would have been based on his 1708 design for a church in Stockholm, but this was never realized. Many other projects, however, were successfully accomplished by the tsar and his immediate successors.

One such is the Church of St. Simon and St. Anna, built from 1731–34 by Mikhail Zemtsov, a striking building with its rusticated quoins (roughly hewn stone blocks at the corners), clearly demonstrating the Italian Baroque influence of Trezzini. Also of note is Korobov's red-and-white Church of St. Panteleimon the Healer, 1735–39, a memorial church commemorating Russia's 1714 naval victory over the Swedes off Hankö, a peninsula in the south of Finland. A mix of Baroque and classical elements, it has a checkered history, but managed to escape demolition and was for a while used as a museum.

During the reign of the Empress Elizabeth work commenced on what remains today one of St. Petersburg's most significant landmarks, the Smolny Cathedral. Built by Rastrelli from 1749 to 1764, its name derives from a site at which tar for naval needs was stored. The actual ecclesiastical name is the Cathedral of the Resurrection, situated at the heart of the complex, which formerly served as a convent. Here, most famously, the empress established the school for the daughters of the aristocracy which until the Revolution forced its closure was Russia's most important educational establishment for young ladies. Elizabeth herself had intended to retire here but her premature death precluded this.

The complex was a vast building enterprise and the marshy site required some 50,000 piles to make it stable, each of which was from four to twelve meters (12–36 feet) in length. As is usual in such major schemes, financial resources were not always forthcoming, despite the fact that the initiative came from Elizabeth, since the wars in which Russia found itself involved took funding priority. Nonetheless, its finished form is one of the highlights of St. Petersburg's architecture. The cathedral's most striking features are its assortment of characteristically Russian onion domes and its truncated apse, its walls painted through the centuries in a pastel blue edged with white exterior Christmas cake–like stucco decoration. Silhouetted against the eastern horizon for miles around, its majesty was recently threatened by the threatened imposition of the new Gazprom tower on the opposite side of the Neva. However, a great public outcry led to the plan's abandonment and the cathedral's profile remains unspoiled. Nowadays it is mostly used for concerts.

Another fine example of St. Petersburg Church Baroque (if less iconic) is the St. Nicholas Naval Cathedral, located in a small park adjacent to both the Griboyedov and Kryukov Canals. Associated with the Russian Navy until the Revolution, it was designed by chief naval architect Savva Chevakinsky and built from 1753 to 1762. A stunning azure structure based on a cruciform plan and richly highlighted in gilt, three of its facades are embellished by imposing Corinthian porticoes. Yet for all its Baroque magnificence, the whole displays a lightness of touch inspired by the playful Rococo fashion. As is typical in many northern Russian churches, the building actually contains two churches, one at ground level for winter use and one on the floor above for use in the warmer months. The principal glory of its interior is the richly decorated wooden iconostasis, full of lustrous icons. Its bell-tower, by contrast, seems to look ahead to the age of neoclassicism which was to become the height of fashion in the final quarter of the eighteenth century.

Unquestionably, one of the most charming and idiosyncratic of St. Petersburg churches of the period is the Church of St. John the Baptist at Chesme, which Yury Felten constructed in 1777–80. Like an extraordinary wedding- cake, it would seem more at home near Sir Horace Walpole's Gothic Strawberry Hill in London than a suburb of St. Petersburg, but then the Empress Catherine the Great was keen on the Gothic Revival.

The Kazan Cathedral, like most Orthodox churches in St. Petersburg, also clearly takes its inspiration from Western Europe, but it does so to a degree which few other churches in the city can equal. It is perhaps no coincidence that Tsar Paul I intended this since he was keen to encourage a reunion of the Roman Catholic and Orthodox Churches. He enjoyed a unique position among the tsars in being made Grand Master of the Roman Catholic Knights of Malta. He thus chose the freed serf architect Andrey Voronikhin, who had proven his artistic skills at the Stroganov Palace (his former owner, and possibly even father, had been Count Andrei Stroganov), to carry out its construction, which he accomplished between 1801 and 1811.

This brick structure, named after the venerated Our Lady of Kazan, is clad in limestone quarried near Gatchina, outside St. Petersburg, and built on a Latin cross plan, while its appearance mirrors St. Peter's Basilica in Rome, with wide Corinthian porticoes and colonnades extending outwards on either side. Its Roman dome, in particular, is highly atypical of Russian Orthodox architecture, while the exterior is enriched with stone sculptures depicting figures from the Bible. Two on either side of the northern entrance, St. Vladimir and Alexander Nevsky, are cast in bronze, a material also used to clad its doors, decorated by images copied from Ghiberti's Cathedral Baptistery doors in Florence. The interior, on the other hand, is more typically Orthodox, with two iconostases painted by Vasily Borovikovsky and Andrey Ivanov from the Imperial Academy of Arts. The cathedral possessed many ancient

Byzantine characteristics such as an *omphalion* (derived from the Greek word *omphalos* or navel, signifying the center of the world in ancient times), a spot delineated by a red stone near the altar on which the tsar was supposed to stand during the service, emphasizing his centrality to the state. Nicholas II, Russia's last and tragically fated tsar, stood here while attending services. A century earlier, John Quincy Adams, later the sixth president of the United States, was present at a liturgy at Kazan Cathedral. In his diary entry of September 27, 1811, he wrote with obvious enthusiasm:

> Went with Mr. Smith in full dress, and attended the consecration of the new church of the Mother of God of Kazan. We were there punctually at two o'clock, and found it difficult to get in, owing to the immense crowd. It was about eleven when the Emperor and imperial family came in... The ceremonies were excessively long, and in very few particulars sufficiently significant to be understood by me. At one stage of it the priests, followed by the Emperor and imperial family, went in procession out of the church, and marched round it, carrying the holy relics, and the sacred, miraculous image of the Virgin to whom the church is dedicated... The priests were in their customary garments, and the metropolitan's mitre was studded with costly precious stones. The choir of singers performed their parts as usual. General Pardo and the Chevalier de Bray soon got weary after the ceremony commenced. Old count Strogonoff stayed until the last half-hour, but was then obliged to retire... The church has been built under his superintendence, as President of the Academy of Arts. It is one of the most magnificent churches that I ever saw.

Impressive though the Kazan Cathedral is, the largest Orthodox cathedral in the city is St. Isaac's, dedicated to St. Isaac of Dalmatia, Peter the Great's patron saint, and built by the French architect Auguste de Montferrand from 1818 to 1858. It was constructed on the site of Rinaldi's earlier cathedral, and parts of the earlier building have been retained within its walls on St. Isaac's Square. The English visitor Sir John Carr noted at that time that Tsar Paul disliked his mother's ecclesiastical tastes and had little sympathy for the architecture of Rinaldi, whose work she so admired: "The late Emperor, disgusted, as I have already explained, with everything which had engaged the care and regard of his Imperial mother, raised in ridicule a little tower of brick, covered with a small dome, on the west side of this temple." Carr also saw little to appreciate in the cathedral as it now stood and commented: "For the honor of the empire, I hope that it will either be altered to the Empress's original design, or pulled down altogether."

Its most imposing feature is its ribbed dome resplendent in gilt, which dominates the city for miles around. The neoclassical building itself is extensively decorated, including red columns, the granite for which was quarried in nearby Vyborg, in Karelia. Especially striking is the malachite and lapis lazuli cladding of the columns which form its magnificent iconostasis. Unusually, the cathedral has stained-glass windows, an unorthodox innovation for a Russian Orthodox house of worship. The stained-glass altar window was imported from Munich and depicts the Resurrection, but was a highly unusual work for a church in Russia at this time since Orthodox tradition rejected the use of stained glass because of its fragility, deemed unsuitable for the long-term preservation of the holy images. On the other hand, the iron and bronze work used to decorate St. Isaac's was produced by the British-owned Baird Works.

The Anglican Church and British Visitors

The Anglican community had had a presence in the new capital as far back as 1721, when a small church was constructed at the English Embankment, serving the needs of British residents including those who had married into the Russian aristocracy, until it fell into disrepair during the upheavals of Napoleonic Wars. In need of repair, it was rebuilt in 1815 by Quarenghi, who gave it an elongated classical facade, shifting its entrance to the side. The front pew on the right was reserved for the British Ambassador and his family and guests. Owned by local Russian Anglican proprietors, often the sons of British Anglican mothers, the Church of Jesus Christ remained in their hands until the Revolution, when the building was confiscated by the Soviet state, its Anglican priest sent to a prison camp where he is said to have died. Eventually it was transferred to the Rimsky-Korsakov Conservatory of Music, which occupies it today. On rare occasions, though, Anglican services, which resumed in 1993, have taken place in the old church.

Many British visitors took a far greater interest in Russian Orthodox churches than they did in the Anglican one. When the author Lewis Carroll (1832–98), famed for his *Alice's Adventures in Wonderland* and *Through the Looking-Glass*, visited St. Petersburg in the summer of 1867, he left his impressions of the city's churches in his diary. If his stories from England show a fondness for the fantastical, he found this aspect in Russian religion too much to cope with. In particular, his preference for Anglican sobriety made him dismissive of ornate Orthodox liturgy. On two occasions he visited the city's most important houses of worship—the Kazan and the St Isaac Cathedrals, he remarked:

> the more one sees of these gorgeous services, with their many appeals to the senses, the more, I think one learns to love the plain, simple (but to my mind far more real) service of the English church.

His student friend at Oxford and fellow academic and traveler, the Rev. Henry Liddon, took an opposing point of view, stating with considerable enthusiasm:

> I cannot understand anybody coming here and saying that the Eastern Church is a petrifaction. Right or wrong, it is a vast, energetic, and most powerful body, with an evident hold upon the heart of the largest of European empires; indeed, a force within the limits of Russia to which I believe there is no moral parallel in the West.

Some might say that the same is true again today, with Russia's post-Soviet Orthodox religious revival in full swing, nurtured by the government both politically and financially.

Religious Revivalism

The second half of the eighteenth century was a period of Enlightenment within court circles, one in which non-mystical, even secular, values had come to the fore, much as they did in Western Europe at this time. Such values were propagated, in particular, by the Empress Catherine the Great. In contrast, St. Blessed Xenia of St. Petersburg appealed to a very different segment of the population. Xenia Petrova (c.1720s–c. 1803) was the young widow of Colonel Andrey Petrov, who himself had been a cantor at St. Andrew's Cathedral on Vasilyevsky Island. Donning the military uniform of her late husband, she gave away all material possessions, devoted her life to looking after the poor and uneducated and hence became a "fool for Christ"—a form of Orthodox asceticism that involves flouting convention. After her death, she was interred in the Smolensky Cemetery, over which a chapel was erected in 1902. Canonized by the Russian Orthodox Church in 1988, processions are still held in her honor and she remains St. Petersburg's most venerated female saint.

As a capital and leading commercial city, St. Petersburg also attracted adherents of other religions, as visitors were quick to notice. In 1869, during the reign of Tsar Alexander II, for example, there were a recorded 5,027 Jews living there despite heavy restrictions on Jewish immigration from the Pale of Settlement. These were largely successful merchants, bankers, and doctors given special permission to settle by the authorities. Muslims, too, were represented in St. Petersburg, with 1,707 there at that time, a small number when the entire population of 614,905 is taken into account. Many of these were scions of noble Central Asian or Crimean families who had been confirmed in their aristocratic status. Others were fur traders or prosperous merchants. Christians enjoyed the facilities of some 247 Orthodox churches, 24 Protestant houses of worship, and 15 Catholic churches. The Jewish community was also catered to with six synagogues. Secular events were less important than religious ones, and so during Lent theaters and concert halls were obliged to shut, a regulation vigorously implemented until the end of the imperial regime. The 1860s also bore witness to an Orthodox revival, which sought to repress growing secular influences from the West, especially those with Enlightenment roots. After the death of Tsar Nicholas I, the Church hierarchy tried to reassert itself and pursued a policy of improving public morals. Sometimes it acted as a censor; in 1860, for instance, 22 sculptures with pagan symbolism adorning the Admiralty were removed and destroyed, the material reused as foundation rubble.

During the 1870s Fyodor Dostoyevsky infused his writings with a deep Orthodox spirituality which made novels such as *The Demons* (1871–72) and *The Brothers Karamazov* (1879–80) profound and complex explorations of Christianity, sin, and human struggle. They also reflect the mounting confrontation in this period between society and terrorism which culminated in the most defining political event of the final decades of the nineteenth century in Russia: the assassination of Tsar Alexander II.

Alexander, the most liberal of all the tsars in the Western sense of the term, failed to stem the rising tide of anarchism and terrorism which permeated Russian society. The goal uniting the various extreme secret societies which came to overrun more moderate democratic groups was the undermining of the very heart of Russian imperial absolutism, and five attempts had previously been made to assassinate him. Many people were killed as a result, but the tsar himself had escaped. On March 13, 1881, however, this murderous dream was finally realized when Alexander—not an oppressive autocrat but the Tsar Liberator who had emancipated the serfs—was finally assassinated. The deed was planned and accomplished by the terrorist group *Narodnaya Volya* (People's Will), which strove to overthrow Russia's imperial regime. Its aim was to put in place a socialist system, which had failed to receive a positive response among the peasantry. The tsar was attacked and killed by a bomb on his way to the Mikhailovsky Manège for a military roll call as was his habit every Sunday.

For most Russian patriots of the time, the tsar's death was a martyrdom, not least because uninjured by the first bomb thrown, which had killed a young boy, he had gone to the latter's help only to be killed by a second bomb. In commemoration of this event the Church of Our Savior on the Spilled Blood (1883–1907) was built on the site of the assassination. Constructed in a national Romantic style characterized by the most lavish of onion domes, it stands on the edge of the Griboyedov Canal adjacent to the gardens of the Mikhailovsky Palace. (It is illustrated on the front cover of this book.) A. A. Frolov, whose mosaic floors adorn the Mariinsky Theater, provided the splendid mosaics for the church. It is an architectural anomaly in the otherwise largely neoclassical city, almost all of whose churches, monasteries, and palaces are Italian in inspiration. Alluding more to medieval Russian church building in the style of Moscow's St. Basil's Cathedral, its lavish use of mosaics and semi-precious stones sets it apart from most others. Yet it attracts more visitors in St. Petersburg than any other church there today. Much of the money to build it (4.6 million roubles in total) came from private donations, despite the fears of Konstantin Pobedonostsev, the procurator of the Holy Synod and adviser to the tsars, that charitable funds would be hard to come by.

The most important religious figure in the environs of St. Petersburg at this time was St. John of Kronstadt (secularly, Ivan Sergiev, 1829–1908). Presbyter and member of the Holy Synod, his deeply spiritual works are still read by devoted Russians, and he has been honored as the only secular priest, as opposed to monks, to have a presence on the Russian calendar of saints. Attached from 1855 to St. Andrew's Cathedral in Kronstadt, he nonetheless traveled to the far corners of the empire carrying out charitable acts, but also earning a devout following among imperial family members, dispensing Holy Communion to Tsar Alexander III on his deathbed in 1894 at the Livadia Palace in Crimea. Some members of the inner circle of ladies, like Anna Vyrbuova, which formed around the Empress Alexandra, consort to Tsar Nicholas II, were especially devoted to him, but his death led to a spiritual vacuum which unfortunately came to be filled by the wayward monk Rasputin. Rasputin's friendship with Alexandra, who was convinced that only he had powers to help her hemophiliac son Alexey, heir to the throne, served to damage her reputation and even that of her husband as well, with dire consequences not only for them but for Russia. John was canonized, first by the Russian Orthodox Church Outside Russia in 1966, and then by the Russian Orthodox Church, in Russia, in 1990. In contrast to that of Rasputin, his reputation is as unsullied today as it was in his own time.

Other Faiths

Despite the Russian Orthodox revival with its fears of atheism, there was a process of religious toleration toward the end of the nineteenth century and beginning of the twentieth in St. Petersburg. This trend was exemplified by Nicholas II's Edict of Toleration of 1905, granting legal status to non-Orthodox faiths. Adherents of Buddhism were among the first to benefit from the proclamation, and their temple in the capital was the first built in Europe. Buddhism had long been respected as a religion as opposed to a sect, a term used even today to describe the non-traditional religions of Russia, and in 1741 the Empress Elizabeth—not otherwise known for her religious liberalism—had recognized it as a legitimate religion within the Russian Empire, where Kamlyks, Buryats, Tuvans and Alataians were its most prominent followers. Still, it was only in 1913, as part of the celebrations of the tercentenary of the dynastic House of Romanov, that the newly built temple opened for worship. Located in the Staraya Derevnaya district on the northwestern outskirts of the city, it was known in Tibetan as the Temple of the Source of the Holy Teaching of the Buddha the All-Compassionate. Its first abbot, Agvan Dorzhiev (1853–1938), a Kalmyk from the province of Buryatia in Siberia, would end his days in one of Stalin's Gulag camps, one of the victims of the repression which targeted religious leaders of all persuasions.

The relation of Russia's Jews to the state had from its very inception been a thorny one. Before the partitions of Poland under the Empress Catherine the Great in the late eighteenth century hardly any Jews lived in Russia. Yet even then the roots of anti-Semitism were to be found. These lay less in matters relating to Jews themselves than in a schism during the Middle Ages within the Russian Church, which had sought to introduce Old Testament rituals into church practice. This heresy had been crushed, but it left a trail of hostility to Judaic practices within Russia for centuries to come. When the so-called Russian Partition occurred between 1772 and 1795, by which Russia seized regions of the Polish-Lithuanian Commonwealth, it suddenly had the largest Jewish population in the world, almost all of whom lived in the Pale of Settlement, an area within the empire in which they were tolerated. Some of these were bailiffs of the Polish aristocratic estates or purveyors of alcohol and innkeepers, occupations looked upon with hostility by large sections of the peasantry and serfs. After the partition, severe restrictions were imposed on where they might live and work. St. Petersburg, as well as Moscow, was off limits unless special permits were obtained for bankers, merchants, and doctors, among others, whose services were considered beneficial to the state. The broad masses of Jewry, however, remained barred. For Jews who embraced Christianity the outlook was different. During the latter years of Tsar Alexander I, Jewish conversions to Russian Orthodoxy were positively encouraged. To this end, the Society of Israelite Christians was founded in 1817 under the patronage of the emperor with the benevolent intention of "providing Jews who have accepted the Christian faith with a peaceful refuge in the bosom of the Russian Empire."

During the course of the nineteenth century the lot of Jews in St. Petersburg who remained loyal to their faith also improved in the general atmosphere of increasing religious toleration. By 1870 they had ten synagogues in the city. That year, Alexander II granted the community the privilege of constructing a new and imposing place of worship, reflecting the high status of the rich merchants, doctors, and others permitted to live in the capital. The Great Choral Synagogue, situated at Lermontov Prospekt and designed by the architect A. V. Malov, was consecrated in 1893 and survived the Revolution and two world wars to remain the city's center of Jewish spiritual life. It is Europe's second largest synagogue, designed in an eclectic Moorish-Byzantine style.

Not surprisingly, many intellectual Jews joined political movements which sought to undermine the imperial system while rejecting the theological tenets and customs of their own religion. This, in turn, led the authorities to see many within their community as hostile to the Russian state. For that reason, anti-Semitism was rife in St. Petersburg, especially in court circles. Anti-Semitic activity also emanated from the political left, since revolutionary journals like *Chernyi Peredel* and *Zerno*, which the authorities attempted to suppress, encouraged it in pursuit of their own agenda—a popular revolution against capitalism. Nonetheless, the pogroms which took place elsewhere in the Russian Empire, like those in Kishinev in 1903 and 1905, never happened in St. Petersburg.

Assault on the Church

The year 1917 seemed to bode well for the Russian Orthodox Church with the re-establishment, after almost three hundred years, of the patriarchate abolished by Peter the Great. It appeared that what had been known as the Babylonian Captivity, with the Holy Synod under undue imperial control, was at an end. As Catherine Merrydale puts it: "Senior Church leaders, including Petrograd's Metropolitan, Vinyamin, were ambivalent, but not implacably opposed to the deal."

Yet soon the real intentions of the Bolsheviks became clear: the destruction of the Church itself and its hierarchy. Lenin himself spearheaded the attack on the Church, writing to the Old Bolshevik political leader Vyacheslav Molotov, later minister of foreign affairs,

> I have reached the firm conclusion, that we must now undertake a decisive and merciless battle against the clergy. We must suppress their opposition with so much cruelty that they will not forget it for several decades. The more... clergy... which we succeed in shooting for this reason, the better.

This the Cheka (Emergency Committee, the first of the Soviet state security organizations) accomplished to so successfully that 2,691 priests, 1,962 monks, and 3,447 nuns were eliminated in Petrograd, among them Vinyamin himself, executed by firing squad in 1922 and subsequently canonized. Many were buried at the Preobrazhenskoye Cemetery, where the victims of Bloody Sunday had been interred, and at the more central Bogoslovskoe Cemetery as well as at Levashovo, outside the city. Countless others would later die in Gulag camps, especially in the Arctic north.

Churches were desecrated. Even that architectural jewel, the Kazan Cathedral, was not spared desecration in the name of the new regime's ideology. As the British consul-general in Leningrad noted in 1931:

> The Kazan Cathedral—a cathedral no longer—is being got ready for 7 November. The text in gilt letters is being scraped off the architrave. Yesterday I could just read "Blessed… in the name of the Lord"; today the inscription has quite disappeared.

It was eventually turned into the Museum of the History of Religion and Atheism.

Another early victim of the demolitions during the 1930s was the city's first house of worship, the old Holy Trinity Cathedral, on a site chosen by Peter the Great and built only four and a half months after the city's foundation. The German Reformed Church, situated on the Neva side of the Moika Embankment, was also targeted. Its belltower was dismantled and the church patronized by so many Baltic German nobles during the imperial era was converted into a workers' club for the postal and telephone services. In 1938 a further 28 eight churches were forced to close and by the end of the year there were only five still open in the city. Near to where the Pokrovsky Market had formerly been located on what is now Turgenev Square, the Church of the Intercession of the Mother of God was partly demolished in 1939. This was followed in 1940 by the demolition of the Church of the Sign, located on the former Znamenskaya Square, now Vosstaniya Square, built from 1794–1804; it made way for planned a metro station. Among its most famous parishioners was the Nobel Laureate Ivan Pavlov, who also sometimes served as church warden there. It was not the only church destroyed in the vicinity: the Oktyabrsky Concert Hall was also built on the site of a demolished house of worship.

Even the Buddhist temple was not spared vandalism. In 1919 it was plundered, its furniture and religious vessels, its tapestries and priceless manuscripts destroyed or dispersed. The abbot suffered the fate of so many of the clergy of all religions: he was sent to a prison camp in Siberia, where he died at Ulan-Ude in 1938.

Countless desecrations of interiors and melt-downs of valuable metals framing and embellishing icons also took place in Leningrad from the early 1920s and throughout the 1930s. With the outbreak of the Second World War, though, some surviving churches were permitted to reopen. This happened not as part of a religious revival but in order to stir up patriotism so as to support the war effort. With the end of the war, however, and the renewed vigor of the anti-religious campaign of Premier Nikita Khrushchev in the 1950s, the closure of churches and persecution of Christians started once again. In 1961 the Cathedral of the Dormition of the Holy Virgin, which had been built on Sennaya Square in the mid-eighteenth century, and had survived the Revolution, civil war, the 1930s demolitions and the Second World War, was finally blown up and dismantled. In its place the unassuming entrance to the Sennaya Square metro station was erected, leaving the square bereft of its most imposing building.

Nonetheless, Orthodox Christianity survived largely underground in St. Petersburg, with only the seminary of the Alexander Nevsky Monastery allowed to function in an extremely restricted form. Even during this dark spiritual period the Church continued to operate, albeit often clandestinely, and Vladimir Putin was secretly baptized in late 1952 at the Transfiguration Cathedral by his mother (his father, a Communist Party member, might have disapproved).

Today's Faiths

In the 1980s churches were once again allowed a degree of operational freedom in the twilight years of the collapsing Soviet Union. It was only in the wake of its final disintegration that a great surge of religious activity once again took place. The Russian Orthodox Church, supported by a temporary tobacco tax granted by President Boris Yeltsin, enjoyed a revival as great as any since its foundation. The Kazan Cathedral was reallocated to the Church authorities and became the mother church of what was now once again St. Petersburg. Many other churches and monasteries were also returned to ecclesiastical administration. Other traditional religions of Russia also benefited. After an interruption of over seventy years, the Buddhist temple of St. Petersburg once again opened, undergoing a thorough restoration. The Russian sculptor Dashi Namdakov was then commissioned to make a bas-relief memorial plaque commemorating the life and death of the Buddhist abbot Dorzhiev. The main synagogue of the city as well as mosques also enjoyed a revival.

Yet it is the Russian Orthodox Church which has most benefited, providing the principal moral and spiritual compass for most of the city's people today, even if only a minority actually attends services on a weekly basis. Over the last two decades, new as well as old churches have been built, restored, and embellished. A saunter through the city, accompanied by the ringing of church bells when liturgies and other services are held, can be a moving experience, making St. Petersburg one of the world's most spiritually inspiring cities. Here is a place in which religious persecution, wars, and civil strife, leading to the death of millions, provided the crucible for a religious revival that believers elsewhere in western Christendom can only admire, and in which even non-believers can take comfort.

This revival has not taken place without secular confrontations. The return of St. Isaac's Cathedral, a state museum from the 1920s, to the Russian Orthodox Church led to serious protests in January 2017 by those fearing that the long established constitutional division of Church and state was threatened. Others were merely opposed to the loss of museum revenue, extracted from the three and a half million visitors who came to the cathedral each year. An anti-Semitic element also reared its ugly head in the issue when some who supported the return of the cathedral to the Church were accused of blaming Jews for organizing opposition. Pyotr Tolstoy, a descendant of the famous author Leo Tolstoy and State Duma Deputy Speaker, allegedly criticized the Jewish descendants of those who "jumped out of the Pale of Settlement" in the wake of the Revolution for undermining the Russian Orthodox Church. He denied the accusation.

10 | Changing Faces
Migration and Social Change

From its foundation, the new capital was a multicultural city which drew its diverse population not only from the four corners of Russia but from most of the countries of Europe. This was a necessity since Tsar Peter the Great needed the assistance of a wide range of highly skilled and innovative individuals from Western Europe's most developed countries in order to encourage culture and technology. One such individual was the Scottish-descended James Bruce (1669–1735), who, having served as a major-general in the Great Northern War against Sweden, was a key figure in the tsar's building of the Russian Navy from scratch; Alexander Pushkin called him the "Russian Faust." He also helped in the establishment of the navigation, artillery, and engineering institutes on which the military depended for highly trained recruits. In order to gather the latest knowledge Bruce went abroad, as Peter had earlier done, "so as to employ masters of the noble arts, which are so needed here." He also corresponded with such luminaries as the German philosopher Leibniz and translated important scientific and academic works into Russian. In recognition of his services, he was elevated to the rank of count, senator, and director of the Moscow Civil Printing Press, which published the calendar which bears his name. This was at a time, it should be remembered, when as one British visitor of the time put it, a printing house was "a great Curiosity in these Parts, for there are few or no Russian Books, of what sort so ever, to be had for Money."

Bruce was also instrumental in enabling Russia to achieve sovereignty over Livonia, Estonia, and Ingria as well as large parts of Karelia, formerly in Swedish hands. Peter recognized his contributions and he was awarded 500 household serfs. As a result, he chose to retire to his large estate near Moscow rather than live in St. Petersburg.

The British profile in the city was by no means restricted to the military sphere. A Scotsman, Dr. Robert Erskine, was appointed court physician to the tsar as well as privy councillor after his arrival in 1706. Highly valued until his death in 1718, he was accorded the great honor of burial at the Alexander Nevsky Monastery. Lesser "heretical" foreigners were buried at the first official cemetery for non-Orthodox residents and visitors by the St. Sampson's Cathedral on the Vyborg Side.

The American Connection

Later in the course of the eighteenth and early nineteenth centuries citizens of the fledging United States of America also began to have a presence in the capital. By then, some Russians from St. Petersburg had been involved in the American Revolution, assisting the revolutionary cause. One Fedor Karzhavin, who was employed in the Admiralty, went west himself and was active not only in the revolutionary movement there but in trade with the new republic.

Some Americans also visited the Russian capital during the revolutionary period. Among the most prominent was John Quincy Adams (1767–1848), son of the second president of the United States John Adams, and the future sixth president of the US from 1825–29. His first visit was as a fourteen-year-old in 1781–82 in the company of the American envoy Francis Dana. As Adams recalled, "nobody… but princes and slaves" seemed to live in St. Petersburg. Yet, despite, or perhaps because of that, it was of all the European cities he had visited "the most magnificent I had ever seen." In October 1809 Adams once again arrived in St. Petersburg, this time as the first minister from the US to the Russian Empire. He took up residence at the Hotel de Londres by Nevsky Prospekt, finally settling in 1810 at 66 Moika Embankment.

During his almost five-year sojourn he kept a diary which sheds much light on his perceptions of St. Petersburg specifically and Russia in general. For example, he was not very impressed with what passed for fairground entertainment. As he wrote on May 5, 1810:

I called upon Mr Harris this morning, and we went together to see the shows at most of the booths on the square of St. Isaac. At the first were a dromedary and two monkeys, a dancing bear, and a couple of poor tumblers, with a man, one of whose legs was deformed, and seemingly jointed like a hand and arm; for he used that foot as a hand, to eat, drink, play upon the violin, with two pairs of cymbals at once, and other like performances. At the second were only dancers on the tight-rope, and tumblers—very miserable. At the third a puppet show... All were of the lowest of public amusements.

It was in St. Petersburg, however, that he enjoyed the most stimulating of intellectual conversations with the conservative Catholic philosopher and diplomat of the Kingdom of Sardinia, Count Joseph-Marie de Maistre, as well as with the Spanish ambassador, General Pardo de Figueroa, one of Europe's leading classical scholars of his time. Adams was also close to the Russian autocracy, enjoying a good relationship with the tsar who, in turn, showed his appreciation in a variety of ways, material and social. This was perhaps just as well, since his salary as minister was hardly extravagant: only $9,000 a year, which included the pay for his ancillary staff of fifteen individuals.

The European Imprint

Swedes constituted one of the largest foreign communities within St. Petersburg, with some 5,164 resident in 1869, many working in metallurgy, timber, and shoemaking industries. There was also a small Swedish mercantile, craft, and industrial elite, especially in the production and sale of jewelry. The most renowned Swede in the capital was the industrialist and oil entrepreneur Ludvig Nobel (1831–88), brother of Alfred Nobel, who later established the Nobel Prize. Ludvig's factory, founded in 1862, was instrumental in advancing diesel technology, and from the income it provided he made charitable contributions to various good causes.

Many members of middle-class German and Finnish communities also resided on Vasilyevsky Island. The former were often doctors, watchmakers, and chemists, while the latter were involved in supplying dairy products to the capital. Others with German, French, and Polish roots lived along Nevsky Prospekt, as well as the intersecting streets near Bolshaya Morskaya Street between the Rivers Moika and Neva. Jewish residents, in turn, usually merchants, lived around Sadovoya Street in a commercial area bounded by Sennaya Square and the Nikolsky Market.

The city's large animal population should also not be forgotten. Vissarion Belinsky wrote in *Petersburg and Moscow*, published in 1845: "The house in which the Petersburger rents his flat is a veritable Noah's Ark, in which you can find a pair of every type of animal." St. Petersburg had become a metropolis of animals; as the twentieth century dawned, it was home to 41,000 horses—one for every six families—and more than 8,000 cows.

It was the British who remained the predominant foreign community in the city, which, by the end of the eighteenth century, was burgeoning. Many factory owners were British and they greatly increased the number of British employees during this period. This was especially true with respect to the Imperial Mint (its machinery British in origin), weapons factories, and other private enterprises. It is said that during the reign of Tsar Paul I their influence in the internal politics of the country had become so great that they played a role in encouraging the tsar's assassination by a court cabal, the reason for which his son, the new Tsar Alexander I, broke relations with Britain for a period.

Typical was the engineer General Alexander Wilson, whose father had assisted the Scot Charles Cameron in his various architectural enterprises, and who, with his brother, had worked at the Carron Ironworks in Falkirk. His iron-framed Alexandrovsk Textile Mill was one of Russia's most important factories, a model of its kind which attracted visitors from all over Europe. Situated on the left bank of the Neva near the Shlisselburg Fortress, it employed children from the Petersburg Foundling Hospital. A playing-card factory was also attached to it, the income from which went to the Dowager Empress, widow of Tsar Paul, who used the funds for charitable purposes. The amenities with which the workers—617 boys and 215 girls—were provided were of the highest humanitarian standards for the time. As one British visitor, George Matthew Jones, noted:

> The dormitories were well ventilated and clean to a high degree; each had a separate bed, of which the blankets and bedding were as white as snow. They have a large play-room, ornamented with plans and models, executed by them, some in superior style.

Yet another leading figure in the industrial development of St. Petersburg was the Scot Charles Baird (1766–1843). One of the country's most powerful industrialists, he constructed the country's first steamship, the *Elizaveta*, which provided a service between the naval city of Kronstadt and St. Petersburg, the monopoly of which he enjoyed for seven years.

By 1827, the British community numbered about 2,500, but, economically and socially, it was not quite what it had been before the Napoleonic upheavals. As Jones observed after visiting in the late autumn of 1822 and following winter, the English Embankment was no longer so appropriately named:

> The quay above the Palace is called the Russian, and that below, the English quay. The latter name is given to it, because the large houses on it were originally built, and inhabited by wealthy English merchants. I lament to say, that very few of them have been able to retain their houses, but have gradually ceded them to the Russian nobility, and, in some instances, to German merchants, while they themselves have been obliged to retire into secondary streets, particularly one called the Back Line.

With a variety of measures taken by the Russian government to the detriment of British firms, many in the mercantile world were now returning home. Even so, Kronstadt retained its highly British profile, Jones writing that "of a thousand foreign vessels which enter, it is calculated 930 are British," while the English church there continued to thrive, supported by its resident priest. Two English-run inns continued to cater for visitors.

Although diminished, the British remained a prominent community throughout this period, even during the height of the Crimean War, when the two empires were enemies. They continued to carry out their business in the capital, irrespective of military action in the adjacent Baltic Sea and Gulf of Finland.

In particular, the British left their mark on Russian high society in the sporting field. They played a major role in the establishment of first the Imperial Yacht Club, in 1846, and later the Arrow Rowing Club. Many were active in other sporting activities, including the Neva Tennis and Cricket Club which was founded just over a generation later. Hockey and football were also popular during the late imperial period and the wide space of the Cadet Corps Square, on Vasilyevsky Island, was the venue for various games.

It was really in the Soviet period that football became one of Russia's most popular sports and nowhere more so than in Leningrad. The Leningrad football club Stalinets was founded in 1925 among metallurgical workers, but had roots in pre-war St. Petersburg, with the British playing a significant role. In 1897 a football match was held on Vasilyevsky Island betwen the local British team Ostrov and the Russian Petrograd. On this occasion the British won 6–0. Another Russian team, Murziinka, was formed in 1914, playing at the newly built Obukhovsky Stadium, known after 1924 as the Bolshevik Stadium. It was from this team that the Leningrad Metal Plant Team or Stalinets evolved, later to merge with the Zenit Football Club in 1939, three years after the latter had been founded at the Bolshoi Stadium. They achieved an early accolade when they won their match against CSKA Moscow in 1944. It took decades for the club to finally win the Soviet League title in 1984, and then the Soviet Cup in 1985.

It is really in post-Soviet Russia that Zenit St. Petersburg has achieved global international recognition, playing in the Russian Premier League. In 2007, 2010, 2012, and 2015, it topped the league after the giant gas company Gazprom took financial control, with the equivalent of over $100 million USD invested in the club and its stadium. Zenit went on to won the UEFA Cup in 2007–08 and its Super Cup in 2008. Among its most notable home-produced players was Andrey Arshavin, who won numerous trophies with Zenit before signing with Arsenal in the English Premier League in 2008–09, and then in Kazakhstan, before returning to Zenit in 2013. Today, the club is accommodated in a brand-new stadium on Krestovsky Island, popularly known as the Zenit Arena, which opened in early 2017. It will host matches during the FIFA World Cup in 2018. Designed by the Japanese architect Kisho Kurokawa, who had previously designed the Toyota Stadium in Japan, it has a capacity of 67,800 spectators.

Fin-de-Siècle City

Turn-of-the-century St. Petersburg was highly cosmopolitan, although not to the degree of the Russian Empire as a whole, in which, according to the census of 1897, the majority of people, even excluding Finland—then a Russian grand-duchy—were non-Russians. So it is not surprising that by 1900 St. Petersburg's 1,418,000 inhabitants were multicultural as those in any great European city today. Although 87.6 percent of the population was of Russian ethnicity, there were many other peoples of various nationalities, including Germans, Poles, Jews, and Tatars, to name but a few. Other nationalities which had formerly played a prominent role in the city were now dramatically reduced in numbers. Resident Swedes had almost halved over the previous half century to 2,980, even if their embassy remained prominently situated at the English Embankment. Finns, both Finnish- and Swedish-speaking, greatly increased in numbers, especially during the winter months when they were not needed for agricultural work at home. Many of these found work in the city's booming construction industry.

Finland's Swedish-speaking elite, on the other hand, arrived in the capital to perform other services. Famed for their scrupulous honesty and military prowess, many worked in government ministries dealing in finance or in the officer corps of the Russian Empire. One especially prominent figure was the Swedish Finn Carl Gustaf Mannerheim. Having first joined the Nikolaevsky Cavalry School in St. Petersburg after an unhappy period at the Finnish Officers' College in Hamina in Finland, he soon was commissioned as an officer in the prestigious Imperial Horse Guards Regiment. While married to a Russian princess in his first marriage he lived at Moika Embankment, where his daughter Anastasia was born. Utterly loyal to the imperial family, he attended the tsar during his coronation on May 14, 1896—many years before his future role in securing the independence of Finland from Russia after the Revolution.

Although the British were by this stage radically diminished compared to their earlier heyday, they retained a sizeable presence, in particular as engineers and in industry. The English Club continued to thrive—even if the overwhelming majority of its members were by now Russian—and the New English Club was established on Bolshaya Morskaya Street, catering for middle-class British and American businessmen. The German community was also in decline despite the construction of a new German Embassy, built in 1911–12 by the German architect Peter Behrens. Its rough, austere granite facade still looms ominously across the road from St. Isaac's Cathedral in the so-called "stripped classical" style which, with the advent of the First World War, seemed a harbinger of the German threat.

Exodus

With the First World War came the revolutions in February and October 1917, and the face of St. Petersburg (renamed Petrograd) changed as never before. International trade came to a standstill and foreign shipping kept its distance. H. G. Wells, who visited the city in September 1920, pessimistically noted:

> The shops have an utterly wretched and abandoned look; paint is peeling off, windows are cracked, some are broken and boarded up, some still display a few fly-blown relics of stock in the window, some have their windows covered with notices; the windows are growing dim, the fixtures have gathered two years' dust. They are dead shops. They will never open again.

Between two and three million people fled Russia between 1917 and 1920. With massive emigration both abroad and internally, Petrograd's population fell dramatically. From 2,300,000 in

1915 it had plummeted to 722,000 during the civil war period. By 1926, however, it had partially recovered, rising to 1,616,000. Natural disasters also afflicted the city during this period. In particular, the second highest flood in the history of Petrograd occurred on September 23, 1924 (following that of 1824). Half the city was under water and around 5,000 buildings were damaged and twenty bridges destroyed. Reckoning in the death by famine, disease, and violence of large sections of its population, it is not surprising that nostalgia for its lost imperial glories dominated the feelings of those who fled abroad or to other corners of what had become the Soviet Union. Yet for many of these the hope remained of returning to their beloved St. Petersburg/Petrograd, their minds still filled, as Vladimir Nabokov put it, with the "animal aching yearn for the still fresh reek of Russia."

His family had been forced to flee in 1919 and settled in Berlin, where the elder Vladimir Nabokov, former head of the Literary Foundation in St. Petersburg, together with his associates Hessen and Kaminka, published the Russian-language daily newspaper *Rul*. They thought that they had escaped the worst of it when tragedy struck during a visit to a political conference; the former liberal politician was shot dead on March 28, 1922, during an incident in which the real target of assassination by right-wing extremists had been Pavel Milyukov, the head of the Constitutional Democrats, who survived unscathed.

The Nabokovs were among countless prominent individuals who took refuge abroad. Nikolai Evreinov, former director of the Crooked Looking Glass Theater, now also fled. So did Prince Felix Yusupov, Rasputin's assassin, who left his homeland on a cart disguised as a peasant with paintings by Rembrandt hidden on his cart. The flying ace Alexander Prokoviev de Seversky also emigrated, eventually settling in the United States, like Nabokov junior. There he took over the leadership of the Seversky Aircraft Corporation, inspired by his earlier career, and was awarded the Harman Prize for Services to Aviation two times.

A renewed exodus occurred for those Russians lucky enough to escape the great purges which took place during the middle and late years of the 1930s, affecting foreigners as well as natives. In what had once been one of Europe's most cosmopolitan cities only a hundred or so British subjects remained—and these were largely Russian-born children of British expatriates, many of whom knew little English. Nonetheless their sense of being aliens remained strong and after British governmental pressure, Torgsin, the Soviet Agency for Trade with Foreigners, agreed to their communal settlement in the so-called English dacha, actually a large house with ten rooms with a glass-enclosed veranda, at Sosnovka on the Vyborg Side, not far from Murino, the village which had been so popular with the British during the summer months before the Revolution. A Mrs. Morley was its matron and saw to it that English was spoken at mealtimes by the dozen or so residents who remained shortly before the outbreak of the Second World War. Photographs of it were published in 1936 in the London newspaper *The Daily Sketch*. Yet the political climate was becoming xenophobic and two years later the dacha was closed down and its last inmates expelled from Russia altogether. By the end of the summer of 1939 virtually all non-Russian citizens had left.

Only in 1954, nine years after the end of the war and following the death of Stalin, did foreigners once again begin to trickle into Leningrad, but today only a small number of foreign residents are western or northern European, with the majority of those from outside Russia coming from Central Asia, working in the construction industry, or Chinese, studying in various universities and academies.

Foreign Investment

During the postwar Soviet period foreign investment in St. Petersburg got off to a slow start. It began during the 1980s with foreign companies setting up and managing new hotels for the tourist trade which began to take form at the same time (see Chapter 11). Among the most prominent of these were Finnish firms which during the 1990s acquired a major role in the market and soon made their presence felt in many other business areas—resuming the role they had played in pre-revolutionary days. The British also returned with major investments in the hotel industry, of which Rocco Forte's

Astoria and Angleterre Hotels are the most prominent examples. US investment in St. Petersburg's economy also became significant, not least in the motor industry, where Ford set up a joint-investment plant to produce cars for the Russian market. Tobacco, too, was a major US target, with R. J. Reynolds investing $120 million in production facilities in 1998. Turkey's presence was, in turn, significant within the construction industry where Renaissance Construction has been prominent since 1993. Chinese involvement has been felt in the significant numbers of students sent to St. Petersburg as well as in the arts, since Russian painting was and remains highly sought after in China. Even more important, however, is its contribution to the building industry. Chinese investors have constructed an entire new residential complex in the Krasnoselsky district, accommodating up to 35,000 residents, known as the Pearl of the Baltic Sea. Building began in 2006 and was largely completed by 2013. This vast complex has the Pearl Plaza at its heart and includes a business center, schools, malls, and a wide variety of cultural venues. A new toll motorway, the Western Speed Diameter, has also helped to develop outlying regions of the city, attracting further investments from a wide variety of overseas sources.

11 | **Consuming Interests**
The Culture of Food, Trade, and Consumerism

F rom its earliest days as a capital city the largesse of the tsars determined St. Petersburg's patterns of consumption. All manner of delicacies and luxury goods were imported for the benefit of the court. Under the Empress Elizabeth, it had become renowned as a glittering capital which vied with any throughout the European continent. As the *St. Petersburg Register*, which published a record of the court's social calendar and other important social events, noted in 1755 with respect to a reception hosted for the British Ambassador by Count Ivan Shuvalov:

> at the conclusion of the meal the honorable guests withdrew to the upper grotto by the hall, where a specially made dessert was placed in the center of a round table. It was graced by: a great mountain confected from diverse ores, minerals and petrified curiosities, precisely copying the mineral collection of His Excellency the Count. Within the summit of the mountain, decorated with allegorical statues, there was a pit, filled with miners at work. A great river issued forth from the mountain on the other side, which flowed into a harbour, in which a number of fully-rigged ships and boats could be seen about to depart on a whaling expedition. A splendid bridge spanned the river and lead to a castle perched on a mountain slope. By the shore, a sail with a flaming light was visible.

The grandiose culinary landscape had been created out of sweetmeats, wines, and liqueurs.

If the imperial tables vied with those of other major European courts, so St. Petersburg's taverns bore comparison with the worst in London. This created a contrast within the city between the luxurious lifestyle of the few and the poverty of the masses which has persisted to this day. James Meader, the imperial gardener at Peterhof, referred to the local *trakitri* (pubs) as "low stinking public houses worse than the worst in St. Giles."

Under Catherine the Great, court life in Russia reached glittering heights and palace festivities showed off not only the sophistication of social fashions but modern technology as well. Lady Jane Cathcart, wife of the then British Ambassador, left her impressions of the "merry" dinner which she attended with the sovereign in a letter she wrote home:

> The foundation of it arose chiefly from the novelty of this way of being served, for when the plates are changed you pull a thong by the side of everybody's right hand which goes underneath the table and rings a bell. Your plate goes down, as all around it is composed of so many divisions like stove holes. You write down upon a slate and pencil which is fixed ready, and what you want immediately comes up. A great diversion was from one table to the other to send something or other that served to laugh.

Most famous of all the aristocrats for his consuming interests was Count Pavel Stroganov. His kitchen in the 1890s achieved fame throughout the courts of Europe, where he was also noted for his musical and literary soirées. His celebrated dish left to posterity was Beef Stroganov, an example of Russian cooking at its best consisting of slices of fillet of beef cooked with mushrooms, mustard, sour cream, and brandy.

It was also during this period that the Yeliseyev dynasty of culinary fame first appeared: Yelisei, the serf gardener of Count Sheremetev, produced a dessert with strawberries for the count's Christmas festivities in 1812, despite the harshness of the winter and the state of war with Napoleonic France. As a result, Sheremetev immediately emancipated him and awarded him a hundred roubles. The following year, Piotr, Yelisei's son, moved to St. Petersburg and after a brief period as a street vendor selling oranges to aristocratic flâneurs began supplying groceries to the those prosperous sectors of society which took an interest in high-quality food and wines. His first premises were at 18 Nevsky Prospekt at the corner of the Moika Embankment, from where he sold "colonial wares from the torrid regions of the world." Later he established his wine cellars on Vasilyevsky Island. He rapidly rose to become the city's most important merchant of luxury foods and eventually purveyor to the imperial court.

This imperial patronage was of immense benefit to the Yeliseyev family, who continued to grow in prominence not only among the aristocratic elite but also those living abroad and foreign visitors to the city. Upper stories were soon added to their premises and their cellars grew to over two and a half hectares (six acres) in area. The eldest son, Sergei Yeliseyev, who had taken over the firm, was given the status of merchant of the first guild, while Piotr Yeliseyev's sons Stepan and Grigory became active in successful commercial ventures, establishing the empire's first private banking house in 1864: the St. Petersburg Private Commercial Bank. Other honors were also granted to them and in 1846 the Senate made the brothers honorary citizens of the city.

The Yeliseyev family were now reaching their financial and social peak, their shops famed through Europe. In 1889 the firm won a gold medal for its wines at the International Exhibition in Paris. Seven years later, in 1896, Grigory Girgioryvich Yeliseyev became head of the family business and within a year the company's turnover had exploded from three million to over sixty-four million roubles. Such wealth enabled them to make their palatial home on the Moika Embankment a showpiece—today it is the Taleon Imperial Hotel—with works by Auguste Rodin, in particular his bronze sculpture of Varvara Yeliseyeva, the wife of Setepan Gigoryevich Yeliseyev, a grandson of the founder.

St. Petersburg remained a city of extremes. On the one hand, large segments of the population, often from the countryside and steeped in poverty, suffered from malnutrition and poor-quality food; on the other, it boasted some of the world's most luxurious culinary establishments, of which the Yeliseyev Food Emporium at 56 Nevsky Prospekt was particularly renowned for its delicacies, an image reinforced by the splendid architecture of its premises. It was built by the Russian architect Gavriil Baranovsky (1902–04, extended in 1906). It included not only extensive space for upmarket food shopping but also a grand theater which accommodated over 400 people when it opened in March 1904. Still in use today as the Comedy Theater, its first production on that occasion was Shakespeare's *Hamlet*. As for Grigory Yeliseyev, he was finally elevated to the nobility in 1913 when his company celebrated its centenary, completing the serf family's rise to the heights of Russian society. Yet a scandal soon plagued the family when the following year the elderly merchant eloped with the wife of a local jeweler. When his wife then conveniently committed suicide, he was free to marry his mistress and both retired to Paris—with significant funds to maintain them—and there he remained until his death in 1949, escaping the Revolution, the civil war, and its aftermath.

Café Culture

By the second half of the nineteenth century, St. Petersburg was increasingly becoming a cosmopolitan center with a rising middle class. In the 1850s the city contained at least 184 restaurants and eating houses, 19 cafés, and 37 pastry shops. This trend continued, and by 1900 there were 1,618 restaurants and more than 710 public houses with beer on tap. Many of their patrons were fond of tobacco, usually in the form of cigarettes, and so at least 311 shops catered for their needs. Bookshops, too, thrived—over 140 in number—not only as places to buy the latest book, journal, or magazine, but as literary meeting places where drinks and food might also be served. Among the most noted was the Literary Café, a patisserie as well as a venue for intellectual conversation not only during the imperial period but throughout the Soviet and post-Soviet years as well, today attracting nostalgic tourist groups from abroad. Located on Nevsky Prospekt, its site was formerly occupied by the Wolff and Beranget cake shop, frequented by Pushkin and Dostoyevsky.

Less cultured tastes were catered for at the many musical venues of a more popular nature spread through St. Petersburg. Frequently the music performed was secondary to refreshments, with proprietors charging inflated prices for alcohol—the real attraction. While statistics demonstrate that alcohol consumption in pre-revolutionary Russia was less than that in such European countries as Germany, France, and Belgium, consumption was far more concentrated on limited occasions, leading to a death rate from alcohol poisoning up to five times that in other countries. Some of these deaths were the result of contaminated spirits produced by an illegal bootleg industry interested in quick profits, not unlike that found in parts of Russia up to this day.

Cafés of the *demi-monde* thrived in St. Petersburg, much as they did in other major European capitals. Among the most elegant, albeit notorious, was the Quisisana, situated on the corner of Nevsky Prospekt and Troitskaya Street (now Rubinstein Street), which became a byword for decadence and debauchery. There was also the Aquarium, one of the city's most fashionable night spots, where lecherous men could watch beautiful young ladies *en déshabillé* while they performed in vaudeville acts or other forms of titillating entertainment. Far more elevated, if still *risqué*, was the Stray Dog, discussed in Chapter 6, where literary figures such as Anna Akhmatova were frequent visitors during the pre-war years.

Revolutionary Austerity?

The First World War, the outbreak of the Revolution in 1917, and the civil war devastated Petrograd. Yet for the cultural elite favored by the new regime, life still had its consolations. The seizure by the Bolsheviks of the reins of state did not mean that for their leaders the days of pleasure were at an end. On the contrary, the writer Georgy Ivanov provides an insight into the life of those Bolsheviks in 1920 who had seized command of the Baltic Fleet in the city. In *Petersburg Winters*, he wrote:

> The magnificent halls of the Admiralty are brilliantly illuminated and well heated. Not habituated to such warmth and brilliance, those invited there mill about the polished parquet floor, sipping spiced tea and nibbling canapés of caviar, proffered on trays by sailor dandies of the Baltic Fleet

For the average citizen throughout the Soviet period conspicuous consumption was not an option. During the heady days of the New Economic Policy, originally proposed by Lenin but abolished by Stalin, a limited and brief return to a market economy was permitted from 1922 to 1928, when newly rich and often corrupt individuals could live it up with flashy cars and money to spend. They were satirized in the novels of Ilya Ilf and Yevgeny Petrov such as *The Little Golden Calf* (1931), made into a film in 1968. For the masses, however, life was a hard drudge. Especially during the Second World War and toward the end of the Soviet period in the 1980s, rationing was the order of the day. Money was not the issue; rather it was the unavailability of goods, with all but essential products difficult to come by. Women and children queued for hours, sometimes days, to acquire basic items. Meanwhile, those of the *Nomenclatura*, the political elite, were usually able to benefit from the system through the allocation of privileges including spacious apartments in the best parts of Leningrad, cars with drivers, as well as domestic appliances, high quality food, and even staff. Those Soviet citizens who received hard currency from abroad during the mid- and late 1980s could use this money at special Intourist shops, which catered for foreign visitors, and where Beluga caviar and other delicacies were sold. Even after the fall of the Soviet Union and in our own time, many people in St. Petersburg, especially the elderly, still depend upon produce grown at their country dachas, where they live during the summer months, for their everyday food.

Modern Tastes

During the years leading up to the Second World War and thereafter, Leningrad had ceased to be renowned as a city of pleasure and consumption. Such hedonism as there was in the Soviet Union was now to be found in Moscow and in the dachas of the ruling apparatchiks. Nonetheless, a few venues from imperial days survived, including the sumptuous Palkin Restaurant on 47 Nevsky Prospect, the Literature Café,, and the restaurants of the great hotels, including the Europa and Astoria. Among newer restaurants, Aquarel at 14 Dobrolyubova Prospekt and Terrassa on Kazanskaya Street are highly popular with the young and wealthy. The Letuchiy Gollandets (Flying Hollander), situated on a wooden sailing ship, appeals to all age groups, and is permanently berthed by the Mytninskaya Embankment and is especially noted for its fish.

Since the collapse of the Soviet Union and the spectacular rise of capitalism and tourism in St. Petersburg, as it has once again become, countless restaurants, cafés, and other watering holes have opened for a brief flourishing only to once again shut as tourism failed to meet expectations, sanctions hit, or the rouble lost value. One such place, a French restaurant on the Moika Canal, even offered its own foie gras from the local hinterland at prices which ran per person into the thousands of dollars, excluding wines. Another, the Noble Nest, in the old tea house of the Yusopov Palace, attracted not only President Putin but also European heads of state. Both have since closed. Some Indian restaurants have also done well in St. Petersburg, one of which, Tandoor, opposite St. Isaac's Cathedral, also welcomed President Putin as a guest. Previously, after the fall of the Soviet Union, almost all the food served in these venues was imported from Western Europe or even further afield.

Today, however, Russian sanctions against European and American imports, in retaliation to sanctions imposed against Russia, have forced the development of a local food infrastructure to fill the gap. Connoisseurs of French and Italian cheeses and cold meats may not be impressed, but the promotion of local ingredients can only be seen as a positive step for the country, and St. Petersburg in particular, in developing its own essential resources.

In any case, its cultural charms are unlikely to fade: with an enviable place on the UNESCO World Heritage List, it boasts over 4,000 historically important monuments and offers the visitor 221 museums, 80 theaters, and 45 galleries and exhibition halls. A wealth of hotels of various degrees of comfort suit all but the poorest pocket, and air connections to all corners of the world make St. Petersburg easy to reach. While most visitors must apply for visas, those arriving by cruise ship are exempted, making that means of access among the most appealing, especially for the older visitor. With its deep-water port, many of the larger passenger ships, like

Cunard's *Queen Elizabeth*, are able to dock quite centrally, while relieving passengers of the tasks of organizing hotel accommodation, transport, and visas. A wide range of travel and tourist guide organizations further provide an excellent infrastructure for the visitor who wishes to see the sights with a minimum of effort and discomfort.

That said, travelers who are more independent need not fear making the effort to explore St. Petersburg on their own, for despite the undisputed difficulty of the language, the city has made itself highly welcoming to the single intrepid visitor as well as those in groups. Many signs are in English and most people are willing to assist the visitor from wherever they may come. About 12 percent of the city's population works in tourism-related industries, according to the Baltic Cruise Association, including 40,000 guides. With some 320 cruise ships visiting St. Petersburg each year, they are not likely to be out of work, catering to 800,000 cruise passengers in 2015 alone, out of a total of five and a half million visitors that year—a figure even larger than the total population of St. Petersburg. As such, it is now in the top twenty of the world's tourist destinations. Not surprisingly, then, tourism has become one of the city's main industries, even if budget tourism, which requires an infrastructure of campsites and hostels, has not yet been fully embraced. A first step was taken, however, when the first motor home campsite, Baltic PARKing, in Strelna on the Peterhof Road on the southern outskirts of the city, opened for business in 2015.

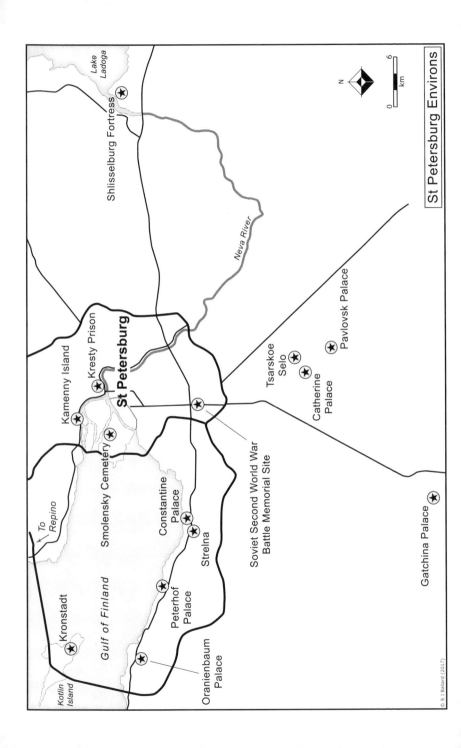

St Petersburg Environs

Lake Ladoga

Shlisselburg Fortress

Neva River

To Repino

Kotlin Island

Gulf of Finland

Kronstadt

Kamenny Island

Kresty Prison

St Petersburg

Smolensky Cemetery

Constantine Palace

Strelna

Peterhof Palace

Oranienbaum Palace

Soviet Second World War Battle Memorial Site

Tsarskoe Selo

Catherine Palace

Pavlovsk Palace

Gatchina Palace

N

0   6
km

© S J Ballard (2017)

12 | Surroundings
The City's Hinterland

istoric St. Petersburg, largely restored after decades of damage and neglect, is ringed by suburbs that are either nondescript or grim, full of apartment blocks, highways, and industrial plants. Yet some places further out from the urban conurbation, in particular to the south and southeast, contain many of the area's most magnificent palaces, parks, and gardens.

The first significant building to be erected in the rural environs of the newly founded capital was the tsar's own mansion at Peterhof, originally built of wood in 1710–11. It possessed few architectural pretensions, but the nearby diminutive stone pleasure palace, Monplaisir, was a different matter. Built by the French architect Jean-Baptiste Le Blond (1679–1719) and the German Johann Friedrich Braunstein, it features a study decorated with *chinoiserie*, one of the earliest examples of this orientalizing fashion in Russia. But it is the Palace of Peterhof itself which is the crowning glory of the site, erected on a promontory with a panoramic view over the far eastern Gulf of Finland. In the beginning Braunstein was responsible for the undertaking, but in 1716 the better-known Le Blond was put in charge and the oak study and Italian Salon, reconstructed after the systematic Nazi devastation during the Second World War, are evidence of his consummate skills in interior decoration. The imprint of other architects can also be felt, for in 1721 a serious fire ravaged Peterhof, requiring a major restoration. This was carried out by another late Baroque Italian architect Nicola Michetti (1675–1758), who had worked under Carlo Fontana while in Rome. Today, therefore, Le Blond's influence is most notable not in architecture, but in the magnificent gardens which he laid out between the gulf and the palace. They incorporate an ingenious hydraulic system which provides water not merely for the vast gardens but also its numerous fountains. Alexandre Benois wrote of these: "Peterhof is the palace of the sea god. Here the fountains are not mere accessories: they are the essence of the place. They are the symbolic expression of the sea's dominion, the mist that rises from the waves as they surge against its shores."

As for the main palace of Peterhof itself, it continued to undergo a major series of renovations, each of which introduced stylistic changes. One was carried out by Francesco Bartolomeo Rastrelli (1700–71), who was in the avant-garde of European fashion when he rebuilt this favored summer residence of the Empress Elizabeth in 1745–55, successfully combining both Russian and Western European late Baroque elements. The two end pavilions and chapel are noteworthy, but Rastrelli's 800-square-meter gilded Great Hall is its pride and glory.

Another architectural gem to be found here is the little Palace of Marly, also by Braunstein. Situated at the western end of the gardens, it is Russia's closest approximation to an English country house of the early eighteenth century, at least with respect to its exterior, as Dutch influences dominate inside. A Palladian English palace, no longer in existence, was also built, one of the most important of its kind in Eastern Europe, designed by Quarenghi. He had studied in Rome and so, not surprisingly, his works are among the most strictly neoclassical in Russia, inspired by a close study of Ancient Greek and Roman ruins in Italy. Its English park, located on the west bank of the nearby lake, survived until the Second World War and has yet to be re-established. Also of note is the Benois Family Museum at 8 Alexandria Street in Peterhof, established in 1988 and dedicated to the dynasty of famous nineteenth- and early twentieth-century architects and theater designers, including Nicholas and Alexandre, whom we have come across several times in this book.

Peterhof was given a new lease on life when in 1832 Tsar Nicholas I made it once again his official summer residence. Yet Anna Tyutcheva, the daughter of the famous poet and diplomat Fyodor Tyutchev, who served there as a maid of honor, was hardly enthusiastic about the place. She wrote,

Despite its magnificent stage setting and the terrible expense used to create the artifice of nature with which one is confronted, the marshy nature of the countryside cannot be escaped. Indeed, it exudes a melancholy mist and the dampness pierces one to the bone. Life is stressful rather than really vibrant here. The Tsarina passes all her days and evenings, in transit, from the Greek Pavilion to the Italian Veranda, from the Swiss Chalet to the Russian Hovel, from the Dutch Mill to the Chinese Kiosk. The entire imperial family and court are constantly on the move, rushing about among these pleasure palaces. We never know where we shall luncheon or take tea. One has to be constantly alert, for there is nothing to enjoy on these forced marches. One is left thoroughly exhausted and stupefied

Suburban Palaces

After Peterhof, Oranienbaum was the most important palace ensemble to be built in the suburbs of St. Petersburg. Initiated by Alexander Menshikov (Peter the Great's protégé) as his country retreat, work was first undertaken there by Carlo Fontana (1638–1714), from 1710–13. It was completed by the German Gottfried Schädel (1680–1752), who had previously worked with another German architect, Andreas Schlüter, famed for the famous Amber Room (lost in the Second World War) at the Catherine Palace of Tsarskoe Selo.

Oranienbaum was confiscated after Menshikov's fall from grace in 1727, and its interior underwent a major redecoration by Rastrelli under the various imperial occupants and their favorites who followed. Its most noted architectural features include the Chinese Palace, built from 1756–61 by Antonio Rinaldi, an example of *chinoiserie* fused with Rococo elements. The ceiling is also adorned by paintings by the Venetian artist Giovanni Battista Tiepolo, the most important painter of the Italian Baroque. Sadly, other major architectural works in the vicinity have been destroyed, and although it is a UNESCO World Heritage site, restoration has been slow. Now only the ruins of Otrada, to the west of Oranienbaum, built for Peter the Great's chancellor, Gavriil Golovkin, evoke the stately splendor which once graced this weather-beaten corner of Ingria.

The third major palace to be built in the southern suburbs of St. Petersburg was the Constantine Palace at Strelna, a name it acquired later through its association with the Grand-Duke Constantine, brother of Tsar Alexander I, who spent a considerable time there from 1808 until his death in 1831. Le Blond was appointed as architect and worked on the project from 1716 until his death from smallpox in 1719. Nicola Michetti carried on until his return to Italy, when Mikhail Zemtsov, who had arrived in St. Petersburg from Moscow in 1709 to assist Trezzini, assumed control. Much of his work draws upon the ideas he had picked up during a lengthy stay in Sweden where he had been sent by the tsar to acquire the necessary skilled workmen. He was also able to take advantage of the many architectural innovations developed there and which he put to good use later in Russia. The hallmark of his work at Strelna is his tripartite arched passages which together form the main entrance to the palace and still today feature in its modern reconstruction. During the Napoleonic Wars a cavalry regiment was quartered at the palace, undermining its fabric, but during the ownership of Constantine, as mentioned above, it was largely restored. After 1917, however, it again deteriorated while it was used for a variety of educational and other purposes. Then, during the Second World War, it was virtually gutted, with only its exterior walls remaining. Today, it has been completely restored as the residence of the President of the Russian Federation in St. Petersburg and is used for important political conferences and international summits.

Perhaps the most magnificent and elaborate of the imperial palaces built near St. Petersburg was the Catherine Palace in the town of Tsarskoe Selo (Tsar's Village) to the south of the city, named in honor of Peter the Great's second wife, the Polish-born Empress Catherine. Originally, Zemtsov and Andrey Kvasov (1720–70) provided the designs, but it was their Russian colleague Savva Chevakinsky who actually began the work before Rastrelli himself took over. He then set about thoroughly altering the design and demolishing a considerable part of what had already been built from 1748 to 1753. It was a vast undertaking, employing 400 stone-masons alone, most of whom were imported from Yaroslavl, a city to the northwest of Moscow famed for its Baroque churches and now known colloquially as Little St. Petersburg.

The Catherine Palace, with its 325-meter (1,065-foot) long facade, rapidly became a symbol of eighteenth-century imperial Rococo opulence, both inside and out: its Great Hall, 48 meters (157 feet) in length, reconstructed along with much of the palace after the ravages of the Second World War, still amazes visitors and guests who attend the public and private events held there through-out the year. But for puritanical eighteenth-century Protestant visi-tors it was a different matter; they found the palace repulsive. The Englishman William Coxe (1748–1828) criticized its "most tawdry appearance," while his fellow countryman, Sir Nathaniel Wraxall (1751–1831), found it to be "the Completest triumph of a barbarous taste I have seen in these northern kingdoms." Few would share this opinion today as visitors from around the world view the Catherine Palace as one of Russia's architectural triumphs. Most would rather agree with Mikhail Lomonosov's ode to its stellar quality:

> The edifice is so splendid
> That it must augment the number of stars,
> Brightly shining in the firmament
> Tsarskoe Selo.

Many architects subsequently contributed to the Catherine Palace complex. Rastrelli designed his famous grotto, located along the shore of the Large Pond. A typical Rococo folly, its molded decorations include exotic aquatic creatures and seashells. Rastrelli, with the assistance of Chevakinsky, also carried out the design and construction of the imperial hunting lodge of *Mon Bijou*, in what later became the Alexander Park, but this has not survived to our day. The Catherine Palace was also renovated under Catherine the Great, with whose name it has been above all associated because of the glittering social everts she held there during her lengthy sojourns. There, at least, she could enjoy a semblance of summer outside the capital, which was not always easy to do. As she herself succinctly put it, "There is no summer in Petersburg, just two winters, one white, the other green."

During this period the German-born Yury Felten built another example of Russian *chinoiserie*, the famous Chinese Summer House (1778–86), a pagoda as much inspired by European Baroque as by China.

The grand staircase and vestibule are also noteworthy, situated within the central block adjacent to the Great Hall. Built in 1780–86 by the Scottish neoclassical architect Charles Cameron (1743–1812), they are embellished with Ionic columns. Cameron also designed and decorated quite a number of important rooms, in particular his Green Dining Room, adorned with delicate stucco reliefs inspired by Sir Joshua Wedgwood, as well as a residential suite for the Grand-Duke Paul, the empress's son and heir. Other work by him included the Cold Baths and Gate Pavilion. He also undertook to redecorate the splendid mansion which Catherine the Great had granted to her favorite and lover General Alexander Lanskoy. However, when the general died in 1784, the work had not been carried out. Rastrelli's Grotto, meanwhile, was given a new prominence by becoming Catherine the Great's sculpture gallery. Destroyed in the Second World War, it was rebuilt in the 1970s.

Of all the work Cameron did in Russia, it is Pavlovsk Palace, built for the Grand-Duke Paul and his consort Maria Fedorovna, with which his name is most associated. In 1780–82 he had already constructed a garden folly, the Temple of Friendship, at the site, but it was his work at the palace itself (1782–86) that was sensational, in particular his Egyptian Vestibule, a form of decoration the Italian architect Giambattista Piranesi had previously advocated in Rome. This was the main entrance hall and its ceiling was decorated by *The Four Seasons*, a work by the Italian artist Carlo Scoti, who was also to work at the Mikhailovsky Castle in St. Petersburg. The most Palladian-inspired building in Russia, Pavlovsk nonetheless failed to please Paul, who obstinately rejected not only his mother's politics but her taste in architecture. In 1789 Vincenzo Brenna, who was assisting Cameron, took over the project in his place. His contributions there included the Imperial Throne Room and extensive Picture Gallery. Further additions were later provided by Giacomo Quarenghi.

Fire devastated the Palace of Pavlovsk in 1803, after which Andrey Voronikhin, otherwise known for the Kazan Cathedral in the city center, was tasked by the Dowager Empress Maria Fedorovna, by now widow of the murdered Tsar Paul, to carry out the restoration. Finally, in the 1820s Carlo Rossi designed its impressive library in a neoclassical style.

Not only the palace but its gardens became an increasingly popular destination for visitors from St. Petersburg. Thus, on October 30, 1837, the first railway line in Russia was completed, linking Pavlovsk with St. Petersburg. Its railway station still stands today and was designed by the prolific Andrei Stackenschneider, a steam locomotive service starting on May 28, 1838.

Another site on the Peterhof Road by Tsarskoe Selo—and one that retains a certain poignancy—is the Alexander Palace, built by Quarenghi for Tsar Alexander I while he was still heir to the throne. Fittingly for an imperial personage, it was embellished with a majestic Corinthian colonnade, the highest of the classical orders. Its interior, however, is late Victorian with heavy wooden panelling. Here Tsar Nicholas II and his family spent much of their time in a relatively relaxed and informal environment, away from the pressures of living in the Winter Palace, and here he was arrested in 1917 after his abdication, a tragic end to the imperial era of St. Petersburg. Its recent restoration recreates the mood and atmosphere of Nicholas and Alexandra's favorite home.

Dachas and Cottages

On the opposite shore of the Neva, on Sverdlovskaya Embankment in the Krasnogvardeysky district, Quarenghi designed the Kushelev-Bezborodko Dacha (1783–84), flanked by curved galleries with pavilions at either end. With its grandeur and elegance, it was one of the most beautiful in the capital but other imposing dachas were now springing up on the periphery of the capital.

The Stroganov Dacha by Andrey Voronikhin was built in 1795–96 along the shoreline where the Chernaya Rechka (Black) river meets the Bolshaya Nevka. A two-story wooden building with a veranda supported by six Ionic columns on the top floor, the center was surmounted by a dome. It burned down in the mid-nineteenth century. Also of renown is St. Petersburg's own version of Toad Hall, a curious building which particularly impressed Lady Dimsdale, wife of Catherine the Great's British court doctor. As she wrote:

> A few days before I left St. Petersburg a Gentleman took me to Hickeri-Kickeri which in English is called Frog-Hall, distant four or five Miles from Petersburg on the Road to Sarsko-Sello. It is a small elegant House, with only one large Room on a floor, the first Room had not any thing extraordinary in it, it was furnished very handsomely [sic] and had a compleat Set of Wedgewood ware, with a green Frog painted on every Piece by the particular Orders of the Empress, as there are a very large quantity of Frogs on the ground, it being a Swamp.

This porcelain collection is now in the Hermitage Museum and the house fell into a state of disrepair.

Conversely, during the middle years of the nineteenth century some dachas near St. Petersburg were built or restored. The private dacha known as "My Property," for example, the country retreat of Tsesarevich, later Tsar, Alexander III, was thoroughly reconstructed by Stackenschneider while keeping as its core Prince Alexei Dolgorukov's original stone mansion. The Leuchtenberg Dacha was also impressive at this time, occupied by Duke Maximilian von Leuchtenberg, the husband of the Grand Duchess Maria Nikoayevna.

Smaller homes, inspired by English-style cottage architecture, also came into fashion, even taking their name. The asymmetrical Cottage (1826–29), built by the Scot Adam Menelaws, is situated in the Alexandria Park near Peterhof, named after Nicholas I's consort, and is one of the most charming examples of English-influenced domestic architecture in the St. Petersburg area, built for the imperial family itself. Its Gothic chapel (1831–32), on the other hand, is German-inspired, a rarity of its type designed by the prominent Prussian architect of the period Karl Friedrich Schinkel.

Dachas in St. Petersburg, and in all of Russia, have for the last 250 years had an immense significance for all sectors of society, creating a *dachnik* culture of outdoor living and gardening. In the imperial period they were mostly grand summer residences in the countryside, where members of the nobility could pass their time away on estates often given as gifts by the tsar. In the years after the Second World War, however, the term assumed another meaning: the Soviet authorities allotted to each factory worker 600 square meters of land in the countryside around Leningrad for the purpose of growing vegetables, in particular potatoes. Thus the dacha, by now a much more modest building, assumed a central role in the life of most citizens in the city. In the post-Soviet era two other types of dacha have made their appearance. Individuals with private means began to acquire such properties in order to amalgamate with the ones they already owned. These became a symbol of the new capitalist order. For those few individuals with even great financial resources, however, this was not enough. They preferred to purchase new estates in the most sought-after areas of the surrounding countryside, creating luxury estates on which they introduced a full infrastructure of plumbing, electricity, and gas. Some even added their own lakes and other geographical features.

The Pursuit of Pleasure

One Jane Vaux is said to have been behind the opening of the Spring Gardens (later Vauxhall) in 1660, London's most renowned pleasure garden of the time. Russia took almost a century, however, to open its first such pleasure garden, inaugurated in 1777 on Kamenny Island. Others soon followed, including one at Ekaterinhof and another at Novaya Derevnya, which was famed for its mineral waters and situated within the Petrovsky Park. The establishment at Pavlovsk was the most elaborate, a large building with an open colonnade and rotunda, which by the late 1830s provided amenities for playing billiards and a restaurant. Gypsy music was a frequent feature of all such places. In December 1839 a Viennese orchestra entertained guests with the music of Johann Strauss. During the day, it played in a specially constructed wooden pavilion, in the evening in the rotunda.

From 1840, the Pavlovsk *vokzal* (the word now means railway station by association) was only open in the summers. Johann Strauss II conducted his orchestra there during the evenings. Tchaikovsky's first public symphonic performance, *Characteristic Dances*, was also held there on August 30, 1865, though the composer himself was not present. The *vokzal* was enlarged in 1860 when the restaurant was separated from the concert hall. Then a new theater, in the popular so-called Russian style by Nicholas Benois, opened on May 18, 1876. Opera, operetta, and drama were all performed there. In Dostoyevsky's *The Idiot*, a number of scenes take place in Pavlovsk, described by the character Lebedyev: "It's nice and high up, and green and cheap and bon ton and musical—and that's why everyone goes to Pavlovsk."

The *vokzal*, so prominent in the summer social life of the city in the middle years of the nineteenth century, continued to thrive into the twentieth century, although with an increasingly middle-class clientele. Pavlovsk's remained the most famous and socially prominent, but the Ozerki *voksal* was also a fashionable venue, accommodating up to 400 people. Its principal wooden building contained a restaurant in which an orchestra performed three times a week. During the Second World War, Pavlovsk's pleasure garden was destroyed, along with many other historic buildings in the vicinity. Yet in more recent years, concerts and other musical events have once again been held in the palace itself and in its surrounding gardens and pavilions.

Some theaters were also constructed in the suburbs. These include the Kamennoostrovsky Theater, situated at the Krestovsky Embankment on Kamenny Island from 1827, famed for its magnificent Corinthian portico of eight free-standing columns. It underwent a major renovation in 1844 by the noted Russian-Italian architect Alberto Kavos. Nicholas I, who lived much of the time at the nearby Yelagin Palace, frequently attended performances to which he enjoyed walking. It functioned exclusively during the spring and summer, with three performances per week, usually operettas, comedies, and other forms of light entertainment. During the later years of the nineteenth century, when the Pavlovsk Theater and others had become more popular haunts, the Kamennoostrovsky Theater fell out of fashion, and by the 1880s it had become a storage space for theatrical props. During the twentieth century it underwent two major restorations and now serves as a theater for television productions and for performances by the Bolshoi Drama Theater.

The brass orchestra of Semyon Naryshkin, composed of serfs, which played at his dacha on the Kamenny Island, now near the residence of the city's governor, was especially famed. Baron Wrangel noted in his book, *The Stately Homes of Russia* (1913), a tribute to the country's soon-to-be eradicated aristocratic world, that when some of the orchestra's members were stopped by the police and asked their names, they replied by giving the musical notes which their instruments played, so linked were their official identities with their music.

Decline and Revival of the Peterhof Road

By the late nineteenth and early twentieth centuries, the Peterhof Road, off which many of the imperial suburban palaces were situated, was already in a state of decline. Factories filled the buildings and grounds of former dachas and that of Prince Sherbatov had become a hospital. Others were torn down, rapidly replaced by other factories, public houses, and even workers' tenements. Some exceptions, however, survived, including the dacha built for the Countess Marie Kleinmichel in 1893, famed for its elaborate tower. So, too, did the dacha of Pyotr Durnovo, a politician and state councillor. An elegant two-story house on the Poliustriovo Embankment (now Sverdlov Embankment), its ten-columned Ionic colonnade made it a highly imposing building. After the Revolution it was given over to the Leningrad Metalworkers' Club.

The twentieth century also took its toll, in particular through the destruction during the Second World War, when many smaller country mansions disappeared. The beautiful neoclassical home designed by Ivan Starov and built for his brother-in-law Alexander Demidov in 1769 was destroyed by the Nazis. But two such stately homes were more fortunate: the diplomat Ivan Chernyshev's "Aleksandrino," located at what is now Stachek Avenue, built in the 1770s and similar to the Tauride Palace, survived, albeit without its wings. It was restored in 1957. Novo-Znamenka, at 13 Chekistov Street, was also seriously damaged during the war but was rebuilt. Originally constructed in the 1750s and 1760s in chateau style by Rinaldi for the statesman Mikhail Vorontsov, it had been turned into an insane asylum in the late nineteenth century, and is now surrounded by late Soviet-style buildings.

During the post-Soviet period the areas surrounding St. Petersburg have enjoyed a revival, with churches, palaces, and dachas restored to their pre-revolutionary glory. These include not only the former imperial residences and their churches as discussed above, restored respectively by the government and Russian Orthodox Church, but elite suburbs, created with private money and provided with urban infrastructures and amenities such as restaurants and schools. These were not created by oligarchs, who in any case tend to live in or near Moscow, but rather by entrepreneurs of the prosperous rising upper middle classes, who, having traveled abroad in Europe and America, have been influenced by the affluent suburbs they have seen there and the money to be made by creating them.

Further Reading

Avrich, Paul, *Kronstadt, 1921*. Princeton, New Jersey: 2006.

Bartlett, Rosamund, *Chekhov: Scenes from a Life*. London: 2005.

Bartlett, Rosamund, *Tolstoy: A Russian Life*. London: 2013.

Beevor, Antony, *The Second World War*. London: 2012.

Belyakaeva-Kazanskaya, L. V., *Siluety muzykalnogo Peterburga* (*Silhouettes of Musical St. Petersburg*). St. Petersburg: 2001.

Benn, Anna and Rosamund Bartlett, *Literary Russia: A Guide*. London: 1997.

Binyon, T. J., *Pushkin: A Biography*. London: 2003.

Blakesley, Rosalind P., *The Russian Canvas: Painting in Imperial Russia, 1757–1881*. New Haven, Connecticut: Yale University Press, 2016.

Brumfield, William Craft, *A History of Russian Architecture*. Seattle, Washington: 2004.

Bunatyan, G. G., *Literaturnye mesta Peterburga* (*Literary Places of St. Petersburg*). St. Petersburg: 2015.

Cross, Anthony, *St. Petersburg and the British: The City through the Eyes of British Visitors and Residents*. London: 2008.

Figes, Orlando, *A People's Tragedy: The Russian Revolution, 1891–1924*. London: 1996.

Figes, Orlando, *Natasha's Dance: A Cultural History of Russia*. London: 2003.

Fitzpatrick, Sheila, *The Russian Revolution*. New York: 2008.

Hill, Gerard, *Fabergé and the Russian Master Goldsmiths*. New York: 2008.

Lieven, Dominic, *Toward the Flame: Empire, War and the End of Tsarist Russia*. London: 2016.

Lieven, Dominic, Maureen Perrie, and Ronald Grigoriev Suny (eds.), *The Cambridge History of Russia*, vol. 1–3, Cambridge: 2006.

Massie, Robert K., *Peter the Great*. London: 2016.

Merridale, Catherine, *Night of Stone: Death and Memory in Twentieth-Century Russia*. New York: Viking, 2000.

Montefiore, Simon Sebag, *Catherine the Great and Potemkin: The Imperial Love Affair*. London: 2004.

Montefiore, Simon Sebag, *Stalin. The Court of the Red Tsar*. London: 2014.

Montefiore, Simon Sebag, *The Romanovs 1613–1917*. London: 2016.

Neverov, Oleg Yakolevich and Dmitry Pavlovich Alexinsky, *The Hermitage Collections*, vols. 1–2. New York: 2010.

Rabinowitch, Alexander, *Prelude to Revolution: The Petrograd Bolsheviks and the July 1917 Uprising*. Bloomingdale, Indiana: 1968.

Rappaport, Helen, *Four Sisters: The Lost Lives of the Romanov Grand Duchesses*. London: 2015.

Sarabianov, D. V., *Russian Art: From Neoclassicism to the Avant-Garde*. London 1990.

Sebestyen, Victor, *Lenin the Dictator: An Intimate Portrait*. London: 2017.

Service, Robert, *The Last of the Tsars: Nicholas II and the Russian Revolution*. London: 2017

Shvidkovsky, Dmitri O., *St. Petersburg: Architecture of the Tsars*. New York: 1996.

Smith, Douglas, *Rasputin*. London: 2016.

Zinovieff, Sofka *Red Princess: A Revolutionary Life*. London: Granta, 2007.

Websites

St. Petersburg Official City Guide
http://www.visit-petersburg.ru/en_saintpetersburg/

An Illustrated History of St. Petersburg
http://www.saint-petersburg.com/history/

Museum of the History of St. Petersburg
http://www.spbmuseum.ru/?lang_ui=en

Taleon Magazine, vol. 1–28 (originally published by Taleon
 Imperial Hotel, St. Petersburg), 2014, at http://www.
 taleonimperialhotel.com/taleon-magazine/

Index